# FIVE DAYS WALKING FIVE TOWNS

## TOURING WINDSOR'S PAST

**Marty Gervais**

**BIBLIOASIS**
**WINDSOR, ON**

Library and Archives Canada Cataloguing in Publication

Gervais, C. H. (Charles Henry), 1946-, author
        Five days walking five towns / Marty Gervais.

ISBN 978-1-77196-178-3 (softcover)

        1. Walking--Ontario--Windsor--Guidebooks.  2. Windsor
(Ont.)--Tours.  3. Windsor (Ont.)--History.  I. Title.

FC3099.W65A3 2017        917.13'32045        C2017-901964-3

Edited by Sharon Hanna
Copy Edited by Allana Amlin
Typeset by Ellie Hastings
Illustrations by Owen Swain

Published with the generous assistance of the Canada Council for the Arts, which last year invested $153 million to bring the arts to Canadians throughout the country, and the financial support of the Government of Canada. Biblioasis also acknowledges the support of the Ontario Arts Council (OAC), an agency of the Government of Ontario, which last year funded 1,709 individual artists and 1,078 organizations in 204 communities across Ontario, for a total of $52.1 million, and the contribution of the Government of Ontario through the Ontario Book Publishing Tax Credit and the Ontario Media Development Corporation.

PRINTED AND BOUND IN CANADA

Photo Credits
ART GALLERY OF WINDSOR: 170; AUTHOR'S COLLECTION: 91, 92, 125, 132, 138, 139, 166, 175, 191, 192, 208, 209, 247; BONNIE AND JEFF GREENACRE: 50; ELINOR L. TAYLOR: 78; JO-ANNE GIGNAC: 31; LIBRARY AND ARCHIVES CANADA: 12; LIBRARY OF CONGRESS: 24, 112, 126, 134; MUSEUM WINDSOR: 189, 190; RICHARD FULLERTON: 28, 32, 33, 34, 36, 38, 41, 43, 46, 54; SWODA: 20, 22, 59, 66, 72, 75, 77, 94, 102-111, 113-119, 128, 130, 131, 135-137, 144, 153, 156, 158, 162, 164, 166, 169, 171, 177, 184-186, 188, 194, 203, 208, 210, 217, 221, 223, 228, 232, 235, 238; TAYLOR CAMPBELL: 17, 19, 21, 34, 35, 37, 42, 44, 48, 52, 57, 58, 65, 67, 68, 73, 79, 80-83, 85, 89, 92, 93, 99, 103, 106, 122, 124, 127, 130, 134, 135, 137, 138, 142, 143, 146, 155, 158-160, 167, 169, 171, 173, 174, 178, 180, 181, 186, 190, 198, 200, 201, 205-208, 219, 222, 224, 227, 228, 230-236, 240, 241, 243, 244; WINDSOR STAR: 10, 13, 18, 19, 21, 23, 24, 27, 29, 35, 40, 45, 49, 67-71, 74, 76, 87-89, 93, 100, 101, 120-123, 129, 132, 136, 142, 145,146, 154, 159, 161, 163, 165, 167, 172-176, 178-180, 182-184, 187, 193, 195-197, 199, 200, 202, 204, 206, 215, 216, 224, 225, 234, 243, 245, 246; WPL: 81, 82, 144

*This book, with its stories and maps and photographs, is for my grandchildren Julien, Sebastien, Calder, Cicely, Lucien, and little Violette, who lives all the way across the ocean in France, a country that sent its children to our south shore that makes up the five towns that we now call Windsor.*

# CONTENTS

# FOREWORD
## By Shawn Micallef

The Freedom Festival fireworks were always a big walking night in Windsor. By necessity certainly—Windsor's a town where you can usually park not much more than a block from wherever you're going—but it was like seeing another Windsor, a city I didn't know. When I was boy, I followed my parents down to the river, and later when I could drive on my own, I'd park and meet friends. A spot to leave the car might be found south of Elliott, Erie, or perhaps even Giles, and to get to the river we might take Mercer, McDougall, or even down mighty Ouellette—all streets I'd mostly seen through the windows of a car. These rare walks were a new kind of intimacy with the geography and crowds of the city I called home. They were cherished walks, but then I got back into the car.

Years later, I moved to Toronto without a car and discovered that city on foot, slipping down passages, along sidewalks, lingering, looking and listening, all things quite hard to do when in a car. On one trip back home, driving along the south end of Drouillard by the Chrysler minivan plant, I pulled over to the side, struck by the sheer size of the factory. I always knew it was big of course and had driven by it regularly, but I didn't know just *how* big it was. So I parked the car and walked around it. (Confirmed: it's big.) Then I walked around the GM Transmission plant before it was torn down, and have continued to walk Windsor on return visits, rediscovering a city I only knew from a distance and at speed, seeing and feeling how it's shaped and how it's put together. Yet, even these walks are only surface explorations.

This book you're holding is a much deeper incision into Windsor. It's an incredibly geographic book anchored in the physical city you can walk today but goes back in time to understand how it got this way. In walking and writing about his beloved city of Windsor, Marty Gervais has given us a social history that is both personal and historic: like all walks with somebody who knows a place well, they're part memoir, part historic record, and a celebration of place.

You might read it, like I did, with Google maps open on your phone, looking up the addresses he mentions on Streetview to see them for yourself, a digital *flâneur* or *flâneuse* along side Marty. Maybe you'll skip Google and take this book to Windsor's streets themselves, reading and walking.

Exploring a city is like wandering through library stacks, picking off random books and poking through them, then looking at the ones adjacent, discovering things by accident. Every block, every lot, every door, and everything a human has touched has at least one story behind it, often many more, and they're connected to other stories nearby. The streets are lined with books waiting to be read. Some of those stories are in here, and they are glimpses of the human network that has created and sustained Windsor.

There are stories here that could have their own chapter, just a nugget or suggestion of something in a paragraph before moving on down the sidewalk. That's how rich this book is and the city streets it travels. Windsor, like any good city worth living in, is an onion that you can keep peeling, finding new layers of life and lives lived. Read and walk on.

*–Shawn Micallef, 2017*

An aerial view of downtown Windsor, Ontario, looking north to Detroit, Michigan, c. 1960.

# INTRODUCTION

The moon lay tangled in a mess of skeletal crooked lilac trees against the sky. Voices in the street frightened me. I was six. I could hear shouting, horns, laughter, foot stomping, singing. The next morning at breakfast my father was smiling and poking at us, asking if we had overheard the revellers. It was New Year's Day, 1952. Those are my first memories of sound in Riverside, Ontario.

Or maybe it was the way we called on friends at their homes first thing in the morning. We'd race up the three-step concrete block porches of those brick wartime houses, and crane our necks to an upstairs bedroom window, and bellow out our friend's name. If you took a moment to scan the neighbourhood houses along the street, you'd see this repeated at other doorsteps—boys standing and shouting out names.

Moments later, our friends would emerge, usually madly wrestling a jacket around their shoulders, and off we'd sprint to a nearby ball diamond or south to the railway tracks that we'd follow east to what was then called, and still is, "Schiller's Bush." Back then, it was a rich forest where we'd build bonfires, and roast weenies skewered on coat hangers, dreaming of being coureurs-de-bois. Today, traces of that original bush still exist along Tranby, nearer to Lauzon. Homes now occupy where we once played.

Today is one of the last days of the old year: December 29, 2015. This winter so far has been kind. Six days ago, December 23rd, Windsor broke a 74-year-old record with temperatures reaching 12.7°C. The previous high was 12.2°C, set in 1941. I am hoping for more of this as I begin my journey through the five towns that now make up Windsor. I realize this is a town of drivers. We don't walk. We ride cars. We ride buses, but not like other towns. Our municipal transportation system pales compared to others. The city-owned bus company, Transit Windsor, for a population of more than 200,000, has 12 fixed bus routes. These are served by 112 vehicles. We didn't open a new bus terminal until nine years ago. The one downtown, sandwiched between University Avenue and Chatham Street, now being redeveloped for the University of Windsor, was built in 1940. Incidentally, it sits atop the Windsor–Detroit Tunnel and the University of Windsor has had to revamp its architectural plans for fear of hitting the exterior of the underground highway to Detroit if it digs any deeper.

The assembly line at Windsor's Chrysler plant, 1953.

For more than a century, Windsor's focus has been the manufacture of automobiles. We build them; we buy them; we drive them. We are drivers. Not walkers. Not bus riders. Six thousand men and women file into our factories that sprawl over 123 acres south of Tecumseh Road to build Dodge, Grand Caravan, and Chrysler Pacifica minivans. These auto workers drive to work. Parking lots are conveniently provided. There's loyalty to the practice of driving to work. These same men and women dutifully paste bumper stickers to their cars to warn the world that if it dares to buy a "foreign car," it is stealing a job away from someone in Windsor. It's the Windsor mantra. Buy domestic. Don't walk. Drive to work.

It's been that way for a long time. The car has been king for so long it's hard to believe it was once otherwise. Windsor has always led the way for the country, as did Detroit. In 1922, for example, Ontario's deputy minister of highways, W.A. McLean, noted in a speech that this city boasted more concrete pavement

for its size than any other city in North America. For our cars. For getting to work. For getting home.

It was also the car that coerced governments on both sides of the river to find a better way of facilitating automobiles traversing back and forth across the border, other than the ferries. The *Border Cities Star* in the 1920s constantly reported complaints of line-ups of cars waiting for the ferry. Editorial writers described it as "intolerable." That was a time when a million passengers crossed the river each month on ferries. Neil Morrison, in *Garden Gateway to Canada*, says he wasn't surprised to learn that on May 14, 1920, some 200 passengers were left stranded in Windsor overnight because they couldn't get on the ferries to take them from the foot of Ouellette to Woodward Avenue in Detroit.

Even transforming our landscape has been a by-product of the car. Until recently, we rarely hesitated when a century-old building was demolished to make room for another parking lot. We favour parking lots. We are the parking lot capital of Canada. Between 1986 and 2016, 43 buildings were bulldozed to make room for more parking lots. Senior City Planner Greg Atkinson told the *Windsor Star*:

> We're used to the landscape now but when you look back at pictures you say, 'Oh, I remember that building, and now it's a parking lot.' So you kind of get a sense for how the cumulative effects really do negatively impact those areas we shop and work in every day... Every year you lose a couple of buildings for parking.

Windsorites frown at parking garages. Indeed, there are probably fewer parking garages in Windsor than other cities our size. In fact, we only have three. By comparison, there are nearly 30 off-street parking lots providing more than 1,500 spaces. Beyond that, the city has installed 1,512 parking metres on its streets, and there are hundreds of private and commercial lots throughout the Windsor area. We want to see our cars. Flatten the geography. Make room for the car. If we're going to walk, we'll do it from our car to the front door. It's not about laziness. It's about daily life. It's attitude. It's tradition. It's the economy. It's what we're all about.

The automobile is part of the reason we have eviscerated our landscape of its history, of its traditions. We are drive-by residents. We don't pause to soak up the scenery. We don't pull over to find if something has changed. We get behind the wheel, and drive to work, head to the mall, go to school, pull into a neighbourhood pub. We don't walk. We fly by.

Walking for health and exercise is something that has come into vogue more recently. We're concerned now with our heart rate and wear watches which track every step we take. Personally, I don't like walking, at least just for the sake of exercise. But I'm bound for this 17-kilometre walk that will take me from the far reaches of Riverside to the farthest boundary of Sandwich. I am exploring what I consider the five original Border Cities, from east to west. Beginning with Riverside, the youngest—annexed to Windsor in 1965—and on to Ford City, Walkerville, Windsor, and Sandwich, which amalgamated into the City of Windsor in 1935. I'm wearing a pair of ankle-high boots,

not particularly comfortable. I don't have proper "walking shoes." I'm not sure it matters. My adventure is to see what's missing. I want to dwell on our history, our culture. I want to re-imagine the ghostly remains of our mistakes in tearing down what our ancestors built, as they fashioned a new life along the river. I want to understand the old neighbourhood. I want to be a part of what has disappeared. I know there will be detours, and the journey will take me up Drouillard Road, into side streets and back alleys of Walkerville, and downtown to Windsor, and all the way past the University of Windsor into Sandwich. Five days. Five towns. On foot. Seeing what remains. Seeing what has been forgotten. Seeing what's been prized, and what's to see in the future, maybe. I want to touch history and understand it. I sense that the best way of approaching this is on foot. It will make me pause, to tarry and linger, and allow the landscape to stand still.

The cars of Christmas shoppers cram into a downtown municipal parking lot at the corner of Ferry Street and Riverside Drive in November, 1955.

13

# Riverside

St. Rose of Lima Church

Marty's Childhood Home

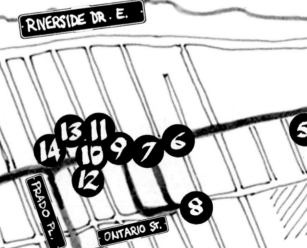

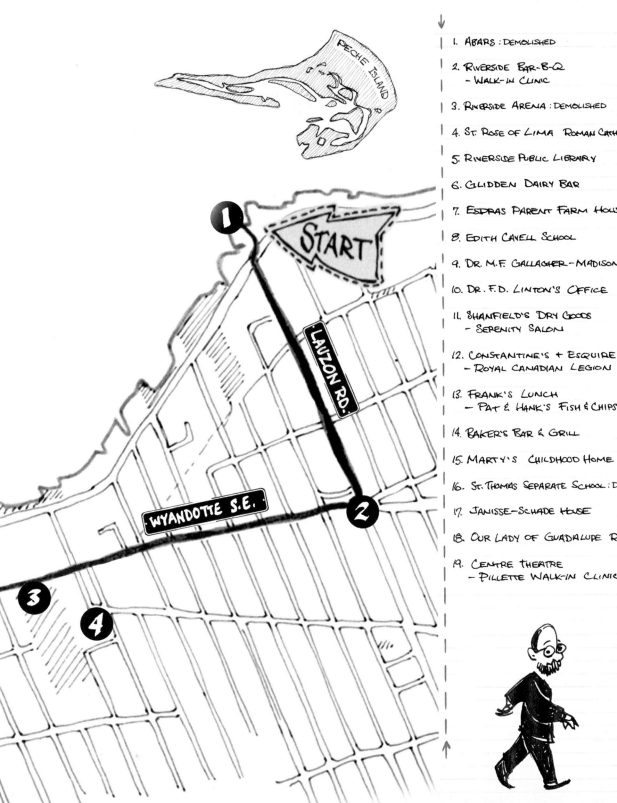

Riverside Library

Our Lady of Guadalupe Church

Riverside Sportsmen Club

Glidden Dairy Bar

# RIVERSIDE
*December 29, 2015*
*5.9 km*

My odyssey starts here, in what's now called Olde Riverside. I hate that term. I despise spelling it that way. This is simply "Riverside," the *younger* sister of the five towns. Before William St. Louis, ancestor to one of the founding French families, led the way to its incorporation in 1921, this area was part of Sandwich East Township. According to historian Neil Morrison, this was "relatively late in the history of the Windsor metropolitan area." Eight years later, some 1,155 families lived there. A decade later, the population had matured to more than 4,400 families. Morrison said this made Riverside "among the fastest growing towns in Canada." It was natural that the western section of the town developed quickly, because it was closest to Ford City, where Ford Motor Company was elbowing for more space. People could walk to work. The truck division of General Motors started up there. So did Dominion Forge and Stamping, and the Canadian Motor Lamp where my father worked. He was 16 when he landed here from Cobalt, Ontario, having migrated like thousands of others, to find a job in Ford City.

As this upsurge in industry was occurring in the late 1920s and early '30s, new homes were going up east of the factories, and many of these dwellings were one-and-a-half storey dwellings, some with wide verandahs. Riverside waned, as did other towns when the Great Depression hit, and the population remained stagnant, with school, church, and home building grinding to an abrupt halt.

## Lauzon and Riverside Drive

I begin at the foot of Lauzon and Riverside Drive. Before me is Abars (7880 Riverside Drive East), a towering three-storey building,

"Olde Riverside" street signs, located from the 5400 to 5900 block of Wyandotte Street East.

closed recently. The last of the roadhouses from the glory days of Prohibition. This ramshackle frame building, dozing at the end of the Drive, actually started up in 1904 and was called Island View Hotel. It was built by Albert Hébert, son of Henri Hébert, a fisherman, who also owned another hotel at the mouth of Little River, east of Lauzon. People always referred to Island View, however, as Abars—really a bastardization of the French pronunciation "Hébert." In Windsor, we regularly anglicize French names, so a street name "Pierre" becomes "Peerie." The fisherman Hébert reasoned that the anglicized name was easier to deal with when he first registered the name "Abars," and his family continued to own the hotel for three generations. Originally it was a stop on a stage-coach line, and the hitching rail at the front remained there for a long time even after the ascent of the automobile. The Hébert family sold the business to the Jacksons in the 1940s, and in 1951, it changed hands again, this time to the Dutka family.

Sprawling behind it today rests a string of collapsing warped and wooden docks that stretch westward, like twisted bony fingers, out into the Detroit River. There was a time when Babe Ruth made his way from across the water to step ashore here and eat and drink and dance with rouge-faced flappers. The Yankees were frequent guests of Madame Hébert. She would sit at the entrance, draped in jewellery, and she'd greet the ballplayers and movie stars and the auto company owners at the door, gladly taking their money. This was the Roaring Twenties when it wasn't

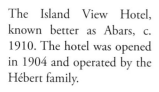

The Island View Hotel, known better as Abars, c. 1910. The hotel was opened in 1904 and operated by the Hébert family.

uncommon to see the likes of mobsters like Al Capone and Lucky Luciano, or movie stars like Lillian Gish and Marlene Dietrich, come through the door. The place was a riverfront jewel. As I stand in front of it today, as we near the end of 2015, the place is shuttered. Its future is uncertain. Some envisage a revival, a bustling pub. City fathers, on the other hand, dream of open parkland. Its owner, the inimitable American business mogul Manuel Moroun, imagined anchoring another bridge here, but gave that up a long time ago when he turned his focus to Sandwich. Since buying the Ambassador Bridge from the Bower Family in 1979, he has set his sights on twinning the bridge. It's clear that he cares nothing for history.

There are those in the city who may not know the roadhouse's past. Its moment in history began with the start of Prohibition in 1920. Like others in the business, Madame Hébert understood how business had to be conducted. She had hammered out an agreement with her rivals—Thomas' Edgewater Inn, and the Rendezvous, both farther east—to protect these colourful establishments from the police raids. The places were wired with a linked buzzer system, so that when the spotters—or boys or men positioned in the upper-storey windows—caught sight of approaching police, the other roadhouses would be warned.

If you look at the old photographs from those days you will notice that the windows on these roadhouses faced east and west, and not so much towards the river. They were designed that way. A long-lost cousin of my mom's from Stoney Point, Ontario, worked for Bertha Thomas at the Edgewater as a spotter. Day and night, this 16-year-old boy slumped in a window facing west. Bertha would send his meals upstairs. He was paid $20 a week, and roomed with another kid his age.

At left is the former site of Abars, at Lauzon Road and Riverside Drive. The Prohibition-era roadhouse, pictured at right in its heyday in the 1940s, was demolished seven months after my walk.

I stand here, gazing at Abars, knowing that there is more to the east, some of it now sheltered only in memory because we have succeeded in subtracting all evidence of its history. That's always been our way, at least until recently. Today we speak of what once was, instead of what still remains. What is there about our population—our forefathers who blindly turned the other way? Did they not care? I don't believe it was genuine refusal, or a conscious decision. We did it without thinking, like someone tossing out clutter from an old desk, never considering its value. We certainly failed to nurture our history; otherwise, we wouldn't have dispatched work crews to get rid of the evidence.

Sometimes it was for expediency. As I wend my way through Riverside, I discover that with progress comes change, and change can also trigger anxiety about the future. If you head along Wyandotte—before 1943, it was called Ottawa Street—you will notice street names reflect the founding French families whose farms stretched from the riverfront to what is now Tecumseh Road. With the explosive development in neighbouring Ford City of the Ford Motor Company, says Riverside historian Rick Fullerton, the fear among these early families was that their lands would be expropriated, and they wouldn't get the value of them. It became imperative to subdivide and sell immediately; otherwise they might be too late. Hence, the farms were broken up. Today, imagine residing on Esdras or St. Louis or Villaire or Prado, and suddenly realizing that your home rests on the soil once inhabited by these farmers, many of whom hailed from either the Normandy coast or Lorraine, close to the German border.

Standing on the Drive facing east, approximately two kilometres away, the shoreline juts out into the river. Tenants in the condos of Solidarity Towers (8888 Riverside Drive East) may be unaware that this was called Drouillard Point in the 19th century.

They may not know the story from 1896, when a tough, handlebar-moustached, German-born roadhouse owner bribed a border guard in Germany to escape the clutches of the Kaiser. Wolfgang Feller found his way to this river, and from the moment he put down stakes, he reigned over 79 acres himself and operated a fish hatchery on that thorny scrubland, Peche Island. Today, all that exists on the island that lies east of Belle Isle and smack dab in the middle of the Detroit River is a small provincial government brick building with a Canadian flag that flaps in the wind. Feller ruled Drouillard Point, running a spirited roadhouse, called simply Wolf's Roadhouse. The place continued for 30 years, until 1926,

Wolf's Roadhouse, at Drouillard Point, c. 1913.

At left is Bertha Thomas' famed roadhouse, the Edgewater Thomas Inn, pictured in 1946. The original inn burned down in 1970. This site is now occupied by Lilly Kazzilly's, pictured at right.

right near the end of Prohibition in Ontario, when he sold it.

Initially, Feller ran this place as a blind pig, but once he acquired a liquor licence, it opened up to a freewheeling alehouse. Prohibition put a damper on it with Abars' Island View and the Edgewater, both nearby, eclipsing his enterprise. That may have prompted Feller to sell the roadhouse and the land for $25,000, to the automobile manufacturers Horace and John Dodge and Detroit City Clerk Robert Oakman. Feller died in 1931, and is buried in St. Alphonsus Cemetery.

A stone's throw away, there is Lilly Kazilly's Restaurant (9550 Riverside Drive East), an infant along the shoreline against the backdrop of a rich and exciting history. This was the spot once occupied by The Edgewater, operated by the iconic and flamboyant Bertha Thomas. Before Bertha, however, the Hébert family actually also owned this property, and managed a small hotel on the spot. Bertha was Riverside's queen. She bestowed her favours on the population. Especially the poor. Her minions distributed groceries to struggling families. Bertha also had a soft spot for orphans, offering gifts of clothing. Every Halloween, Bertha threw a party for all the kids in Riverside.

*Maclean's Magazine* in 1953 described Bertha and her roadhouse this way: "Bertha was buxom, beautiful, full of personality, a Canadian counterpart of Manhattan's Texas Guinan. Her meals were good, her drinks were good, her band was lively."

Several years ago, I met a 99-year-old woman, Dorothy Lavallee, when she lived at

A young Bertha Thomas, at right, with a companion some identify as her lawyer, c. 1920s.

A postcard showing the interior of the Edgewater Thomas Inn, dated 1944.

Devonshire Seniors Residence, and she told me all about working with Bertha Thomas. She had an album resting on the bed beside her, and when I flipped it open, there were photos and old clippings about this woman who was born in California, but came to live with her family in southwestern Ontario.

Hers was a story of working in the hospitality industry—restaurants and hotels and bars. Dorothy landed a job at the Edgewater and toiled under the tutelage of Bertha. She said this eccentric philanthropist ran her supper club with an iron fist. Each day began the same, with Bertha making the waitresses line up outside the kitchen for inspection.

"She would check our shoes, what we were wearing, our hair, everything," said Dorothy. "If something wasn't right, she'd tell you. You had to be on the ball. You did what you were told. She didn't miss a thing."

While Dorothy resented the woman's strict ways, she carried the skills she learned at the

Edgewater to Phoenix, Arizona, where she managed a few clubs. Eventually she would return to Windsor to take over Bertha's old inn, then owned by the Klein family. Dorothy said the restaurant had fallen on hard times, and had lost a lot of money, but her management brought it back. "I had that place hopping," she said. What she had done was what Bertha had always done: infuse the staff with discipline, pride, and high standards.

To most people, Bertha was a mystery. She lived on the second floor of the roadhouse in a lavishly decorated apartment. Upstairs were also some private rooms and, according to Dorothy, the politicians and those "in the money" would make their way to see her. "I know this, because I had to bring the whisky up there," said Dorothy. She suspected these patrons might have been connected with those managing the booze operations in Detroit and Chicago. Rumours of Al Capone coming there are well-founded, she said, but she never saw him.

Bertha was vigilant in monitoring the comings and goings of the law. Most of the time, she had the police in her pocket. It permitted her to operate unencumbered, and if it meant escorting the occasional vigilant police officer out the door, she would do it herself—or make sure that he was accommodated. She'd snap her fingers at waitresses to fetch steaks and frog legs. "She treated them royally," said Dorothy. "They didn't give her any trouble."

However, Bertha had good reason to worry. Occasionally, even though she doled out bribes to police and judges to keep them away from catching her in the act of serving liquor and carrying on with organized gambling, a zealous sergeant might take it upon himself to conduct a raid. Dorothy said the staff instantly knew what to do. When the lights flashed on and off, they would jump into action, dumping their trays, leaving the carpeting in the roadhouse damp with champagne. Dorothy said: "If the carpets could talk, you would never understand them—they would be drunk with all the booze we poured into them."

At one point, Bertha was sentenced to three months in jail, but never served that term. She managed to wriggle out of it. Her lawyers acknowledged that indeed there was alcohol content in the floorboards that had been ripped up, but it wasn't from patrons dumping their glasses into the thick carpeting. Instead, they argued that the alcohol was part of the chemical ingredients in what was painted over the planked floor. The case was thrown out of court.

Farther along the river, roughly a kilometre away, stands the Riverside Brewery—a tall, red-brick building facing north. The faded lettering proclaims its tie to the Roaring Twenties. One of the 29 breweries that sprang forth in the 1920s in the heyday of Prohibition, it was there to serve Americans. Its foundation set down as close to the American shoreline as it could—hugging the edge of the Detroit River. From its loading docks ferried "The Taste Tells," while its owners were reaping dollars hand over fist. There's a lovely advertisement that shows a family picnicking outside with mom and dad and all the children kicking back with a few brews. A family that drinks together, stays together.

The Riverside Brewery, which still stands at Riverside Drive East, near Sandpoint Beach, in 1926.

Riverside Brewery wasn't one of the more successful ones. Indeed, it ran into trouble about two years after it opened in 1926. It was started by J.F. Kirsch, who was the former owner of the local Yacht Club. It appeared that the brewery would do well initially because it had lured Otto Rosenbusch, brewmaster for the Stroh Brewing Company of Detroit, to join it as an investor. Riverside Brewery made it even more convenient for export when it managed to convince authorities to establish a federal government export dock right at the edge of the Detroit River.

Peche Island was less than five minutes away, and so boaters could easily whisk the contraband over there before finding a covert way of conveying it into Michigan.

Business tycoon and founder of Canadian Breweries Ltd. E.P. Taylor picked up control of Riverside Brewery in 1935. He already owned the British American Brewing Company in downtown Windsor, and the reason for buying it was to shut it down. Then he quickly sold off Riverside's assets for $27,000. As one writer noted in a history of the brewery, "On a blustery day in 1935, with white caps on the Detroit River… the brewery dumped what was left of their products, including the contents of their bottled beer and ale, into the Detroit River."

Derelict cottages that fronted the Detroit River were temporarily declared unfit for human habitation in the early 1950s. This area is now Sandpoint Beach.

A view of Peche Island, taken by the Detroit Photographic Company, c. 1900.

Adjacent to the former brewery is Sandpoint Beach. For years, up until the late 1960s, a succession of derelict cottages fronted the river. I lived in one of them briefly in the spring of 1969, fending off constant flooding. I had a clear view of Peche Island to the west —its eastern extremity is exposed to the current. But when I lived in that clapboard shack, I knew nothing of the mystery and intrigue that surrounded this quiet place. Though it has never been able to raise itself into a proper tourist site, Peche has never been considered part of Riverside—at least not in any legal way. Riverside people, however, regarded it like a foster kid, a part of the family.

As far as the mystery behind it, there's plenty to wonder about, if you believe the lore. The island is supposedly cursed. At one point, it boasted of thriving subsistence farming, but as soon as the Walker family muscled their way into owning it, exiling the Walpole Island-born Rosalie Drouillard, the place was damned. Not long after coercing the widow Drouillard into this deal, Walker's lawyer, Willis Walker—who cunningly engineered and handled all the legal work—dropped dead of a heart attack. He was 28 years old.

Local historian Elaine Weeks in *The Walkerville Times,* however, believes jurisdiction has plagued the island from the beginning of time, or so legend intimates. No one discerned that when the lands were transferred to the Crown in the late 18th century, when the French inhabited this area, the Aboriginal population slyly and conveniently excluded it. They kept this slice of paradise as a fishing spot. That fact did not prevent the island's first farmer, Jean Baptiste Laforet dit Tenor, from settling there about 1800. In his diary, surveyor John A. Wilkinson reported meeting Laforet in 1834. He noted the farmer had been there for 34 years. Others argue that Jean Baptiste Laforest (the "s" was eventually dropped) had ownership of the island as early as 1780. He had been awarded this for his service as an interpreter and guide to the British Army. Jean apparently moved to the island, raised a family and farmed. If this theory is correct, the first white person to be born there was Jean Mary Laforest in January, 1781.

The Laforet family continued to live there for a hundred years, sharing it with the native people who inhabited its western extremities. According to Weeks, the family secured ownership from the native people in exchange for livestock. Nevertheless, in 1857, Peche Island was formally transferred to the Crown. However, Weeks says this deal was never taken seriously because according to a report from Essex County Council in 1873, most considered the Laforets the island's defacto owners: "Their ancestors having been in possession for a long series of years, and having always regarded the place as their home, and considered that they would be awarded at least squatters' privileges in respect of the said island… the island may if sold, be sold to the said Laforet or Teno family…"

The last of the Laforets to live there were Leo (grandson of Jean Baptiste) and his wife, Rosalie Drouillard. She was the daughter of a native interpreter, and was known for weaving and selling straw hats in Detroit. She and her husband farmed and fished, and staked out four acres for themselves in 1867 at the time of Confederation. In 1870, Windsor businessman William G. Hall entered the picture and acquired 106 acres, all the lands of Peche except for the four acres owned by the Laforets, at a price of $2,900. When Hall died in 1882, his executor sold the island with its fishing privileges to Hiram Walker's sons, who bought it as a gift for their father. Benjamin Laforet, a descendant of Jean Baptiste, disputed the purchase. He claimed that he and his brother had a one-third interest in a parcel of that land. The case was settled in Benjamin Laforet's favour and he received a cash payout. However, Leo and Rosalie still lived on their four acres, creating a problem for the Walkers.

When Leo also died late in 1882, Walker's thugs strong-armed Rosalie and her sons to sign the land over to the Walker family. The whisky company men slammed down $300 on the table, giving her no choice, and set an eviction notice for the spring. This was 1883. During the winter, an intruder spoiled the family's winter stores. Rosalie, however, managed to survive through the spring. But before leaving, she knelt down on the land, and cursed the Walkers, and the island. According to Weeks, the words she uttered were: "No one will ever do anything with the island."

Never anticipating trouble ahead, Hiram Walker built a 40-room estate, dug canals, introduced electricity, set up a golf course, planted hundreds of trees and a peach orchard, and erected an elaborate greenhouse. This was accomplished in an effort to develop not only a retirement home, but to lure cultured high society to its shores where he would create a resort. Instead, his wealthy friends rushed to Belle Isle, farther upstream.

An early photograph showing Rosalie Drouillard with her son, Alex Laforet.

Hiram finally gave up, fell ill, suffered a stroke, and handed over the island to his daughter, Elizabeth, who quickly incurred the wrath of area residents when she refused to give them the peach harvest. Instead, out of spite, she dumped the fruit into the Detroit River.

In 1907, Elizabeth rid herself of the island and the estate. She was tired of ferrying executives and family back and forth across the river. She sold the mansion to Walter E. Campbell, owner of the Detroit and Windsor Ferry Company. He told the *Detroit News* on November 11, 1907, that the massive and elaborate Walker Estate would be converted into "a temporary pavilion." He envisioned creating "one of the one of the finest island summer resorts in America." Instead, Campbell died suddenly, in the mansion on the island, only months after buying the property. Still owned by the ferry company, the island lay abandoned for years, all through Prohibition. In 1929, lightning struck and the mansion burned to the ground. The foundations of the estate can still be seen on the island.

All attempts of transforming Peche Island into a viable resort failed miserably. The Bob-Lo Company eventually took it over. Some contend it was their way of deterring a future competitor for its own highly popular amusement park near Amherstburg. Bob-Lo held on to its ownership until 1956. From that point on, the island fell under the ownership of a series of others, all to no avail. There was a brief moment in the late 1960s when a businessman attempted to set up a zoo, and actually set up an operation to house bears and cougars and rare birds. When it failed, he shut it down, but not before opening up the cages and letting the wildlife free. In Riverside, people tell the story of a bear running down Wyandotte one early morning. In 1974, the province acquired the island and turned it into a provincial park. The City of Windsor stepped in to gain control of the island in 1999 as a municipal park, but has done nothing to develop or enhance it.

Farther along to the east was The Rendezvous. Nothing remains of that Roaring Twenties roadhouse with its false walls and hidden vaults. An entrance gate that opens up to manicured lawns and stylish residences reads: *Rendezvous Shores.* Few in that subdivision likely realize that this was once one of the most popular dining places in Essex County. It was one of the few establishments where you

could dine on fresh pickerel, perch, and frog's legs. Staff continued to serve those old "shore dinners." The sprawling restaurant, with its spacious ballroom floor, hearkened back to the 1920s when its lights never went out until the wee hours of the morning.

In between the two former roadhouses—the Edgewater and the Rendezvous—is another Riverside institution: the Riverside Sportsmen's Club (10835 Riverside Drive East). The place has been on this site since 1946 when hotel entrepreneur Danny Bell (a big name in the hotel business during Prohibition) started it. He was the first president with Clyde Hyde as secretary/treasurer. The club purchased the property from Riverside Drive to the CNR tracks, and the money to buy it was raised from raffles and 50/50 draws each month. The original building was constructed by Guido Fantin

The Rendezvous Hotel, pictured here in an undated photograph, is now the site of an upscale subdivision, Rendezvous Shores.

The Riverside Sportsmen's Club, pictured here in the late 1940s, was originally surrounded by swampland that regularly flooded.

and Murray Russell. Originally, the Riverside Sportsmen executives held club meetings at the Rendezvous. Their organization's aim was to promote conservation and to nurture junior sportsmen. In 1960, the company extended its quarters, adding a 2,400 square-foot hall. This meant selling off a major chunk of its land. Originally, it owned 34 acres.

At the time of the purchase, right after the war, the site of this club wasn't such a steal because the land was swampy. It necessitated trucking in more than 2,000 loads of dirt. As a matter of fact, there is a 1940s photograph

Riverside Bar-B-Q was located at the northeast corner of Lauzon Road and Wyandotte Street East. Today, this spot is occupied by a walk-in clinic.

of the club, nicely reflected and surrounded by what appears to be a lake.

*Lauzon and Wyandotte*

I have reminisced on these stories from along the Detroit River long enough. It's time to start walking. I travel south on Lauzon until I reach Wyandotte. Turning, I venture west. Across the street, on the south side, at the corner of Lauzon was the former Riverside Bar-B-Q. It was housed in a low building with a canvas awning. Now, there is a walk-in clinic (7885 Wyandotte Street East) in its place. Not far from there, on the same side of the street is Roma's Pizza House (7805 Wyandotte Street East). I wondered if it was somehow related to the old Roma's Bakery that used to be a few doors down from Frank's Lunch in the Almina Building near Prado and Villaire.

I am now venturing into childhood, my life as I remember it in Riverside, though I rarely, if ever, reached this fringe of the town. I left

Riverside in the late summer of 1958, when my father's company, the Canadian Motor Lamp, moved part of its operation to Bracebridge, Ontario. My neighbourhood—situated in that corridor that ran between Pillette and Jefferson—was farther west. Growing up there I gleaned little of our history. I lived during the Cold War. I knew the face of Eisenhower. I knew the exploits of General Patton. In school, we studied the American Civil War, memorized the presidents of the United States, and coloured in countless maps of the United States in geography. We heard Senator Joe McCarthy's "Red Scare" radio broadcasts, tuned into Fulton Sheen and got on our knees on the kitchen's linoleum and prayed the rosary with this American bishop. I'm confident in saying that few Canadian children growing up in the 1950s ever felt the same way that we did at this end of the province. Our lives were tied to Detroit.

Like a thousand other kids in the Border Cities, we were politically conscious. The Korean War flashed nightly on our black and white television sets. It was as much our war as it was the Americans'. Russia was our enemy, too. As a Catholic, we marched in May Day parades, paralleling, and protesting the parades in Moscow Square. Our rally with floats and banners streamed down Ouellette Avenue, saluting the bishop and praying for peace. We were called the Blue Army after Mother Mary, as opposed to the Red Army. Meanwhile, our neighbours dug bomb shelters, and every Saturday afternoon we heard the air raid warning sirens blaring across the Detroit River.

We feared the end of the world.

Then, Russia suddenly got closer with the orbit of the 184-pound Sputnik satellite in October 1957. I recall the commotion over this silver rocket, and to this day believe that I observed it glide over Riverside. I sprinted out to the vacant lot adjacent to our house on Prado to peer up at the sky after hearing a radio announcer report that it had been sighted. I swear that I spotted this sliver of silver glint as it sailed high above our house. I'm not sure anymore if I simply imagined this, but an

Young Catholic girls march in Windsor's ninth annual Mary Day parade up Ouellette Avenue in 1957.

**Soviet Russia's Satellite Now Circling Earth**

Skies the Limit
SUNNY, WARMER
6 a.m. 44, 4 p.m. 61
Low tonight 42, high Sunday 65
See details, P. 6

**The Windsor Daily Star**

Late Sport
Churches P. 8, 9
★★★★
Theatres, Amusements P. 12, 13

The Canadian Press—Associated Press—United Press—Reuters—Associated Press Wirephoto

VOL. 79, NO. 29    2 PAGES    WINDSOR, ONTARIO, CANADA, SATURDAY, OCTOBER 5, 1957    Authorized as Second Class Mail Post Office Department, Ottawa    SIX CENTS

article by Paul Dickson called *Sputnik's Impact on America* held out hope that it was true. He claimed, "Not only could you hear Sputnik, but, depending upon where you were, it was possible to see it with the naked eye in the early morning or the late evening…"

That was the era in which we lived. And so when it came to our heritage, sure, we might touch upon Jacques Cartier, and the coureurs de bois, but no one ever spoke about the St. Louis family and the farmers whose soil now abounds with homes and churches and businesses. No one ever confided to me the tale of Louis Villaire dit St. Louis, a man raised in the seminary, but who turned away from being ordained. Here was someone of great piety, according to writer Irene Hare in *Our Town: Memories of Riverside, Ontario 1921–1966*. So "saintly" was he that area people called him St. Louis—which is where the family name comes from.

Louis Villaire dit St. Louis, a soldier with the French army, settled at the mouth of Turkey Creek at LaSalle in 1749—not in what is now Riverside. As part of the French Government's offer, he was also awarded one cow, a hoe and an axe, 20 bushels of wheat, and 80 roofing nails. It was pretty clear what he had to do. And he went ahead and settled there. Louis St. Louis, Jr., however, his son, was the one

who 31 years later forged that deal with the native peoples, gobbling up 300 acres from the Detroit River straight south into the wilderness into what is now Riverside.

When the British defeated the French, the original deed, or transfer of ownership to the St. Louis family, apparently made with the Ottawa First Nations people was signed by Chief Francis Macouse with a mark of notched sticks. He shows the boundaries of the farm as extending from Riverside Drive to Concession bordered by Villaire and St. Louis. Louis literally built himself a palisade there, and was the first settler to clear the virgin forest for farming. There were no roads then, simply a trail in front of his house, mostly made by him or his First Nations neighbours. There was also the Detroit River. The shoreline in those days often flooded, leaving it swampy and low, and sometimes the surrounding land impassable. Today, if you wander down Villaire, St. Louis, or upper Reedmere on the west side, you would be trespassing on his original farm. This was my old neighbourhood. This is where I grew up, went to school, and farther to the west, attended Our Lady of Guadalupe Church and the former Centre Movie Theatre. This was my world.

Back to Louis Jr.: he was 79 when he died. His son Francois inherited the homestead

A St. Louis family reunion in 1895, showing Leander's farmhouse, which still stands today at 7075 Riverside Drive East, though heavily renovated.

in 1826, and the tales that surround him are legion. One in particular, which would have thrilled me as a boy, was how the young Francois was nearly executed by Aboriginal warriors when he allegedly killed one of their ponies. The younger St. Louis somehow managed to negotiate his release by offering his accusers a substantial store of supplies. In time, he came to be their friend. Indeed, they turned to him in times of setbacks. He was their "saint."

Francois' home is long gone, but parts of it may have been incorporated in the home at 7075 Riverside Drive East. At least parts of the original log foundations. Not that you can actually see them, but they're there, or at least, that's the common belief passed down from one generation to the next.

Francois was among a few of the French population to join General Brock as an officer, along with others from his family, during the War of 1812. In 1844, before Francois died, he purchased additional property for his son, Leander, further east between St. Rose Avenue and Isabelle Place. Leander's farmhouse, built in 1850, still stands today at 7075 Riverside Drive East, but originally it was on the site of 6945 Riverside Drive East. Leander moved it, piece by piece, with horses and logs. He did this so that his own son, Alexander, could build a house in 1880 at 6945 Riverside. That particular two-storey building was still standing up until a few years ago. The property, though not considered a part of Windsor's heritage list, even though its history dates back to Leander's original homestead. But there is nothing there to indicate it. Windsor City Councillor Jo-Anne Gignac, whose great, great, great grandfather was Francois, was "heartbroken" when the house that Alexander built was demolished. "It was magnificent, its stone foundation brought from Amherstburg and beautiful wide board floors cut from our trees, it must have been a massive undertaking."

As for Leander's house, now sitting at 7075 Riverside Drive East, much of its original features, with its broad front porch, have been masked by renovations over time. The porch is entirely gone. Jo-Anne Gignac reiterates the belief that the original logs from Francois' fortress still exist "at the core of 7075 (the living quarters which was expanded overtime) by the time it was moved…" She gave me this rare photograph of that rambling house built by Leander. It shows a family reunion from 1895. You can barely recognize the original. Leander, by the way, may have been successful as a farmer, but he was also wily real estate man as far back as the 19th century. By the time of his death, he had acquired 320 hectares of Sandwich East property.

Another figure who proved to be prominent in the St. Louis family with the founding of Riverside was Leander's grandson, William, who inherited the original family farm that was situated between Villaire and St. Louis on the south side. Like his father, who had political ambitions and served on township councils, William pursued a similar career. He was better educated and knew how to reach a consensus among people. This led to making Riverside a town, separate from Sandwich East Township. It also resulted in William becoming the new municipality's first mayor in 1921.

During the 1920s, the family sold off much of its holdings from the original farm lot for new home construction. Brothers Alphonse and Alfred St. Louis also donated a parcel of land to the diocese to build St. Rose of Lima Church. The building of Riverside Arena too, has its roots in the St. Louis family. It came about one hot summer day in the 1950s, when Leo St. Louis, Cliff Chauvin, John Dunlop and Ray Adam were relaxing on the steps of the town hall. The four got talking, and suddenly began dreaming up the idea of building an arena. "They dumped change from their pockets into a tin cup to get the ball rolling," writes Hare. The group managed to lure Ford Motor Company and Hiram Walker into making major donations, as well as securing commitments of building materials and time from local construction companies.

## St. Rose and Wyandotte

This brings me farther west down the street, another two kilometres. Walking this route

Riverside Arena was built in 1956–57 and demolished in 2011. The former site of the arena sits at 6755 Wyandotte Street East.

in these wintry months is the best, because it's easier to size up the landscape, trace the outlines of the steep rooftops of the wartime houses, and identify the schools, churches, and new apartment buildings. It's disconcerting to see the vast vacant area where Riverside Arena (6755 Wyandotte Street East) once stood. Construction on that building—really the first municipal arena in the Windsor area—started in 1956. It was opened a year later. I personally have no recollection of the place, except in more recent years when my own sons played hockey in tournaments there. I did play baseball with the Riverside Tigers, a house league team, in the open fields that lay behind the rink, or before there was an arena there. I can't forget the day the coach wheeled up to the grassy field in a sprawling *Forward Look* De Soto, flipped up the trunk, and start tossing cotton t-shirts and

ball caps to us. There's a photograph seen below, from the 1950s marking the involvement of the Riverside Firefighters who put up the money to run this Pee Wee Baseball league. I vaguely remember the group shot being taken that day. I was using my older brother's fielder's glove, and it was far too large for my hand. I can't for the life of me pick out where I am in that picture. I am probably stuck behind someone.

Standing on that empty lot today, right across the street from the Metro grocery store, I see the blunt steeple of St. Rose of Lima Catholic Church (891 St. Rose Avenue) rising above a clutter of homes and the school of the same name to the west of it. I served mass at that church from time to time in the 1950s, but always on loan from Our Lady of Guadalupe Church farther down Wyandotte. St. Rose was an offspring of Our Lady of the Lake parish

Pictured at left is me in my Riverside baseball jacket, age six or seven. At right, members of the Riverside Minor Baseball Association (including myself) wave at the camera in this 1950s shot.

at the foot of Drouillard and Riverside Drive, or as it has always been known, Holy Rosary. With the population moving eastward, Father F.X. Laurendeau of Holy Rosary petitioned the London Diocese bishop to permit him to set up a new parish in Riverside. Alfred St. Louis, Alphonse St. Louis, and Eugene Mailloux stepped forward to donate the land.

At right is St. Rose of Lima Catholic Church, located at 891 Rose Avenue. It closed in 2011.

Below, a Model A travels down St. Rose Avenue in 1926, in this view looking south to Ottawa Street from Riverside Drive. St. Rose of Lima Catholic Church, two years after opening, can be seen in the background.

Blonde Contractors of Chatham built the church that was designed by the renowned local architect John Boyde. He opted for a red-brick Romanesque structure with a 60-foot-high entrance tower, with double wooden doors with a crucifix design, limestone panels, and central arched stained glass windows. The interior, in keeping with the overall design, has a domed ceiling. At the laying of the cornerstone, some 2,500 turned out in June 1924. The first mass to be held there was November 16, 1924.

St. Rose of Lima is significant to Riverside. It was the first church of any denomination to be built in the town since incorporation. When it opened, its membership was 150 families. By 1951, more than 1,000 families were on the church rolls. Such growth prompted the start of Our Lady of Guadalupe in 1951, and later, St. John Vianney and St. Thomas the Apostle.

I have seen photographs from that period. One from May 1926 shows St. Rose Avenue looking south from Wyandotte—then known as Ottawa Street. A Model A is cruising towards the camera. St. Rose sits at the end of the street. Nearly adjacent was St. Peter's School, situated northeast of the church, and behind the school there is a tree-less, empty, endless stretch. Today, that school is gone, but St. Rose School has been there since 1953. It likely borrows its name from Sister St. Rose, who taught at the former École St. Louis, the area's first separate school, then located on St. Rose Avenue, and dating back to 1895. Or maybe it's from the church itself. Sister Rose was the first sister of the Order of Sisters of St. Joseph to work in the schools in Riverside. The convent in those days was closer to Our Lady of the Lake church. According to Fullerton's *Our Town: A History of Riverside*, "on occasions when the weather was so inclement as to prevent her from returning to her convent in the evenings, the home of Alex St. Louis… was always a secure shelter." This seems incredible, because the distance between the church at the foot of Drouillard Road and the school isn't any more than a five-minute car ride today.

## Victor, Patrice, Jefferson

As I continue towards Jefferson, there is Riverside Public Library (6305 Wyandotte Street East) at Victor and Wyandotte. But before being placed here, the town opened a library at St. Mary's Boulevard and Wyandotte in the former public utilities building. That was in 1955. I remember it well, because I signed up for a library card right after the official opening. I was nine years old. The first book that I borrowed was Mark Twain's *Huckleberry Finn*. I remember that because my brother owned a copy of the book and wouldn't let me read it. I carried the library book home proudly, and brandished it dramatically in his face. I also had that sense that I had joined a club, that I was part of something. It may have been the advent of awareness about books that I had never felt before.

Above: town officials break ground for Riverside's first standalone library, located at Wyandotte and Patrice streets, in November 1954.

Left: Isabelle Place and St. Rose Avenue street signs.

Names of the streets have always fascinated me. Except maybe when I was a boy. Back then, I am certain that I never cared, never gave it much thought. Heading westward along Wyandotte, Victor Drive, for example, derives from Victor Reaume, brother to Patrice Reaume, one of the original French settlers.

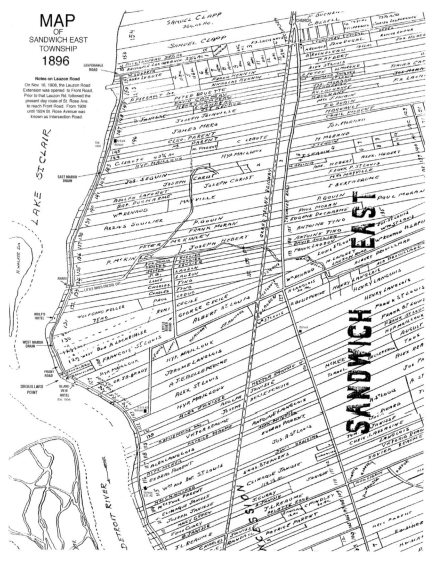

MAP
OF
SANDWICH EAST
TOWNSHIP
1896

Notes on Lauzon Road
On Nov. 16, 1908, the Lauzon Road Extension was opened to Front Road. Prior to that Lauzon Rd. followed the present day route of St. Rose Ave. to reach Front Road. From 1908 until 1924 St. Rose Avenue was known as Intersection Road.

This map of Sandwich East Township from 1896 shows the pattern of French ribbon farms that were established along the Detroit River in the 1700s.

The same rationale applied to so many others. Like Isabelle Place that I've just passed, a name chosen to honour Isabelle Belleperche, wife of Adolph J.E. Belleperche, also one of the French pioneers. Janisse Drive also dates from the early 19th century French settlement. There was

Joseph and Clinaque, Tom, and Charles, whose farms were opposite Belle Isle. Later, A.O. Janisse, trying to emulate Orville and Wilbur Wright's famous 1903 flight, built himself an airplane, and according to Morrison, intended to fly it in August 1911 from the Canadian shore to Belle Isle. Right across the Detroit River. As far as anyone knows, he abandoned that flight, but it may have been Janisse who "stirred the hearts of Harrow residents when 'an airship floated gracefully over the section, heading southwest.'"

On the other hand, some streets bear no connection to the French. Bertha Avenue was named for roadhouse owner Bertha Thomas. Jefferson was the choice of Kenning Real Estate Co. of Detroit, which oversaw the development of that street and wanted it christened after the downtown boulevard across the river. Matthew Brady Boulevard referred to the doctor of the same name. St. Paul was after the reclusive and scholarly Paul Le Duc's, one of the most colourful—and maybe least known—figures in our history. His love for education led to the building of the long-forgotten Edith Cavell School.

Le Duc owned the property at the foot of Reedmere Road, where the first steam ferry boats used to stop to collect the supply of wood needed for keeping the vessels operating. This pipe-smoking, eccentric area pioneer, who never married, was also friends of Horace and John Dodge. So close, in fact, that the Dodges offered to buy his home on Reedmere Road. Irene Hare, in an article about Le Duc in *Our Town: A History of Riverside*, claims that

Dodge handed Le Duc a blank cheque, signed with his name, and told him to write "whatever amount" he wanted on it. Le Duc apparently turned down his wealthy Detroit friend, and remarked that there wasn't "enough money (in the world) to buy this place." Fullerton wrote: "This was said, not in a spirit of bravado or of belittling the millionaire's fortune but merely pointing out he so loved the home of his ancestors… every sold and well-seasoned board that had gone into its construction.

Reedmere is one name that eludes everyone. Fullerton pointed out that often it's linked to a castle, a place in England. Really, there's no known connection, except maybe to the English language. At one time, the area around the present day Reedmere was perpetually flooded from a creek that ran between Reedmere and St. Louis. The name "reed" was derived from the tall grasses, or reeds, that lined that brook. And the term "mere" apparently comes from an archaic English term meaning "a standing sheet of water."

The streets in Riverside running north and south, however, do reflect the seigneurial system of farming laid out by Cardinal Richelieu and the French monarchy when its soldiers invaded North America.

The names, for the most part, represent the original land grants awarded by the King. As in Quebec along the St. Lawrence, these narrow farms stretched ribbon-like from the river. The physical layout was designed this way, partly to encourage transit. The river became the highway, the most efficient means of transportation.

Now when you stroll this stretch, either along Wyandotte or Riverside Drive, you will notice that the distance between the streets is short, sometimes enough for only one or two houses, but never more. That explains the design of Windsor as a collection of north/south streets with few thoroughfares to transport one from east to west. E.C. Row was a breakthrough when it was finally finished in 1983. Up until then, the only two efficient ways of crossing the five communities was to take Tecumseh Road or the Drive. Otherwise, you were faced with the stops and starts of smaller avenues that ran into dead ends at parks.

The original settlers arrived here in the 18th century to clear the land and put in their crops. In time, they were permitted by the French crown to subdivide these farms and grant deeds to sons and daughters.

All that's left of that history is a handful—maybe a dozen—of original farmhouses from the French period. If you take Patrice north of Wyandotte to the river, at the corner of

An original French farmhouse, the Patrice Parent house at 4371 Riverside Drive, was built in 1859 and still stands today.

this street and Riverside is the Patrice Parent House (4371 Riverside Drive), a two-storey wooden clapboard home with a front gable. It was built in 1859. It is one of Windsor's earliest French homesteads, according to *The Canadian Register of Historic Places*, which provides a single source of information about all historic places recognized for their heritage value at the local, provincial, territorial, and national levels. The Patrice Parent house was situated on Farm Lot #108. According to the Register, it is "illustrative of the French farmsteads which once dotted the Detroit River shoreline… it displays vernacular rough-hewn timber construction and is supported by log joists." The house is Georgian in structure with a front gable.

### Glidden and Wyandotte

I'm getting ahead of myself. Still on the south side, I come upon Glidden Dairy Bar (5989 Wyandotte Street East), still bearing that Coca Cola sign and advertising Sealtest Ice Cream. The store borrows its name from its location at the corner of Glidden and Wyandotte, but the origins of naming the side street, says Fullerton, came not from one of the early settlers, or from some real estate agent, but from an obsession that the real estate developer had with automobiles, especially the once-famous Great Motor Race of 1905.

John Lundy was the president of the Essex County Automobile Association, and he was the one who suggested naming the street after Charles Jasper Glidden, who had worked with Alexander Graham Bell. This American financier and great supporter of the automobile donated a silver trophy for the winner of the 1,100-mile race through New York and New Hampshire. The motor event that began in 1904 and was called "The Glidden Tour" was intended to raise awareness of the new roads being built in the United States. In that competition, some 34 four-cylinder automobiles, like the British Napier and the Pierce-Arrow, were used.

Of course, I knew nothing of that when I lived in Riverside. I'm sure those stepping into the Glidden Dairy Bar today could not even guess at such a connection. Or would know anything about Charles Glidden, for that matter.

The other thing I knew nothing about, was that at one time—right after the First World War—Glidden was known for its nearby orchard. It was not uncommon for boys in the neighbourhood to string up rope and create an outdoor boxing ring here, says

The Glidden Dairy Bar is still operating today, recognizable from its "Coca-Cola" signs.

historian Natalie Atkin, in her piece, "From Learning to Living: Edith Cavell School" for the *Times Magazine.*

The store itself has been there since the 1950s, when Riverside was going through its post-war boom years. New home construction was rampant. Whole streets were being developed. This was the start of the "baby boom era." It was the age of the car, of rock and roll, of social and technological advancements never seen before, of economic growth, but it was also the birth of suburban communities. Riverside illustrates this perfectly.

Morrison's history explains it this way, pointing out that with the Second World War, the Border Cities was engulfed with a massive influx of men and women seeking jobs in the manufacture of trucks, ambulances, gun carriers, and machine guns. Domestic car production itself was discontinued, and you couldn't even buy a new car until a year or two after the war.

This population explosion, coupled with the return of soldiers from the battlefields, meant the Border Cities suddenly faced an acute housing crisis. The Liberal Government recognized this during the war, and introduced housing projects as early as 1941. By the end of the 1940s, the federal government had ramped up efforts for a public housing program for low-income families with costs and subsidies shared 75% by the federal government and 25% by the province. This led to the creation of Wartime Housing Ltd. (later, Central Mortgage and Housing Corporation) in 1946.

In effect, it created an early housing boom in Riverside that persisted well into the 1950s. The town really came alive in this period. As a boy, I remember scavenging at building sites that were scattered all over the neighbourhood. At the end of the day, the carpenters would return home, but always leave behind their tools and lumber. That's when my buddies and I would invade these places, and lug away dozens of two-by-fours and nails to make tree houses and forts. We never thought we were doing anything wrong. For us, it was the era of opportunity, and neighbourhood democracy.

Today as I wander down some of these streets, I notice these cookie-cutter wartime homes—very few of them brick—mostly clapboard, though now sided with aluminum or vinyl, all from after the Second World War. These houses had steep roofs and shallow eaves. They were called "Victory housing."

In Riverside, however, in addition to these wartime structures and the occasional larger two-storey brick home with a verandah and a dormer, you find a collection of low, odd-shaped, diminutive dwellings, these being assembled either by independent contractors, or in some cases, by the homeowners themselves. They might have gone up during the war, or immediately after it. My father and my grandfather, for example, constructed their own abodes on George Avenue from massive wooden crates garnered from factories along Seminole.

With the rise of home building also came the need for new infrastructure. Richard Fullerton explains how drainage was so unpredictable in parts of Riverside that it was not

Newly constructed war-time houses on Isabelle Street, south of St. Rose Avenue, 1953.

uncommon for areas nearer to Lauzon and Wyandotte to be flooded, usually following the spring thaw. Local residents were often seen "travelling to and from the streetcar stop… aided by canoes rowboats and hip boots." The biggest flood occurred in March 1952 when the river surged over the low-lying areas east of Jefferson. The town banded together to sandbag the shore to foil further losses from the three-foot waves. Riverside set into place more than 10,000 sandbags, and its mayor, Robert J. Bondy, son of a shoe salesman, and upon his election in 1951, the youngest mayor to be elected in Canada, petitioned the federal government for assistance. The floodplain was more than a mile deep inland. Windsor Mayor Art Reaume ushered in help from the Windsor Fire Department.

Coupled with the growth of suburbia, or this urban sprawl, came the era of the car, the romance surrounding it, and the reliance upon it. Julia Biris in *Suburbia, the Automobile and Obesity,* says although the car was popular before the 1950s, "it was during this decade that the automobile really became a 'necessary' component of Canadian life… Living in the suburbs was made possible by the automobile and paved roads which linked suburban homes to essential services in the heart of the city."

Flooding on Lauzon Road, looking south towards Wyandotte Street, in 1947.

In short, it meant getting to and from work.

Again, Riverside was the perfect candidate. It was right next door to automobile production, the headquarters of car making in Canada. And it had the space needed for a workforce looking for a place to live. Indeed, Riverside had sweeping empty fields, eager and ready for development. This gave opportunity to real estate agents, builders, and tradespeople. Many street names reflect this, having been named after the developers or the sons or daughters of these builders. For example, Homedale Boulevard refers to Home Real Estate Co. Two other streets—Christopher Drive and Alan Crescent—were the names of family members of Isack Construction Company. Thompson Boulevard derives its moniker from Kaiser, Thompson and Mills Real Estate Company.

The 1950s was marked by the rise of the building trades. Riverside-based construction companies included Ray Allan on Reedmere, Bolohan Construction on Menard, Deschamps Plasterers at 307 Fairview, Isack Construction at 3310 Riverside Drive, Gosling and Lamoureux at 252 Matthew Brady, John's Home at 281 Ford Boulevard, Krogh & Sons at 84 Buckingham, Frank Wetzel at 3905 Riverside Drive, and Riverside Plumbing at 441 Jefferson.

The Esdras Parent farmhouse was built in 1852 on the riverfront and was moved into its present location at 827 Esdras. Its front entrance faces north towards the Detroit River.

## Esdras Place

I now take Esdras Place, one block and just a few shops away from Glidden Dairy. I make a left turn onto this street whose name is derived from Esdras Parent, son of the original French settler Laurent Parent. You are probably going to miss a rather nondescript white frame house on the west side at 827 Esdras. Its entrance faces north, rather than east like all the other houses on the street. That's when you realize at some point in time, this was because this building sat alone on this plot of land. As it turns out, this was Esdras Parent's original one-and-one-half storey wood frame farmhouse, in a typical Classical Revival style

with a main entrance flanked by windows and clapboard cladding. According to *Canada's Historic Places*, it is "an important remnant of early French farmstead settlements along the Detroit River." The house's original placement actually was on the riverfront when it was built in 1852. Esdras' father, Laurent, settled the land around 1800. According to *The Canadian Register*, "The original Parent farm is associated with the 1838 Battle of Windsor, purportedly having been the landing spot of about 140 'patriots,' prior to their march into Windsor during the Rebellion of 1837–38. The invaders were quickly routed and hightailed back across the Detroit River, abandoning firearms and other items that the Parent family collected and kept." The family moved the house to its present location in 1913, and subdivided their riverfront land for urban development. In 1959, the Parents sold the house, which by the way, is of log construction with hand-hewn beams, 15-inch planks and hand-forged nails. The rear section was built about 1890.

All very interesting, but you wouldn't even guess at its past as you walk by. I was tempted to knock on the door to inquire if the owners knew historical importance.

Continuing along Esdras brings me to the dark-brick former Edith Cavell School (5595 Ontario Street) at the intersection of Esdras and Ontario. When I lived in this neighbourhood, it was Riverside High School. But the Edith Cavell building that you see today wasn't actually the first to serve the area. Pre-dating the original two-room Edith Cavell School that opened in 1919 was another, white-frame building

An early photograph of Edith Cavell School, which still stands, but was converted into condominiums in 2002.

situated at 957 Ford Boulevard. Its replacement right after the First World War on Esdras and Ontario was named for the British nurse who was sentenced to death by the Germans for providing refuge to British, French, and Belgian soldiers. The property for the school was built on land belonging to the farm of Gilbert Parent, and his wife was named the school's first principal. Additional classrooms were built in 1936 as the neighbourhood grew. From that point on, the building went through a variety of transformations, but its importance to Riverside really was felt during the 1920s and also during the Depression, when it served as a place of community recreation involving dances, card parties, and film nights.

Riverside United Church (881 Glidden Avenue) also started its congregation in the school before building directly across the street. That structure still stands.

Natalie Atkin, in writing about this, described the neighbourhood in which this school was put, as marked by a series of creeks that snaked through Homedale, Jefferson, Glidden, and Ford. In the spring, the area often flooded. Housing development back then was mostly north of Wyandotte, but Ford workers toiled at night building new homes for themselves with the help of hurricane lamps.

Edith Cavell went through many transformations. It morphed into a high school and was renamed Riverside High in 1956, but when the community built a new Riverside High School in 1964, it reverted back to being an elementary school. Unlike so many in Windsor's past—this building was saved from demolition in 2002 when it was converted into a 20-unit condominium. The exterior is much the same as I remember from the late 1950s. As you pass by this august building, you can still read the school's name.

## Reedmere Road and St. Louis

I wind my way back to Wyandotte, and now I'm at the corner of Reedmere. The second floor of this building, now housed by a gift shop called Madison's (5850 Wyandotte Street E), was the office of a long-time Riverside dentist, Dr. M.F. Gallagher. He was someone whose impact upon me was subtle yet profound. Unlike my siblings, or my parents, or for that matter, my teachers, this new, young dentist encouraged me to prattle on and on, to spin tall stories, often prodding me for details that I delivered without hesitation. Gallagher listened. He'd stand back, bemused by my efforts to please with the most confounding tales. I lost track of him when we moved away. In a curious way, I think he started me on writing, though I never realized it until much later, when people ask what were your influences. This man. I got to see him quite a bit because I was the cavity kid, but it was also because of some early—and regular—orthodontic work.

The other influence in my early childhood was Dr. F.D. Linton whose office and home was a block away at the corner of St. Louis. The entrance to his practice was at the side, facing St. Louis. Tim Horton's (5720 Wyandotte Street East) moved into that spot, but has since closed. I lived in fear of this cigar-chomping Doc Linton even though there was nothing intentionally menacing or intimidating about him. As a matter of fact, he made house calls to deal with fevers or gut aches, and was often swinging into our driveway on Prado and climbing the front steps with a large black leather medical bag in his hands. But whenever I was at Doc Linton's office, I was entirely lost in the bizarre and peculiar medical calendars and charts that adorned the place. It was a dark office, lit by a single desk lamp, but somehow the doc would find a way to do a proper exam. The only annoying thing, as a kid, was to put up with all the cigar smoke in your face. Hardly healthy. But then we didn't have such concerns. We may have been told that smoking was bad for one's health, but no one ever spoke of cancer. It seemed more like an excuse to keep cigarettes out of the hands of teenagers. The laws, too, were different then. My neighbour, Joanie—a former flaper from Prohibition—was forever dispatching me to the corner store to pick up a pack of *Player's* for her. I was maybe seven or eight.

The second floor of Madison's Gifts, at the northeast corner of Reedmere and Wyandotte Street East, used to house the offices of Dr. M.F. Gallagher, my dentist.

One of the most famous of men of medicine in the world, however, lived farther north along Reedmere. This was Dr. Henri Breault. He raised his family at 36 Reedmere. The Tecumseh-born Breault, who died in October 1983, was the man who created the first child-proof prescription container. It was something that he was driven to do because of the number of cases that he dealt with in Emergency at Hôtel-Dieu. His daughter, Rosemary Breault-Landy, told me how her father arrived home shaken and shocked at the death, or near death, of a child from having swallowed pills. This happened countless times, and the University of Western Ontario graduate swore he would find a way to stop this. Breault eventually became Chief of Pediatrics at Hôtel-Dieu, and continued his research into the manufacture of these safe prescription bottles.

As early as 1962, Breault established the Ontario Association for the Control of Accidental Poisoning, and in 1967, finally succeeded in the adoption of a cap design known as "Palm N Turn." It was quickly endorsed by the Ontario College of Pharmacy. Breault noticed the number of incidences of poisoning drop by 91 percent from 1,000 per year in the province. Breault, quite rightly, was inducted into the Canadian Medical Hall of Fame in 1997.

My memories of the man, however, have more to do with his daughter. The two of us were classmates at St. Thomas Elementary. A few years ago, I spoke to her about her father, and she recalled how the dining-room table of their house was cluttered over with an assortment of prescription bottles with which he

Dr. Henri Breault demonstrates how to use his invention, the "Palm N Turn," a safety cap for prescription medication bottles, in 1965.

had been experimenting. From time to time, Breault would hand one to Rosemary, then barely a teenager, to try, and if she successfully managed to open it, it was tossed aside.

Now before you reached St. Louis, there was someone else of notoriety who served the area well and that was Henry Shanfield. His Shanfield's Dry Goods store was at 5780 Wyandotte Street East, now a barber and beauty salon. He was a man of immense generosity, and cared deeply for Riverside. Not originally from Riverside, Shanfield moved here in 1927, having learned the retail business from his father, a merchant. It wasn't until after the war, when Shanfield served in the Navy on a sub-chasing frigate that sank U-boats, that he opened up his dry goods shop on Wyandotte. While living here, he also ran for political office and served as alderman for Riverside. Shanfield

Shanfield's Dry Goods, owned and operated by community leader Henry Shanfield, was located in Riverside until it moved downtown in the '60s. This storefront currently houses Uptown Barbershop & Hair Studio and Serenity Salon.

was behind building the Riverside Arena, and fought hard on the town council to see that its parks were improved and maintained. It wasn't until the mid 1960s, about the time Riverside joined Windsor, that Shanfield moved downtown, opening up a fabric store.

This curious figure in our politics was best remembered for riding his bicycle, which stemmed from a profound concern for the environment. Shanfield continued his civic involvement when Riverside joined Windsor. He ran for city council before serving on the Windsor Utilities Commission. He also served as president of the former Downtown Business Association, and was a director of the Children's Aid Society. Some suggest his biggest achievement was almost single-handedly

acquiring Peche Island for Windsor. He spent close to 40 years trying to make this happen. This was typical of him, and the obituary in the *Windsor Star* said he "always championed the underdog and fought against vested interests." Shanfield died in 2003.

Another fellow known to many Riverside people nearby is Chuck McIntosh. He used to own McIntosh Paving, and chances are the church parking lot that you pull into, or the one at the school, or the office building downtown was done by his company. Decades ago, he was also honoured as Businessman of the Year. Chuck's story is that of a politician, or a doctor. He was a Riverside boy who worked hard, married his sweetheart, started his own business, raised a family, and put in 12-hour workdays, arriving at his office a little after six in the morning. He was lucky to be home before nightfall. I spoke with Chuck in October, 2010, at his Riverside Drive home at the foot of St. Louis, a stone's throw from his childhood home. I'm not going to bother making my way along St. Louis to the Drive to where his home is. My memories of that interview serve me well. Chuck was 81 when I sought him out. His reminiscences ran deep to the wide-open fields of Riverside and the bonfire burning nights in the old neighbourhood ballparks. Chuck was there long before I was born. He was there before the housing boom of the 1940s, and he knew everyone, including the cigar-chomping Doc Linton, and Esquire, the barbershop nearby, where everyone solved the problems of the Cold War. He knew Henry Shanfield, and shopped at the nearby grocery stores and ate at the local neighbourhood diners. This was Riverside in its heyday—a time when anyone could telephone the mayor at home and bitch, or meet him for coffee, or sit down and banter with the police chief.

As Chuck got older, and started his own business, he would bump into these fellows at the Riverside Tavern for coffee every morning. That, he pointed out, was the real council meeting. That's where the deals of the day were sealed. All with a good degree of repartee. This was small-town grassroots politics—simple, uncomplicated, down-to-earth, and things actually got done. All of that changed when Riverside was gobbled up by Windsor, said Chuck. And it was never the same.

When Riverside was annexed by Windsor in 1965, it helped to triple the size of the Border Cities. As Doug Schmidt wrote in the *Windsor Star,* the city became "the proud new step-parent of 58,500 new citizens, turning itself into Ontario's No. 4 city." There were bitter feelings at the time, especially among the older generation. Former Mayor Mike Hurst, who grew up in Sandwich East, recalls the anger his own father had over the earlier annexation of Sandwich, East Windsor, and Walkerville in 1935.

Schmidt quotes Hurst as saying, "We call it the A-word—it certainly is a word that creates a lot of interest and captures everyone's attention."

That period in the 1960s was dominated by former Justice Gordon Stewart. He hailed from Riverside, and was among the best civil and criminal lawyers during the 1950s. He put in his bid for town politics and ran for a seat on Riverside Town Council in 1954. Two years later, he was elected mayor. It was a time of great expansion, and his efforts paid off in the building of Riverside High School and the new sewage treatment facilities. But Stewart vehemently opposed the movement to swallow up his beloved town. He campaigned vigorously, but lost that battle. He quit as mayor in 1964. The following year, however, he agreed to serve as Windsor police commissioner, a job he kept until 1975. In 1965, Stewart was also appointed a provincial magistrate.

Chuck McIntosh remembers Stewart and that period of time. But he likes to harken back to when municipal politics was a lot simpler, more straightforward, and more in touch with people.

"It wasn't perfect," acknowledged Chuck, but there was trust and people were honest with one another and cut through the red tape of municipal politics.

"We grew up when hard work was pounded into you. And I worked all the time. Did everything, and got a job at Walkerville Dairy, and was up at 4:30 a.m. and rode my bike to Walker Road. All that money went to my mom."

That's the way things were. And when you bought a car, you paid cash, Chuck recalled. He told me how he once he had his eye on a brand new $1,250 dark metallic-blue '51 Ford with maroon gabardine seat covers, and only had $250 saved in the bank. His mom finally lent him the balance. Then every week, a portion of his wages was deducted for his mom—it took him a year to pay off that car.

Ironically, Chuck had nowhere to go with it, because he couldn't afford the gas. It sat idle in the yard until he could scrounge a few pennies to get it running. Chuck, however, never pined for the old days of the 1950s, but when he strolled the old neighbourhood streets of his childhood, he recalled those years when few families locked their doors.

"I laugh when they say everybody left their doors open because at my house, my mother locked our door, but only to make me come home. And when I got home late at night, I was skinny enough to crawl through the milk chute."

Nobody has a milk chute anymore. If they do exist, they're sealed up. In those days, right up to the early 1960s, milk was delivered to homes. So was bread. So was ice. Back then, garbage collectors hauled the metal trashcans from the rear of your house to the truck. You didn't put them out at the curb.

"Was it a better time?" I asked Chuck. He smiled that smile that made it pretty clear: What do you think?

## St. Louis and Wyandotte Street

As I stand here at the corner, I realize it was a defining place for me growing up. The Legion now sprawls and stretches all the way across that block, and the confectionery shop, Constantine's, is long gone from where it was at 5645 Wyandotte Street East. In the 1950s you entered it from St. Louis. It was around the corner, in the same building as Esquire Barber and Beauty Shop where Clarence Janisse was legendary in cutting hair. The candy store, however, was our world. We called it "Cooties." The counters were smothered over with squarish cardboard containers of black balls, licorice pipes, Sugar Daddies, Cinnamon Toothpicks and Turkish Taffy. Most

The Royal Canadian Legion, Branch 255, sits on the southern block of Wyandotte Street East, between Villaire Avenue and St. Louis. Constantine's Confectionery and Esquire Barber and Beauty Shop were once located in this spot.

disconcerting was the cat which stepped lightly over these boxes as if they were minefields.

I learned politics from Clarence next door in the shop that smelled of a mixture of Lucky Tiger hair tonic, Sandalwood shaving cream, mixed with Pinaud-Clubman aftershave with its hints of orange, jasmine, and lavender. I'd look over at the large trademark jar on the mirrored counter and see Clarence's collection of combs and scissors sitting in that translucent blue liquid Barbicide. The sweet smell of the place went with you when you stepped outside Esquire. Hair shiny and slicked back, feeling clean and manly, you were now ready to take on the world.

But as you slumped in Clarence's chair, you were also getting a political education. It wasn't difficult to eavesdrop on the grousing about Korea, about Eisenhower, how Nixon might be the next president, or why Paul Martin ought to be the country's next prime minister. I flipped through the *Archie* comic books, waiting to get "my ears lowered," pretending to pay attention to the cartoons,

but actually listening about the possibility of a war with Russia. The face of Nikita Khrushchev scared me. The men who descended upon this barbershop seemed to have an inside line on what was happening. Their grumblings fuelled my paranoia. the *Windsor Daily Star* seemed to support what I was hearing in this cramped barbershop, just a stone's throw from my Prado Place house. This was the hood, my place in the world. A candy store, a barbershop where the only choice was a buzz cut, and Frank's Lunch across the street at 5622 Wyandotte Street East, now Pat & Hank's Fish and Chips.

## Villaire and Wyandotte

Frank's Lunch looms large in my memory, because as a kid, I used to slip pennies into the slots of its machines and twist the crank and watch gumballs fill my hands. More importantly, and nearly tragically, when I was

Wyandotte Street, looking east towards St. Louis Avenue from Villaire Avenue, in 1963. Note Frank's Lunch at left, and Constantine's Confectionery, and Esquire Barber and Beauty Shop at right, where the Royal Canadian Legion Branch 255 is now located. It was directly in front of Frank's that I was hit by a car.

five, I ran between two parked automobiles in front of this coffee shop, and was hit by a passing car. From what I was told, I was catapulted 50 feet onto Wyandotte. I can't forget the scream of the siren in the ambulance, and later returning home to 228 Prado. As my father drove up the driveway, I lay bandaged on the back seat, staring up at the branches of the trees to discover that my brothers had constructed a treehouse.

I was always fascinated by this lunch spot at Frank's. As I got older, I used to study the behaviour of those men with floppy wool caps sitting at the lunch counter, and how they would ogle the curved nyloned legs of demure women tellers from the Canadian Imperial Bank of Commerce at the corner of St. Louis. These ladies would slip in for coffee, and when they left, the men would guffaw, and mutter things I really didn't understand.

Of course, there was Baker's (5570 Wyandotte Street East) right at the corner of Villaire on Wyandotte. a breakfast and lunch joint. It's been there since the 1950s. It has gone through various owners, but still

Baker's Bar and Grill first opened as a dairy bar, and expanded in 1962 into a full-service restaurant. It is pictured here in the early '60s and is still operating today.

retains the name. I often stop in for breakfast. Across Villaire, still on the north side, is the Almina Building. Both played pivotal roles in my growing up. First, the upstairs apartment above the storefronts was where my buddy Rocky lived. He was raised by a single grandmother. I learned my first swear words from him. We would double-ride his bicycle through the neighbourhood and hunt for pop bottles to cash in so we could buy candy. Rocky was always in trouble at school. He smoked at 12. I lost track of this wild, free-wheeling kid when I moved away, but years later I discovered this street-wise boy with a foul mouth became a Detroit cop.

Baker's was special. It brings back lots of memories, the first being the time my mother sent me there to pick up something for her. The incident says a lot about the era. I was maybe 9 or 10, and my mother handed me a folded-up note, and told me to take this with a handful of change to Baker's. She also instructed me to hand the note to "the lady" in the store, and warned me not to read the message. Of course, on my way there, I reviewed what she had written and frowned. I figured my mom had made a spelling mistake and when I handed the note to the sales clerk, I apologized for what she had written, telling her that my mom's first language was French and she couldn't spell. I said, "She wants a box of Kleenex." The female clerk looked at the note, and nodded, then fetched a squarish box that was covered in brown wrapping paper. I sauntered on home. A few days later, I spotted the same box in the bathroom, with the brown wrapping pealed back. I peeked inside, and pulled out a white pad, then read the lettering, "Kotex." I didn't have a clue what this was.

But the story that still moves me to this day about Baker's is one that I wrote for the *Windsor Star* in September 2007. It was about my childhood memories of this place, and a woman called Mary, and my wondering about whatever happened to her. I never believed I'd see her again. When my family moved away from Windsor, she had told me I looked like her long-lost son. She showered me with favours whenever I stopped in, giving me an extra scoop of ice cream, handfuls of O'Henry bars, bubble gum, anything I desired. She was like a favourite aunt. I never knew anything about her, and it may be because I truly never listened to her. I always wished I had.

Right after writing about her in a newspaper column, I received a four-line e-mail. It arrived like a dove on my shoulder, telling me she was the woman in the column, that she was still very much alive, that she was 86, and she'd love to see me again. I sat by the phone all morning waiting to phone her, feeling incredibly nervous. I hadn't seen her in 49 years. I turned over and over those last moments in my mind when my parents dropped me by Baker's to say goodbye in 1958. That morning, she hugged me, and handed me $5.

That was so long ago. I figured she was long dead.

And while my life has taken numerous turns since then, the story of this remarkably kind-hearted woman with red hair, who believed I was the spitting image of her son, never left my thoughts. It is a story I have shared countless times, often when I meet people at Baker's for breakfast.

Now finally, here I was, driving to her house in Riverside's east end near today's Riverside High School. She asked that I not reveal her last name. I didn't know what to expect when I rang the doorbell. I didn't have to think about it for long, because when this lively woman opened the door, she cupped my face in her hands, and kissed me on the cheek. She said she had waited a lifetime for this moment. Believe me, she still had red hair and green eyes, and a smile that opened doors and windows everywhere. As it turned out, Mary, too, never ceased relating that same story about the boy from Riverside who looked so much like her son. And years ago when she spotted my photograph with my *Star* column, and read about me living in Riverside, she turned to her husband, Don, and said, "That's the boy!" Mary said, "I wanted to call you so many times, but never did." Still, she continued to tell the story of the kid from Riverside. What irony. There we were, both seemingly worlds apart, spinning the same tale to people everywhere. Now we were face to face.

Mary was 38 when I knew her. Slim. Good looking. A single mother making ends meet in the midst of a recession in the 1950s. Getting $35 a week from an ex-husband before finally landing a job at Baker's. The grimmest period in her life. That might explain why the day I strolled into her store was the one bright spot in her life.

"That first day you came into Baker's, I thought you were my son. Same age and fair hair. I was so certain, I looked out the window to see if my ex- husband's car was there dropping you off. You were so shy, so polite. There were days when I'd look for you, because it made me feel good. Then when you left, I was so sad."

The son I resembled was living with an aunt. He had had rheumatic fever and a heart murmur and the hospital had wanted to keep him. However, her ex-husband's sister, who didn't have children of her own, offered to keep him at home, and did.

"You thought he had died because I told you he wasn't with us anymore," she explained.

One of the original cast iron streetlights of the Town of Riverside, located in the 200 block of Prado Place, the city's first Heritage Conservation District.

As it turned out, with the custody battle over the children (she has three others), and his illness, Mary never got to raise that son. He's healthy now, and lives in Windsor. "You don't know how many times I have told this story to people," she said. "I don't think anyone believed me."

Believe it now, I told her.

After my story appeared, I received a note from Bonnie Greenacre, who wanted to hear more about Riverside, and told me she grew up "literally… at [her] father's gas station at Villaire and Wyandotte." This Imperial Oil station was owned by Jack Baker. He also owned the original Baker's, but it was Fred Baker who actually ran the dairy bar. Bonnie's aunt Marge and her mother Sylvia worked there for years.

## 228 (942) Prado Place

A block away is Prado Place. I lived in what was then the 200 block, all through the 1950s. This was on the south side of the street. Today, the north side is the 200 block, and runs from Wyandotte to the river. In December 2005, Windsor established the city's first Heritage Conservation District (HCD) on the north side. This was done to preserve "a streetscape that is unique in the City" with its mid-island landscaped design. The street still boasts of ten original Town of Riverside street lamps along the block, the only cast iron streetlights that remain in Riverside. The north side was a different world, even back then. It was leafy, gentrified, exclusive. Long gone from the north end of Prado was the three-storey C.H. Millard mansion with its curved verandah. It is said the place was haunted. Built by the wealthy American Joseph Canniff, and in 1904 sold to J.L. Hudson, the place was burned to the ground in the 1920s and made way for the development of what is Prado Place today.

The south side was punctuated by a mixture of rooming houses, wartime homes, and makeshift dwellings. My cousins lived a few doors down from us. As I mentioned earlier, my father and his brother, Clay, built that house from factory crates. It was a one-storey ramshackle place, set back deep on the lot. It was eventually torn down to make room for a newer home.

An interesting fact about Prado on the south side was that it was originally called Lillian. It was at that juncture that there existed a "town tap." Robert F. Watson, in his piece about Riverside in Fullerton's book, recalls a public waterspout that was used by the neighbourhood. He writes there was "a community tap located between Lillian and Edgewood [now Villaire]… Some came to do their laundry right on the site for there were no wells in the town. Others carted in buckets and tubs."

Memories of that street, and the pursuits of my older brothers, played vividly for me when I saw the movie *October Sky*, the story of the Rocket Boys. In the vacant lot next to our house (942 Prado Place), my brother Bud had thrown up a tarpaper shack that served as an observatory, and fashioned a powerful telescope whereby he could examine the surface of the moon. The Sputnik fired up his imagination, and soon he was working on his own rocket in our dad's garage. He cleared out the wirey pigeon cages, scrounged metal from a scrapyard, and got use of a lathe down the street. Then with the aid of various substances pilfered from Corpus Christi's (now Brennan High) chemistry lab and gunpowder supplied by Lever's Drugs, Bud constructed a thin tube of a rocket. My role was to hunt down a mouse in the field to be used as a suitable passenger to ride in this rocket. He was emulating the Russians who had sent Laika, a stray dog found in the streets of Moscow, into orbit in Sputnik 2 in November 1957.

My dad knew nothing of this experiment. He lounged in the living room reading the newspaper, or hugging the Zenith radio tuning into the Friday night fights, completely unaware of our activities. This was the Cold War. A fridge cost $150, a TV $300. We watched *The Price Is Right, Queen for a Day*, and *Howdy Doody*. We watched the nightly news to see who was winning the war in Korea. The airwaves were dominated by Elvis and Pat Boone. We feared intercontinental ballistic missiles. We heeded the words of Joe McCarthy, who was hunting down communists and perverts in every sector of society. We needed to do something. We needed to put a rocket into the night sky.

That summer evening in 1958, my brother launched this missile. My dad and mom were lazing on the front verandah, oblivious to the

St. Thomas Separate School fronted Thompson Boulevard, but was located in the centre of my neighbourhood. The back faced Prado Place, across the street from my childhood home. The school, now demolished, has been replaced by housing.

plan. The rest of the neighbourhood knew. At least all the kids. We scurried to the empty lot next to our house, and observed Bud removing a lumpy mouse trapped in his coat pocket. He slipped it smoothly into a tiny chamber, and shut the lid. He advised us to back up, and we did, and we parked ourselves alongside the lilac trees near the driveway. Bud set the switch, then stepped back. The fizzle stretched to an eternity, then suddenly there was an explosion, and the tiny rocket burst into the twilight, blasted over a neighbour's house, and soared higher and higher before lightly plummeting like a wounded hawk and toppling on the roof of St. Thomas school. In that instant, we became the Rocket Kids of Prado Place.

Back then, we believed in neighbourhood. We owned it. We didn't join organized sport—we organized it ourselves. Baseball tournaments, road hockey games, boxing matches, poker games, marbles, and

even sword fights with pine swords. And, of course, we set off rockets.

Everything revolved around St. Thomas Separate School, which actually faced Thompson Boulevard. The school was not named for the "saint," but rather for Thomas Parent, of the original pioneer families that settled there. In the 1950s, we were always in the schoolyard. We had no need of committees. No need for fundraisers. Or lawyers. Or parents. We made our own decisions. Took our own measures. And when the school was demolished years later while I was working at the *Windsor Star*, I wrote that if this were 1957, "and push came to shove, we would have never let this happen."

I was a terrible student, and struggled from one year to the next, but looking back, St. Thomas was pivotal in my education to become a writer. It was because of Sister Mary of Perpetual Help, its principal, who taught Grade 6 and art, that I gravitated to books. There was that supreme moment in late afternoon when she would dim the lights in the classroom, order us to remove everything from the tops of our desks, and tell us to sit and listen. She would quietly open a novel, and begin reading, and we sat transfixed, completely taken up with the story at hand. None of us fidgeted. None of us joked, or parried secretly with one another. We were adrift in the story. She read to us Thomas B. Costain's *The Silver Chalice*. This quiet, unfettered moment of being absorbed in words turned my attention to following that urge, the idea of spinning stories, getting caught up in the imaginary lives of others. In a way, it's what I was already doing in the schoolyard—telling tales, making my friends believe the unbelievable. The priest may have called these lies. I, instead, regarded them as real. Those afternoons in the shadows of that classroom at St. Thomas with my head lowered, was the beginning of writing.

In those years, so says Dean Kouvelas in a piece called "On Being: 'A Riverside'" in Fullerton's *Our Town: Memories of Riverside,* the town was "a twinkle in our eye…a state of mind… what legends are made of…Riverside was its own entity. It had its own identity, its own memories and its own legacy for all those who shaped her history and, to some, extent, her future."

Kouvelas recalls the place where I lived until I was 12. His description of the 1950s and 1960s was of a "town [that] was safe to walk in… We had the same values and the same tolerances. Riverside was good natured, easy going, simplistic…" True enough, the town reflected the times. Most families had two or three children, usually spaced about three years apart. There was only ever one car in the driveway or on the street, one television in the house, and one radio. It was also a time when nobody locked the front door, and where yards were rarely fenced off. As Kouvelas says, "If it sounds like the 'Cleavers,' you've got the picture."

There was neighbourhood pride. Each clique had its own ragtag bunch of boys that made up a baseball team. Entirely democratic. And we'd rival others—dividing line to the east was Jefferson. We'd duel with those boys, and there was a fierce competition to show them we were champions, though we often got our butts kicked.

This neighbourhood pride extended to our parents. Every Labour Day, our moms and dads would gather near the baseball field at St. Thomas and build a raging bonfire. There would be makeshift tables laden with hot dogs and marshmallows. As kids, we'd cavort in the failing daylight, roasting hot dogs, laughing and downing Vernors. Today, someone would alert the fire department. Back then, it was neighbourhood. It was family. It was celebrating the end of summer, the beginning of a new school year. This was where we grew up, where we were shaped, where we learned to cope, where we learned to be who we are today.

Today, resting on top of my desk at home is the school recess bell that Sister Mary of Perpetual Help used to ring. She, or a chosen female student, would perch on the edge of the steps at the back of the school, and clang this brass bell, signalling us to return to class. A former principal of the school gave it to me after St. Thomas was closed. It's really all that's left of that neighbourhood school.

Ours was a different time. The Second World War was still fresh in the minds of our mothers and fathers. As kids we were intrigued with the stories, certainly, but it was the spoils of war that fascinated us beyond anything else. Some of my buddies had fathers who had returned from the battlefields of Europe with Nazi armbands, photographs of Hitler, German Lugers, even bits of German uniforms. It was embarrassing to hear from my mother how my father never went to war—he worked in the munitions factory on Seminole, manufacturing shell casings and machine guns. This was all rather convoluted to explain to my friends, so when they asked about my father, I told them that he was a spy. And when they pressed me for evidence, I cleverly said, "Spies don't wear uniforms." Now, they were in awe. But I couldn't leave it at that—I now informed them that my father was still a spy, and that he worked for Eisenhower. That sent them over the moon. From that point on, my pals would walk nearly in slow motion in front of our house to take a studied long look at my father, who sat there, like any ordinary man, reading the *Windsor Daily Star* and drinking *Labatt 50*. And every day, he would leave the house, and head to work at the Canadian Motor Lamp, just like anybody else, but to me and my friends, he was spying in the factory. At 9 years of age, I didn't know about real life industrial spies. Years later at the *Star* I interviewed a woman, who coincidentally had worked at Canadian Motor Lamp like my father, and she told me how the RCMP had raided her father's house the day after he died. She recounted how when she arrived at the family home, she found the police hauling out cardboard boxes of files. Eventually, after countless telephone calls and letters, she was informed that her father had been a corporate spy working for them in the factories.

Another figure from that time that dominated the street was Joan Girard, a long-lost cousin of former mayor Art Reaume. She was one of us. Not at all like any of the other moms. She'd play a stack of 45s of Elvis and the Everly Brothers and dance the *Chicken* with us in the afternoons. Joan was our mentor, friend, teacher, and a mom who taught us the value of storytelling. She could make you laugh. She was Catholic and was raised by nuns, but stopped attending Mass years earlier. When we asked why, she never said—except maybe she was also raised by gangsters. And when Joan told me this, she'd bat her big eyelashes and smile, and swing out her hips.

I was best friends with her son, Rick, and her daughter, Candy. As kids, we'd congregate on her back screened-in porch, and spend whole afternoons watching the flicks hosted by former actor Bill Kennedy, who hosted the once-popular *Bill Kennedy at the Movies* from CKLW in Windsor. Joan would lap up all the stories of the movie stars—all the gossip, dirt and glamour. Then she'd enlarge upon these for us, helping us imagine the lives of these heroes, and make us feel in our bones the wonder and mystery of the world around us. The wartime house she lived in was directly across the street. Her backyard faced St. Thomas School. I learned so much more from her in that three-bedroom house: to dance, and hear music in a way no other kid on the block could appreciate, how to read a racing sheet, and pick out the names of fillies that ran in the Kentucky Derby. And we studied the finest moves in poker instead of the usual kid card games like Go Fish and Old Maid. More significantly, we gradually figured out how to make everybody believe our lies. The essence of storytelling.

## Ford Boulevard

Back to Wyandotte. I move west to Ford Boulevard, then head north along that street to the river, and there is the Janisse-Schade House (5325 Riverside Drive East), a place that was built in 1928 at the height of a population boom during the Roaring Twenties. This two-storey, red-brick Colonial Revival style house, situated at the corner of Ford and Riverside, has a prominent central gable-covered entrance porch supported by a pair of Doric columns. It is on Windsor's heritage list. This was Eugene Janisse's house. He was president of Janisse Realty. His was the first house built on the south side of Riverside Drive between Ford and Thompson. Janisse sold it to H.L. Schade, president of Sterling Products and the Bayer Company, in the mid-1930s.

## Pillette Road

I head back to Wyandotte. I'm not sure when I became an altar boy, but it was a large part of my life in Riverside. I rose early with my brother, Bill, and would hotfoot it along Ontario Street to Our Lady of Guadalupe (834 Raymo Road). Father Dill was the pastor; his assistant was Father John Mooney. Morning mass. Each day

without fail. We'd enter by the side door at the back of the clapboard church, and slip on cassocks and surplices, and file out into the sanctuary of this long narrow building, which is now behind the newer A-frame church that was designed by Robert Langlois and erected in 1962.

After serving mass, my brother and I would make it back home for oatmeal, toast and hot chocolate before heading off to school. I never knew the new church. I studied Latin in the basement of the old church's rectory. By then, it was Father Quenneville instructing us. Catholicism was part of everyday life. Our teachers were Catholic. Our best friends were Catholic. Even the movies we went to see had to be approved by the

The Janisse-Schade House, located at 5325 Riverside Drive, on the corner of Ford Boulevard, was built in 1928 and is still privately owned.

Legion of Decency, ratings that were posted on the bulletin boards at the church entrance. Ironically, the newer building that opened in 1963 is on the Heritage list for Windsor, but the older frame building—still there—has more history. It isn't on the list. Probably because it is far from unique architecturally speaking. After all, it was thrown together as a prefab, in keeping with the wartime housing development that was happening in the neighbourhood. The neighbourhood itself was white Anglo-Saxon. Not much diversity at all.

Our Lady of Guadalupe opened Christmas Day 1951. It cost parishioners $35,000. The diocese hired a London, Ontario lumber company to build this 40" by 110" church. Footings were put in Thanksgiving Day, 1951, and construction began November 1. Fr. T. G. Dill and his assistant initially resided at the back of the church, but this proved inadequate, so the church built a rectory at a cost of $40,000 to house the priests. The church was deemed necessary because of the overflow from Holy Rosary and St. Rose of Lima, and with the sudden growth of Riverside.

Across the street from Our Lady of Guadalupe is McDonald's and a walk-in clinic, but when I lived there, this was the location of the Centre Theatre (4900 Wyandotte Street East). My Saturday afternoons were spent in that theatre. Fifteen cents for a movie; 10 cents for popcorn. As kids, our mothers ordered us immediately after the movie to head to the church for Saturday afternoon confession, a story I have told often. I've written about it in poetry—how one afternoon I filed into line along with my brother, Bill. I was barely six. In those days, the queue for confession was lengthy, and you never left it for fear of losing your spot. I was squirming from having to pee so badly. Despite being so desperate to get into that confessional box, I figured I could hold it long enough to tell my sins to Father Mooney, and still get out and use the bathroom. At long last, I was inside, when the grated panel slid open slowly, I immediately began with that time-worn prattle, "Bless me, Father, for I have sinned…" Except at that very moment, I couldn't hold it anymore—and uncontrollably started peeing my pants. My words turned to panic. *Bless me, Father I am peeing in your confessional.* The priest, straining to understand me, asked gravely, "How many times have you done this, my son!" To which I responded, "I'm

The original Our Lady of Guadalupe Catholic Church, built in 1951, still stands behind the existing, in-use church on the corner of Raymo Road and Wyandotte Street East.

A view of Wyandotte Street East, looking east from Lawrence Road, showing the Centre Theatre on the north side. On the south side of Wyandotte are: East Side Cycle Shop, John F. Burns Dry Goods, Albert W. Reid & Sons Hardware, and the Royale Tavern.

doing it right now!" I then bolted from the confessional, holding my wet crotch, running from the church and all the way home. I was certain I was going to Hell.

Those thoughts go with me now as I stand at the corner of Pillette and Wyandotte. They call this Pillette Village. That annoys me. Yet it's maybe a way to engender identity, something I think was ingrained when we lived here. For me, this was Riverside. As a boy growing up there, we didn't regard boundaries in the same way as others did. We saw neighbourhoods. Our allegiances were clear. It was respect, a recognition of the order of things, an understanding. Riverside, though very much a part of the larger urban settlement along the south shore, was like a small remote town. We didn't need to go far for help—it was right next door at the school, the gas station, the beer store, the church, or the town's municipal office. Everybody knew everybody else. There was trust. My mom would leave a handful of coins in a cracked teacup in the milk chute for the milkman. People parked their cars and left them unlocked. Workmen put down their tools on the worksite, and left them overnight. You might inadvertently lean your bicycle parked against the wire backstop at the school ball diamond, and wander home without it, but it would be there the next morning. Tree houses were left untouched. We were guardians of the neighbourhood—each and every one of us.

In a way, the porches and verandahs that I speak about were part of the landscape. Our moms and dads sat in those large wicker chairs and monitored the street before us. Not like spies—I don't mean that. It was in our nature to not let anything escape our attention. Today, instead of wiling away summer afternoons on their verandahs, people now congregate just a few feet inside garages with the doors open. They slump in lawn chairs, and drink beer, read the paper, barbecue. Mr. and Mrs. Front Porch has been replaced by Mr. and Mrs. Open Garage Door. But it's not with the same vigilance. It's not the 21st century term—"Neighbourhood Watch."

I know it sounds idealistic, nostalgic even. But as a boy of four, I remember once harassing my mother to stop the bread man for donuts. Her refusals quickly led me to swipe *Monopoly* money from my brother's game to fool the bread man into giving me sweets. Just in time to catch him on his route, I marched out to Prado brandishing a fistful of *Monopoly* money. He must've smiled when he spotted the colourful denominations. Without hesitation, he filled a bag with donuts and handed it to me. Figuring I had fooled him, I tore off down the driveway, past the screen door, and raced down the basement stairs. Of course, when my mother noticed me digging into this bag, she didn't buy my story. She made me stand beside her while she frantically rifled through her purse. I will never forget how she glared at me. She was certain that I had pilfered the change in her purse.

I tell that story, and others, because it says something of the time. It was an era of caring, of belief in one another—as idealistic as that might sound. In some ways, things were easier, less complicated. Handing me the donuts maybe made this guy's day. I wasn't just another nameless customer. We were a good Riverside family. Why not make an exception? There are stories of the Riverside Police returning suddenly-in-trouble young teenage boys to their parents for a good scolding rather than arresting them for some misdemeanor. And advice was never far away. Sometimes it came from a local politician, or a war vet, a nurse next door, or the Catholic priest. My father, for example, wrestling with my oldest brother's wish to join the Navy, eventually turned for advice to Father Dill. This was in 1956, eleven years after the end of the Second World War, and only three years after the Korean War. All my father could envision was losing a son. He had lost four cousins in the disastrous Dieppe Raid during the Second World War fourteen years earlier. The priest was the only educated man that my father knew. The advice was simple: let him join. And my brother did, along with his cousin who lived a few doors away on Prado. I remember the two of them shipping out from the docks downtown at the Detroit River. I was there to bid goodbye.

Ours was a different time in the 1950s and early 1960s. I wasn't there when the town became part of Windsor. That happened January 1, 1966. I was working in Toronto. It didn't really affect me. I knew nothing of Riverside's politics. But the people in

Riverside continued to identify themselves as being from that place. I wondered how my father felt that day in the new year when Riverside came under the official jurisdiction of Windsor. Did he believe the old values from that period would vanish? Today as I stand at Pillette and Wyandotte, it is a different world. The Centre Theatre is gone. McDonald's now looms high above in its place. Brennan High School nearby has edged its way to crowd the walls of the old church building. Tattoo parlours and pizza joints have invaded the area. And Glengarda—that fine old Ursuline convent built in 1919—has been swallowed up entirely by high-rise condos. Gone is its elegant, Italianate-style bell tower. Gone is the religious order, and its influence over the landscape, over the population. Maybe, gone, too, are the values we once held. Maybe neighbours no longer know neighbours. Maybe it's awkward to knock on someone's door to ask for help. I'm not sure. I live in a different part of the city. In my own end of town, it used to be that this elderly Italian woman cared for the nearby residents. No one needed to check the municipal calendar around the time of a civic holiday to see if it was still yard waste day, or the day for recycling, or garbage pick-up. She knew. She'd drag out the bins, and then everybody else would do the same. I also used to watch her make her way down the street with a pot of hot chicken broth for an ailing neighbour, knowing he couldn't get out anymore. Or patiently taking the time to instruct a teenage boy on how to prepare pasta. She reminded me of what it was like in Riverside. It was not uncommon for Henry Shanfield to bend to the pleas of a man starting a new job, handing him a clean shirt and trousers, knowing the dry goods store bill wouldn't get paid until that first paycheque. That's what it was like. Maybe it was that camaraderie, that small town ethic, that sense of neighbourhood, or maybe it was bound up in the way people felt during the war, that sense of belonging, of losing one's loved ones. Whatever the reason, there's one thing I'm certain of: in old Riverside, that sense of community was real.

# Ford City

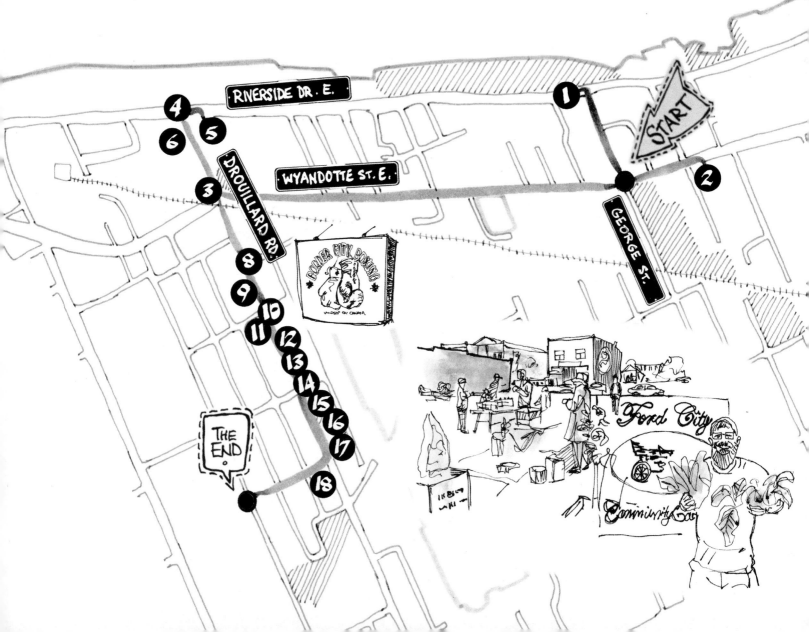

## Ford City Town Hall c. 1964

with *Our Lady of the Lake Roman Catholic Church* *
& *Ford Power Plant stacks*

[* later, Holy Rosary R.C. and still later Water's Edge Event Centre]

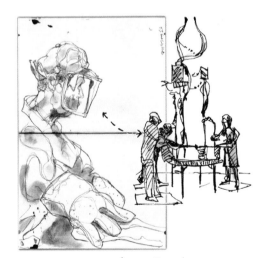

## Generations Sculpture

Drouillard at Whelpton

with detail from the artist's sketchbook.

Drouillard Road c. 1950

Ford Model-T Assembly Line

Bishop Fallon

Walkerville Wagon Works

# FORD CITY
*January 11, 2016*
*4.6 km*

The second part of this odyssey of the five towns is Ford City, bounded on the east by Pillette Road. Every Saturday morning from 1954 to 1958, I crossed that line from Riverside into Ford City by bus, getting off at George Avenue. I didn't know anything about boundary lines; it didn't much matter. Life for me revolved around piano lessons. I'd head down to Holy Rosary Convent, then owned by the Sisters of St. Joseph, at the foot of George. Conservationists in Windsor now call this building the Frank H. Joyce house after its original owner. Its address is 3975 Riverside Drive East.

And that's where I'm headed now. Starting at Wyandotte, I make my way north on George Avenue, anticipating this sprawling Tudor Revival mansion, with its tall and decorative chimneys and iron gates encompassing the property. Originally, it was designed by George Masson of the Sheppard and Masson architectural firm, built for industrialist Frank Henderson Joyce in 1926. The mansion boasted of a five-car garage and servants' quarters. In 1937, the property was sold to Thomas E. Walsh who owned an advertising agency, whose biggest client was Chrysler. He sold the property to the Western Ontario Broadcasting Company—now CKLW—but when the neighbourhood protested the notion of having a radio station operating next to their homes, the media company leased it to John Bankhead, the U.S. Vice-Council in Windsor. The Sisters of St. Joseph, seeing the need to accommodate its growing religious order, finally bought the building in 1952. John Boyde was ushered in to draw up the blueprints for a new south wing and organize renovation of the main house.

Built in 1926, the Frank H. Joyce House, at 3975 Riverside Drive East, was Holy Rosary Convent when I took piano lessons there from Sister St. James in the 1950s. I would slip in the back door, visible at the rear of the building, pictured at right.

Today, I pause in the open parking lot at the back of this expansive building, now owned by the Académie Ste.-Cécile. There's the door where I'd slip in, ever anxious to see Sister St. James, the severe piano teacher. I feared her every Saturday morning. She knew instantly if I had slackened off in my daily practising and held nothing back in her criticism. She only ever complimented me once, when I took the Royal Conservatory exam. Sister St. James had stationed herself just outside the dark oak door, listening to me as I played for the examiner. When he left, I heard her talking to the Conservatory official. Finally, she appeared, looking defeated. She told me that I had fallen one mark short of getting first class honours. She held a tiny gold pin between her thumb and index finger and said, "This is what you would've received if you got first class honours." She paused, "He was wrong. You deserved first class honours, and that's why I'm giving you this pin." My only compliment. In that instant, it taught me something about perfection, about hard work—to know within myself just how good I could be. That lesson, I will never forget.

The Henkel Home, pictured in 1918, once stood at the southeast corner of George Avenue and Riverside Drive.

Today, only the ghosts of those sisters remain in my memory. The nuns moved out in 2006. Other sisters, who taught at St. Thomas Separate School, also lived there. A good friend, and former sister who used to reside in this convent, is poet Mary Ann Mulhern. She recalls her room—each sister had her own—with just a bed, a desk, a chair, a lamp, and sink. Spartan. Twenty-five nuns housed there. Mondays to Fridays, they would fan out to schools all over the city.

Holy Rosary Convent abounded with characters. One nun had nicknames for all the sisters, including one who was christened "Kissy face" because she was so pretty. Another nun, who made tea for the others at meals, would occasionally forewarn a select group from filling their cups from a specific teapot, which was brimming with dandelion wine that she secretly made. But none compared to Sister Menard, who had a bizarre preoccupation with "crashing funerals." Unlike the others, she didn't go out to teach, and so took every opportunity to see the secular world. Her ticket to freedom was a funeral—in particular, any deaths from French families. Sister Menard kept an eagle eye on the obituaries in the newspaper, and whenever she spotted a French name, she would invent an excuse to attend. Often, she pretended she was a long-lost relative or close family friend.

Before leaving the convent, right across the street at George and Riverside Drive was the once sumptuous summer home of Robert Henkel who owned Henkel Flour

Mills in Detroit. His ivy-covered home sat on a piece of property that extended all the way to Wyandotte and had a fence to mark its privacy. The Henkels sold the property around the time of the Second World War and it was used by the Frontier Badminton Club, who leased it out for weddings and receptions. Eventually, it was torn down to make room for more housing. The only remaining element is the name of the adjoining street: Henkel Place.

Also at the foot of George Avenue, along the riverfront, was the East Windsor Bathing Beach (also called Ford City Beach). It was closed after excessive dredging of the river, done to permit sea-going freighters, caused treacherous currents. Before that, during the 1930s, the docks extended out into the river, and this bathing spot, which stretched out between Strabane Avenue to the west and Rossini Boulevard to the east, was among the most popular in the area. In the 1920s, Ford City had made tremendous efforts to reclaim the land here, and created a 200-foot sandy beach for its residents. Today it is Alexander Park, named for former Canadian Governor General Harold Alexander of Tunis.

I turn and head back south along George Avenue, returning to Wyandotte. Upon reaching that thoroughfare, I head two blocks east to pause in front of a 19th century farmhouse at 4219 Wyandotte Street East that has always fascinated me. It belonged to Stanislas Janisse, and was built in 1877. The house, with its extensive verandah, stands out because it has nothing in common with any other building near it.

Left: The East Windsor Bathing Beach, at the foot of George Avenue, was a popular spot in the 1930s. Today, it is Alexander Park, pictured below.

The Stanislas Janisse House was built in 1877. It sits at 4219 Wyandotte Street East and is still privately owned. Note the house number, indicating the house's historical significance: "est. 1877."

The owners have marked its importance with a plaque at the entrance declaring its age.

I turn around and walk west on Wyandotte, heading towards Drouillard Road. At one time, travellers along this route could ride electric streetcars between the towns. That may account for the wide thoroughfare along Wyandotte. The stops were situated in the middle of the street. When the streetcars disappeared, so did the medians.

### Drouillard Road

When I reach the viaduct and underpass where the street dips down into an area that is sometimes flooded, I turn north to the river. This viaduct, constructed in 1930 and 1931, was prompted by the tie-up in traffic on these roads with the railway crossing. It joined Ford City, then called East Windsor, to Riverside and permitted an uninterrupted flow of traffic. The construction of these viaducts was

done by the unemployed on welfare during the Great Depression. They were paid with meal tickets and coal vouchers.

This is Drouillard Road, effectively the main street of Ford City—the town's name, of course, originating with the birth and development of the car company that set up its Canadian headquarters here in 1904.

As one travels farther along Drouillard, it becomes clear that the only ostensible design that was imposed upon this once bustling community is the governing presence of the car. Rosemary Donegan, who curated an exhibit on Ford City at the Art Gallery of Windsor in 1994, wrote: "The plants themselves were built on a north-south axis, like two thick industrial spines, parallel to Drouillard and Walker. Drouillard was the main street and centre of the working-class…" Town fathers failed to synchronize development, and houses sprung up in the neighbourhood helter-skelter around the plants. Railway tracks crossed over streets, taking precedence, all leading to and

The Drouillard Road underpass, looking north, c. 1931. To the right, this artwork, installed on the southeast corner in 2016, welcomes motorists into old Ford City. It is part of an effort to tie the neighbourhood's identity to its heritage with Ford Motor Company of Canada.

from the factories with no regard for residential neighbourhoods. As one walks Drouillard Road, or dips west to Albert Road, the buildings and streets betray the haphazard manner in which this community grew. Homes were thrown up, built from heavy-duty crates and discarded lumber. My father built two homes from the salvage of those crates. So did hundreds of other families.

Former Windsor archivist G. Mark Walsh in *Archivaria 29* describes Ford City at its time of incorporation in 1913, as being "little more than a shanty town for industrial workers." On the surface, that's why it was regarded unfairly by the other river communities. At its core, he said, was a municipality of predominantly French Canadians, whose ancestors dated all the way back to the surrender of Detroit. Many of the pioneer families there worked for John Askin and his partner Angus Mackintosh in their North West Company. The young Ford City, however, was attracting immigrants, mostly from Eastern Europe, with its promise of manufacturing jobs. The other river towns were not particularly keen to attract this population growth, hence they made little effort to accommodate them. By 1928, Ford City's population hit a staggering 16,000. The town attempted to keep pace with suitable infrastructure, boasting six public schools and a main retail thoroughfare. A year later, its ambitious politicians switched the name to East Windsor. People, however, still called this community of some 1,600 acres "Ford City." Even today people call it that.

As the writers of *Postcards from the Past* state, the rise of Ford City was "meteoric, propelled by the coming of the automobile." Next door was Walkerville, but Hiram Walker set the tone for that municipality with meticulous planning and measured growth. In comparison, Ford City was driven by necessity. The Architectural Conservation Advisory Committee on Ford City states that in hindsight, it was clear that "Ford City had grown too fast." The frenzied growth, combined with the lack of urban planning and vision, was not sustainable. Moreover, the boom-to-bust narrative that haunts this community is directly tied to the company that gave it its name: Ford of Canada. And that is no more keenly felt than from where I am now standing, at the foot of Drouillard Road, looking towards the Detroit River.

This aerial view of Ford Motor Company of Canada, c. 1952, displays the haphazard layout of old Ford City, with housing interspersed around the plants. Drouillard Road runs north-south through the middle of the photograph, intersected by railway lines. Ford Plant One, now demolished, dominates the foreground at the riverfront.

It is hard to imagine that this empty, grassy space was once a booming factory—the birthplace of the automotive industry in Canada. Gone from the riverfront, except for the towering Ford Power Plant, is the massive window-lined automobile assembly operation built in 1912: Ford Plant One. Ford Motor Company sprawled alongside the Detroit River on what was reclaimed land. Fifteen-foot metal lettering spread out over 450 feet with the words *Ford Motor Co. of Canada* could easily be read by our neighbours to the north. I remember the demolition crews working through the winter of 1969 to tear down the long, vacant building. I was six years old when Ford started pulling its assembly operations from Windsor. It also moved its head offices to Oakville by 1954—only fifty years after the Canadian company's humble beginnings in a refitted wagon works on this very spot.

Ford Motor Company really started in March 1904, when Henry Ford teamed up with Gordon McGregor whose father, William, founded the Walkerville Wagon Company. William McGregor was a savvy businessman, having made his fortune selling horses to the Union Army in the United States during the Civil War. Later he would open a bank, a real estate company, a mill, a fence company, and of course, the Walkerville Wagon Works. William also ran for political office and served as Warden for Essex County and as a member of Parliament from 1874 to 1896. William's son learned much from him, and Gordon handily took over management of the family business in 1901. Two years later, he became its president. That was the year William died. In January 1904, Gordon told his brothers that the future was the automobile. He said, "There are men in Detroit who say every farmer will soon be using an automobile. I don't see why we cannot build them here in the wagon factory."

That was the spark that led to the creation of the Ford Motor Company of Canada.

It was McGregor who initiated the negotiations with Henry Ford in March 1904, along with a group of other Windsor businessmen.

Ford Motor Company of Canada started producing cars out of the old Walkerville Wagon Works, pictured here in 1904, shortly after the car company was founded. A sign over the entrance reads: "Ford Motor Company of Canada Automobile Manufacturers."

Their pitch hinged on the fact that the tariff on component parts was less than on assembled American automobiles. Ford is described by historian Neil Morrison as a "struggling inventor" who needed an infusion of cash and the moral support for his vision. He found that with McGregor. The negotiations to set up Ford Motor Company of Canada was struck at The Exchange, now known as the Victoria Tavern—not the one that now exists at 400 Chilver in Walkerville, but in a building situated behind it.

Car production at the former wagon works factory in Walkerville started October 10, 1904. That fall, 17 employees working around the clock turned out 117 of the first cars ever to be built in Canada. This was the Model C. According to the Ford Motor Company's own history, the operation was rudimentary:

> ...the cars were assembled one by one as the parts were ferried by wagonload across the river, and often they were delivered to the factory by horse and cart [...] In those days the Canadian plant depended entirely upon American sources for parts and supplies. Sometimes a vital nut or bolt fell down through a crack in the floor, delaying production until a replacement part arrived from Detroit. Sometimes, too, production halted while the general manager took to the road as sales manager to sell the last car built. Proceeds of that sale were needed before the company could purchase parts to build another car.

Ford Model 'T's come off the line at Ford Plant One, c. 1913.

Four years later, the classic Model T went into production in Canada. The plant Ford was using was constantly expanded with new assembly line techniques, with conveyor belts being introduced in 1913. The *Walkerville Times* describes those early years as "the springboard from which ensued the most vibrant growth of a manufacturing industry which Canada had ever seen."

The agreement that McGregor ironed out with Henry Ford was the right to market the automobile to others in the British Empire, taking advantage of the preferential tariffs. This soon led to the Canadian division of Ford owning subsidiaries in South Africa, New Zealand, and Australia. Exporting cars overseas started as early as 1905. The first of these was shipped to Calcutta, the second to New Zealand.

The Ford Motor Company operation soon outgrew its original wagon works building that sat on a site that had first been owned by Jenkins Shipyards, and later a grape sugar refinery. A new building—Plant One—was completed in 1910. Plant Two was erected in 1922 farther south, in the heart of Ford City, and this was followed by another plant in 1937. The Power House was put up in 1923, and the legendary Albert Kahn, leading industrial architect of the 20th century, designed it.

Ford workers numbered 1,400 by 1913. Their wages then were $4 an hour and they had a 48-hour work week. No other place in the country could boast such good pay. This, naturally, caused an influx of workers, mostly landless farmers from all across the country, but also from parts of Europe—Romanians, Ukrainians, Serbians, and Italians.

Ford of Canada caused an explosion in the industry, and soon the Big Three were coming to the south shore of the Detroit River. Chrysler started in 1925, followed by Maxwell-Chalmers, on St. Luke Road. General Motors

took over the Fisher Body plant on Edna Street. By the 1920s, the municipality was booming, and building paved roads and schools.

However, McGregor never fully saw this vision of the world embracing the car the way it did. He was 49 when he suddenly took ill and died—either from an old injury, cancer, or a rare blood-vessel disorder, the cause is contested. But the result of McGregor's efforts to establish an automobile industry in Ford City was the creation of an urban environment, or zone that saw the workforce gather around the factory, say Mary Baruth and Mark Walsh in *Strike: 99 Days on the Line*. They wrote that "life was hard but good… Ford City grew to be one of the most industrialized areas of the 'Border Cities'… [and] one of the best places for American automotive companies to locate in order to gain access to the markets of the former British colonies."

What is not remembered, or even talked about, were those early years when the car was still an unfamiliar site on the streets. The horse and buggy were more common. According to Morrison's history, "apparently little was affected at first by the motor vehicle." The bicycle in some ways was more of nuisance than the automobile. People adopted a penchant for joy riding on the wooden sidewalks. Police responded to the outcry among the population with an organized crusade against such violators. In May 1900, 14 were arrested, including the police department's own inspector. Windsor's Chief Magistrate, Alexander Bartlet, fined each of them $1.50 and let them off with a warning. However, this ambivalence towards the automobile wouldn't last.

This postcard from 1911 shows a typical streetscape, here on Sandwich Street (Riverside Drive) and Ouellette Avenue, featuring the most common forms of transportation: horse and buggy, streetcar, and bicycle.

Sandwich Street and Ouellette Avenue, Windsor, Canada

In 1904, a new federal law was passed to address the growing problem of horses being spooked by passing cars: "If your horse is afraid to face an automobile on the road, hold up your hand and the driver of the motor vehicle must stop and assist you to pass." Soon, the "devil wagons" were taking the bicycle's place as the subject of the public's ire. Indeed, the *Amherstburg Echo* in August 1906 bemoaned, too, what had evolved with the bicycle, suggesting that those good times were over, and that now, this vehicle was being used mostly for business purposes. The editors wrote: "Say, what has become of the lady bicycle rider? A few summers ago, she was in the public eye to a very large extent. Now she is an exception rather than a rule." In Ford City, the critiques and fears over the coming of the car were tempered by the promise of prosperity—and the gamble payed off. The car was here to stay.

## Drouillard and Riverside Drive

I am getting ahead of myself. I turn around to make my way south past what used to be Our Lady of the Lake Catholic Church *(2879 Riverside Drive East),* commonly known as Holy Rosary. During Prohibition, an illuminated cross on its steeple, bought and paid for by the parishioners, was a beacon for the rumrunners crossing the river at night after dropping off contraband liquor to Michigan customers. The Romanesque-style building with its twin dome bell towers, designed by the Williams Brothers, is really the second church structure on this site. The first, built in 1884, burned to the ground

Our Lady of the Lake Catholic Church, better known as Holy Rosary, was built in 1907-8 and now operates as an event venue, Water's Edge, pictured here.

in 1907 when sparks from a nearby train set the church on fire. The new edifice was built at a cost of $45,000 the following year.

It is a place of tremendous history, none more dramatic than the so-called 'Battle of Ford City.' Nine years after the new building was opened with all the liturgical fanfare, English and French-speaking parishioners were reduced to stone-throwing and running at each other with sticks and shovels, over the rumour that the Irish bishop, Bishop Michael Francis Fallon, had appointed an anti-French priest.

I imagine that infamous moment in 1917, but why all the fuss? Why such extreme reaction? It stemmed from Bishop Fallon's harsh and unyielding opposition to bilingual schools in Essex County. Fallon argued that Ontario was an English-speaking province and that "boys and girls going out to fight the battle of life must be equipped first with English." Scholar Jack D. Cecillon argues that Fallon believed "the only way to improve the quality of education… was to allow instruction in one language only…"

The reaction from this part of the province—where there were still rich pockets of French Canadians—was immediate, especially when Fallon closed three area French language schools. Sisters of St. Joseph nuns didn't take it kindly and readily reported to the newspapers that they were now "forbidden to teach in that [French] language…" That's when the pastor at Our Lady of the Lake, Father Lucien Alexandre Beaudoin, stepped into the fray. Outraged at Fallon's interference, he accused the bishop of prejudice and wanting bilingual schools to shut down altogether. Fallon denied it, but there was no refuting his statements, according to Cecillon. The bishop had said time and time again that bilingual schools "left children illiterate and completely unprepared for life in the industrialized world."

A young Father Lucien Alexandre Beaudoin, the beloved priest of Our Lady of the Lake parish from 1891 until his death in 1917.

Letters from Essex County priests flooded the desk of Pope Benedict XV, demanding that Fallon be removed from office. Even the Quebec Curia joined the controversy. One cardinal went so far as to draw up a list of possible replacements and forwarded these to the Holy Father. The Quebec press, including renegade journalist Henri Bourassa, seized upon this fiery revelation and denounced Fallon. Pope Benedict finally was drawn into the controversy and penned apostolic letters in an attempt to bring reconciliation.

Fallon was furious, and reacted by forming a diocesan tribunal—where he acted as judge and prosecutor, as well as accused—to deal with this defamation of his character. As a result, he managed to get the priests who had signed the petition to retract their statements. Three local priests refused: Rev. Pierre Loiselle of River Canard, Pierre L'Heureux of Belle River and Napoleon Saint-Cyr of Stoney Point. The latter priest was expelled from the diocese and was denied his pension, while the other two were suspended.

The real target was Fr. Beaudoin. Fallon went after him with a vengeance, trying (unsuccessfully) to get the Ford City priest to take full responsibility for the controversy. As Cecillon writes, Beaudoin "refused to play the scapegoat." Rome finally stepped in, ordering Fallon to cease in his actions against the priest. However, the impact on Beaudoin was severe, and left him in terrible health. By 1916, the 54-year-old pastor was reduced to using crutches to carry out his parish duties.

As I stand in the parking lot at Riverside Drive and Drouillard and study this tall riverfront church, I begin to glean the pent-up rage over Fallon's indiscriminate actions. Just before the riot in 1917, the bishop toured his French-speaking parishes to denounce and belittle those disobedient Franco-Ontarian priests for tarnishing his image from the pulpit. Instead, Fallon only further embittered these parishioners.

The infamous standoff that put our Lady of the Lake on the front pages of newspapers all over Canada was set into motion by the death of their beloved pastor. Beaudoin had been suffering from phlebitis and died August 18, 1917. Cecillon believes that upon Beaudoin's death, the parish had become "a powder keg… The potential for catastrophe required a simple spark." And that was ignited at the funeral mass for Beaudoin, held on August 22. Parishioners discovered that among the clergy attending that mass was Rev. François Laurendeau, their newly appointed pastor, the same one who had served on Fallon's "notorious tribunal."

That's when the trouble accelerated. Immediately following the funeral mass, parishioners raided the presbytery, and seized Laurendeau's suitcases and belongings, and tossed them on the front lawn of the church. That's when the blockade formed, preventing the new pastor from re-entering his new residence. The

Our Lady of the Lake, c. 1913. Note that the church presbytery is visible just behind the church building.

demonstrators then crowded the sweeping front steps of the church. Laurendeau was forced to change from his liturgical garb into his clothes out in the open. He then fled the scene, and the angry mob quickly assembled into a defiant standoff. The dissenters then issued an ultimatum that unless Bishop Fallon replaced Laurendeau, they would continue to blockade the property.

The situation only worsened when Fallon fired back, threatening to shut down the church permanently if its parishioners didn't accept his appointment. It came to a head on September 8, with the police marching in to break up the blockade. They were surprised to be facing some 3,000 protesters ready to do battle. And

## WOMEN EMULATE THEIR RUSSIAN PROTOTYPES IN FORD CHURCH RIOT

Battle Has All Thrills
and Frills of Real War
On a Modified Scale

This September 10 headline in the *Evening Record* reveals French-Canadian women as instigators in the 'Battle of Ford City.'

The embattled Bishop Michael Francis Fallon is pictured here in 1920, during Assumption College's Golden Jubilee Celebrations.

A 1920 portrait of Father François Laurendeau, who served the parish from 1917 to 1942.

as soon as someone fell at the hands of the billy club swinging officers, a full-scale riot ensued, completed with bricks, stones, shovels, broken bottles, and even knitting needles used as weapons. Cecillon said the fiercest rivals to the police came from the French-Canadian women in the ranks of the protesters. They were described by the *Evening Record* as "sharing the will of the Russian Regiment of Death." They blockaded the doors to the rectory porch, and adamantly refused to permit Laurendeau, or anyone, back inside. The riot lasted for twenty minutes, resulting in several injured and nine men arrested.

That story is probably one of the most dramatic chapters in the history of the London Diocese. As for poor Father Laurendeau—the one who sat on that hated diocesan tribunal that slapped the wrists of these rebel priests—he had pleaded with Fallon not to send him to Ford City, sensing the trouble that would ensue. He also petitioned Pope Benedict XV to replace him, but instead the Vatican threatened parishioners with ex-communication if they did not accept him. As it turned out, the priest wound up being regarded with much love by parishioners, and membership rose by leaps and bounds under his direction. But in that first year, following the fracas in Ford City, many parishioners stayed away from attending mass. Laurendeau finally found their trust. He stayed until 1942 as their pastor.

Bishop Fallon continued his stormy reign until 1931, his name cursed in most French-Canadian homes in southwestern Ontario—including ours. My maternal great uncle, Rev.

Henri Baillargeon of Stoney Point, Ontario, had been personally blocked from entering St. Peter's Seminary by Fallon. He was forced to attend Le Grand Séminaire de Montreal instead. Furthermore, he was never permitted to serve in the London Diocese, but was assigned to the Detroit Archdiocese. Windsor-born writer Michael Power, who considers the controversial bishop his specialty, agrees that Fallon stirred up "a public row a day [...] the public loved or loathed him, venerated or vilified him." This Irish firebrand bishop also set his sights on Hôtel-Dieu Hospital in Windsor, threatening to replace the French-speaking sisters with his own hand-picked nuns. In the end, he did not, but he did refuse the hospital religious order's request for his approval of their new mother superior. Instead, Fallon dispatched to them an Irish nun from Kingston to take over. Unfortunately, this woman only spoke English, and as a result, was alienated among the community at Hôtel-Dieu where the predominant language was French.

Still, this is the same Catholic bishop who opened 18 new parishes, decorated St. Peter's Cathedral in London, and built St. Peter's Seminary. Sadly, says Power, the issue he raised over bilingualism was "played out in operatic passion and paranoia," both at the provincial level and at the Vatican.

The church's history echoed large with Larry Horwitz, entrepreneur, politician, and head of the Downtown Windsor Business Improvement Association. He bought the place in 2015, knowing full well it needed a new roof and an air conditioning system.

*Windsor Star* columnist Gord Henderson noted that Horwitz saw it "still as a magical place" that "oozes history." More importantly—and this is key to what I have held for years—"If Horwitz can figure out a way to keep this vital piece of Windsor's mostly obliterated heritage safe from the wrecker's ball that would be a huge win for the city." And it was.

The church has been saved, and now serves the community as Water's Edge Event Centre. And yet, much of the history around it has vanished. In addition to Ford Plant One on the riverfront, the Ford City Town Hall, once at the southeast corner of Drouillard and Riverside, and the Ford City Post Office, are gone from the landscape. When the Town Hall, a landmark from the 1920s, was demolished, it was turned into a parking lot, and for years, it served a thriving church.

This postcard from 1925 shows Our Lady of the Lake, the Post Office two doors east; and the Town Hall in the foreground with a peaked roof. The Ford Powerhouse and Ford City Public School can be seen in the background. While not pictured, Ford Plant One was directly across the street.

Frederick B. Taylor's *Looking South Over Windsor,* commissioned by Seagram's of Canada in 1951, shows Ford City from the perspective of the roof of Ford Plant One.

I now make my way south along Drouillard Road, my body bent to the wind. Snow flurries now. But this does not deter me. I am beginning to see the shape of what was once a thriving town. As I walk, I recall a stunning painting by Frederick B. Taylor that gives you the sense of this community as it existed in those early days. His depiction of Ford City was called *Looking South Over Windsor* and was one of 22 paintings commissioned in the early 1950s by Samuel Bronfman, president of Seagram's of Canada, as part of the *Cities of Canada* project. Its view shows the rooftop of

the Ford plant on Riverside Drive, as well as the church and the town hall. You can also see the power plant down the street.

Taylor was best known for his urban street scenes, but also of war industry workers. This artist, who, incidentally, was the younger brother of brewery tycoon E.P. Taylor, developed a keen interest in painting while attending McGill where he studied architecture. It was in the wartime period that Taylor put his focus upon Canadian industry, with paintings that depicted the life in the harsh conditions of the factory. He was so passionate about this that he pushed and arranged for his paintings and etchings to be exhibited in factory lunchrooms and union halls.

What is interesting about Ford City—from the point of view of the artist—is this relationship between the residents and the industrial presence. Rosemary Donegan, guest curator of a Ford City exhibit in 2014 at the Art Gallery of Windsor, argues that the major reason for the wide appeal of industrial images is the "complex and contradictory relationship artists and the public had to mass industrialization in this period." She reveals that while industry and machinery were celebrated in art, specific locales were almost never revealed because industrialists rarely permitted access to their factories. There was an exception, a significant one: Yousuf Karsh, perhaps the greatest of 20th-century portrait photographers, ventured into the Ford plant in 1951 to photograph the workers as part of the car company's annual report. Ken Saltmarche, former head of the Windsor Art Gallery, said Karsh had "come close to immortalizing the working man." Donegan says the photographs in many ways are like "movie stills in their formal composition and direct gaze… the photographs of the young workers evoke the sexual and smouldering intensity of a James Dean or Marlon Brando."

I never knew the subtle complexities of this industrial landscape and its citizens when I was growing up. I was warned about this neighbourhood flanked by the steel and brick and the row upon row of slanted tinted and grimy windows. High crime. Avoid the quarter. I was also conflicted in my loyalties because my cousin, David, grew up on its streets, and was forever in trouble with the law. His name was well known to *Windsor Star* readers. His father, Gilbert, lived in a modest frame house farther up the street, next door to the rundown church. The place is still there. My uncle would sit on the front steps chatting with my dad about David, who was at Kingston Penitentiary. Years later, I bumped into David at a family reunion. "I never really knew you," I said. He smiled, then remarked, "Well… I was away at summer camp a lot." Congenial. A nice guy. His life had been turned around after all the forays into crime. In Kingston, where he made his home, he became someone of high regard for his outreach to convicts and addicts. His reputation was that of Father Charbonneau in Windsor, the man who founded Brentwood. When David died, there was a huge funeral in Kingston to celebrate his work.

## *Trenton & Drouillard*

I climb the slope from the underpass. The place at the top of the hill on the east side is the International Tavern (928 Drouillard) and the road running east from it is Trenton, which dead-ends onto a Ford Motor company gate. I'm not sure of this place. I haven't ever stopped in, but have always been curious.

I move farther along. I'm not surprised to find a ghost town. The street is no longer brimming with business, as it did in the past. One would have been hard pressed to find an empty retail outlet anywhere in the late 1940s and early 1950s. Today, buildings are abandoned, run-down; but a bright light is that there is a community garden on Drouillard Road. The same has happened in Detroit. In the midst of boarded-up edifices and vacant lots, small agricultural ventures are springing up, even in the downtown core. The Ford City Community Garden (971 Drouillard Road) is hard to miss.

International Tavern, located at 928 Drouillard Road.

The Ford City Community Garden was opened in 2010, as part of an initiative to "enrich the lives of urban residents."

The community garden is colourful, plentiful, abundant—a symbol of hope. It tells the world there is a reason to be here, to not give up. Former *Windsor Star* writer Frances Willick, who wrote extensively about Ford City and its past and future, interviewed an elderly woman who revealed that a shared garden on Drouillard wasn't unusual, considering the history of the street. Willick wrote:

> That garden will bring back memories for one woman who has lived in the area for about 70 years. The 86-year-old remembers Drouillard during the Great Depression when residents farmed carrots, cabbages, and onions in

a community garden between Seminole Street and the train tracks. "After Halloween, you could take stuff from anyone's gardens," this woman said. "Of course, there was nothing else left after Halloween—maybe some beets or something.

This elderly woman recalled Ford City humming once more by the 1940s, with grocery stores, hardware stores, bakeries, dry goods shops, doctor's offices, an appliance shop, a shoe store. There wasn't an empty store to be found. "Now, she doesn't venture out much," says Willick. "Gone are the days of walking home at midnight after the community dances, or taking off to Toronto without even locking the front door."

Standing in the garden and turning around to face north, there on the wall overlooking this place is a mural, one of 36 that adorn this street. Called *Pioneer Spirit*, it tells anyone who pauses here something about the history surrounding Ford City. This one reaches back to the 1700s, when French settlers farmed those narrow strips stretching from the Detroit River for more than a mile south. In the 1820s, Francois Drouillard acquired a ribbon farm, then just east of where Drouillard Road is today. In fact, together with the neighbouring Maisonvilles, he allowed for a 'right-of-way' for the development of Drouillard Road in the 1860s.

Across the street from it on a brown-brick building is a giant mural of Margaret Sidoroff, a three-time world champion boxer whose life was this street. She trained at Border City Boxing, and eventually was one of its owners and trainers. The mural displays the pugnacious slouch of the female boxer who was never defeated in her amateur run and who fought all over the world as a pro. Today, Margaret teaches in the Essex County school system. Before going into education, Margaret was a teen counsellor and was regarded as a role model for Drouillard Road children, sharing with them her skills and encouraging them to pursue excellence. I remember photographing her on a steamy late spring afternoon. I marvelled at how her hands flew against the speed bag, and that intense, mesmeric stare she gave the moment.

## Whelpton and Drouillard

A stone's throw away is an old bank building on the northwest corner of Whelpton and Drouillard. If you enter from Whelpton, and climb a long flight of stairs, you will find New Song Church (993 Drouillard Road) has its administrative offices there. This was once the office of Floyd Zalev, a Windsor lawyer. In a way, it was also his home. He was there every day. I remember him well. There was no one in the city who knew real estate properties better than Floyd. If you mentioned the address of the street that you lived on, he would pause, roll his eyes up, as if he was about to read it off a list of city lot numbers, then he'd spew out its details from exactly where your house was located, names of previous owners, cite the builder and the original selling price. He was a walking encyclopedia of Windsor's real estate.

Top: Drouillard Road, c. 1930, looking north from Charles Street (Whelpton Street). Visible storefronts include Provincial Bank of Canada, J.A. King Dentist, Harry's Place, and T. Dubensky's Dry Goods.

Left: The Champs Mural, on the side of 993 Drouillard Road, features Margaret Sidoroff and Al Delaney, two boxing greats who hailed from Ford City.

Top: The Provincial Bank of Canada in 1931 now houses New Song Church, pictured at right. At one time, Floyd Zalev's offices were located on the second floor.

And so it came as no surprise that in February 1987, this legendary real estate agent registered the sale of an East Windsor home at 10:52 a.m., and that particular transaction ensured it had a place in Essex County history. The deal was the one millionth land registration recorded at the Windsor registry office. Eric Mayne, writing in the *Windsor Star* on February 7, 1987, described Zalev as "calm, cool, taking the occasion in stride." Apparently, Zalev proclaimed it "just another milestone." Even the new owners were unaware that the

sale had made history until they were contacted by the *Star*. Zalev also registered the first deal when the registry moved in 1977 from its original location, at Sandwich and Brock streets, to its present location at 250 Windsor Avenue.

The first transaction registered in Essex County was in 1796, and recorded the sale of a large lot located at the mouth of the Detroit River from William Caldwell to Susan Baby. Local historian Larry Kulisek said Caldwell was a frontiersman and Loyalist who battled the Americans during the Revolutionary War. Baby was Caldwell's mother-in-law, and the mother of one of Windsor's founding fathers, François Baby. Caldwell sold the plot to Baby for 2,500 New York pounds, one of several currencies in use at the time.

As I move down the street, I'm in the heart of Ford City. Besides the old plant gates, the sculpture and mural at Whelpton and Drouillard is an intimate reminder of the presence of the Ford Motor Company operations. This is across the street from the bank building at the Ford City Parkette. This metal sculpture, by artist and Ford journeyman Mark Williams, represents the generations of Canadians who built this city and put Windsor at the forefront of the world when it came to building cars. The wall mural of the yellow 1949 Ford Tudor represents the lifeblood of the Ford factory, rolling off the assembly line to join the more than three million vehicles built at Ford Plant One.

Today, I look at the park, and standing in the cold is an assembly of people waiting for the soup kitchen to open. It is early, but they are hungry. They stamp their feet in the cold. The wind has picked up, and light snow is falling. Willick, in writing about the Ford City neighbourhood, observed that Windsor was perhaps "the Canadian city most devastated by economic collapse and cuts in the auto sector, [and] this is the most visibly wounded neighbourhood."

You don't need to look far to see that. As I said, the former bank building now houses this evangelical church. It also accommodates a cafe. Breakfast, lunch, and dinner are served here each day. Friday nights are the community supper, and it brings neighbours, the homeless, the unemployed, people from all over the area. There's a prayer before dinner, but no one is pressing anyone to recite it. The church is open to everyone. This isn't the time to preach. It's a time for good deeds, respect, paying attention to the needs of everyone. Or as Pastor Kevin Rogers told the *Star*, it's a time "to come together, grab a bite and have a chat." The bearded, pony-tailed preacher has spent years now working in this neighbourhood and has seen Drouillard Road residents "living on the edge."

The Ford City Parkette at the corner of Whelpton and Drouillard features the "Generations" sculpture by Mark Williams.

> I never have a boring day. I love people that are colourful and that wear their heart on their sleeve. Among the poor there's a lot of honesty. There's a lot of sharing and looking out for each other and generosity. So, for me, I just feel that that's probably where Jesus would have hung out. And that's where I want to be.

Willick says that despite its reputation for crime, drugs, and prostitution, "this is a neighbourhood of small graces and big dreams, where residents seed wildflower mix in their city parks and where everyone—including the criminals, the "crackerjacks" [crack addicts] and the prostitutes—is invited to the dinner table." Still, Willick's article caused an uproar in Ford City when it appeared. Marina Clemens, executive director of Drouillard Place, penned this to the newspaper:

> For long-time residents and those of us who have worked in the area for over 30 years, the overall tone was degrading and the focus was on the addictions that some of our people struggle with, with very little mention of the services that are available in the area. Where were the pictures of our flower gardens, the beautiful, well-kept homes along Hickory, Albert, Henry Ford and St. Luke streets, the numerous murals and the sculpture at the Whelpton parkette? Not sure where Frances got her stats for the value of homes but according to other sources

homes have been selling for the asking price even in these difficult economic times. Again, where did she get her information that the Drouillard area was the most visibly wounded neighbourhood in this economic collapse? The parks staff have told us that our Drouillard Park has less vandalism than the parks in South Windsor, Forest Glade and the Ganatchio trail.

Pride. Dignity. A fierceness that defies all else. That's what you find on this street. I experienced it myself when I led a group of students to Drouillard Road in 2013. We moved the classroom from Dillon Hall at the University of Windsor to Atelier Virginanne. I spent four wintry months operating out of this small art gallery with a dozen journalism students whose job was to write stories and produce a documentary film on Ford City. We covered every square inch of the street from the evangelicals to the strip bar farther south, towards Tecumseh Road.

Dawn Trottier, one of those young student journalists who joined me, recalled that experience in the *Windsor Star*, admitting she had lived in this city all her life, but had never been to this neighbourhood. Preconceived notions prepared Trottier for a part of the city as a haven for "drugs and prostitution… The truth is, sure those things happen here but they also happen all over Windsor. Drouillard Road is a district with a rich history that somehow stalled after the downfall of the Ford Motor Company plant."

She instead encountered "community and home." She wrote:

For an outsider like myself, I couldn't see why someone would want to stay on Drouillard Road, let alone be proud to live on Drouillard Road. I understand it now. When the rest of the city 'forgot' about Drouillard Road, the community was bound tightly with a shared belief that the area was still home and could eventually thrive again. It's almost like a small town feel in a big city where everyone knows each other and helps each other out.

*Windsor Star* columnist Anne Jarvis believes the area is "vibrant." In a 2014 piece she describes the neighbourhood this way:

It's the modest red brick storefronts, the mom and pop shops that sustained the neighbourhood. It's the churches with gold and silver onion domes, the cultural and social centres. It's the murals and the sculpture proudly depicting the heritage of the birthplace of the automobile in Canada. Mostly, it's the feel of a close and once-thriving community… Drouillard Road: It's one of the funkiest streets in Windsor, and it's finally beginning to get its due.

Jarvis noted that there has been a small resurgence with a printing company, auction house,

This mural, "Shift Change," found at 998 Drouillard Road, is copied from a 1950 photograph of Ford workers by Fred Lazurek.

tailor, restaurant, and artist studios, all opening since 2010. The new owners of Maisonville Court retirement home plan a $6 million renovation, and as mentioned, Holy Rosary has been transformed into a banquet centre. Things are changing.

The problem with Ford City, and I think, Sandwich, too, is that people come and go, see the place, explore it, then depart. They rarely return. For me, Ford City is where my family got its start. My father initially lived on Albert Road, and walked to Seminole where he worked at the Canadian Motor Lamp which was producing 4,000 headlamps per day. That company started with 20 employees in 1913, but by 1929 boasted of 400 workers. This was life in Ford City. A bustling, fast-paced town whose population growth sprung up around

these car companies and smaller feeder plants. Eventually, people like my father moved away. In our case, it was to Riverside.

With this growth, the population's demographic in Ford City changed too. Up until the 1920s, it was predominantly French-Canadian, but during the 1930s, Eastern Europeans began to settle here, mostly from Poland, Romania, Russia, and Serbia. One such family was the Lazureks. They came right after the First World War. Theodore Fredrick Lazurek, or "Fred" as he came to be known, wasted no time in finding a job in Ford City. He became a photographer like his father, and worked from a home studio on Drouillard Road. His subject was life in East Windsor. A large mural of him covers part of the south-facing wall of Brown's Breaktime Lounge (1118

Drouillard Road) farther along Drouillard, near Richmond. Those honouring him state:

> Enthralled and inspired by its cultural diversity, Fred saw Ford City as a true community where everyone knew and cared about each other. A free spirit, unconcerned with fame or fortune, Fred was obsessed with recording images, taking delight in commonplace scenes like a group of boys hanging out at the Temple Theatre, or the neighbourhood knife sharpener on his daily rounds.

One such iconic image of his takes up most of a wall at Whelpton. Called "Shift Change," copied by Steven Johnson, this photo by Lazurek displays workers parading out at the end of a day, exhausted and hungry, and the gates out of which they spill is the Ford Motor Company Whelpton gate.

The image is important, too, because of the history it tells of the street and the workers. It was here in this neighbourhood that the labour laws we have today were thrashed out and fashioned. It is because of what happened here that unions all over this country can now pay homage to the men and women who put their future on the line when they stood up to the powerful forces of Ford Motor Company. It wasn't accomplished without a fight.

It all started in the midst of the Second World War. The United Auto Workers Local 200 negotiated and signed an agreement to represent Ford workers. The company had wanted a "committee" to do this when ordered by the federal department of labour. In January 1942, the UAW started negotiating on the part of Ford workers, and by November, organized a wildcat strike in response to Ford's plan to hire women for the line, but paying them 60-70% less. Local 200 effectively won wage parity for women, the first such gain for women in Canadian history. However, when all was said and done, Ford settled on not hiring women at all, and did not until 1977.

Three years later, the famous 99-day strike took place, and from that point the labour movement in Canada was never the same. The story of that formative event is documented in *Strike: 99 Days on the Line* by Mary Baruth and Mark Walsh. The company had wanted life in the plant to return to what had existed before the war, but workers weren't about to turn back the clock. As Baruth and Walsh state, "The Canadian UAW and indeed the entire Canadian Labour Movement did not see the end of World War II as a time to surrender."

Negotiations stalled, and Ford workers were ready to hit the street with "all of corporate and unionized Canada...watching," write Baruth and Walsh. On September 12, 1945, 11,000 Ford workers went on strike and stayed out for 99 days. The strike—seeking dues check-off, job security, medical benefits, better working conditions and decent wages—was historic. It established the principle of union security through compulsory dues check-off, where employees, regardless of whether they were union members or not, were obligated to pay union dues. This was called Rand Formula, and without it, organized labour would not be where it is today.

Early on in that labour incursion, workers shut down the company's powerhouse, thereby cutting off the heating system to the plant. With winter approaching, the pressure was mounting to procure the union's accord to turn it back on. Finally, the local police commission overruled Mayor Art Reaume, and ordered the police to move in and restore power. It wasn't very effective, because the police, say Baruth and Walsh, were not strike-breakers but "were sympathetic to the strikers." Indeed, "they went through the motions of trying to break the picket line but nothing more than a shoving match took place." The strikers themselves were conscious of this, and when they wielded two-by-four lumber, they used these to push away the officers rather than hit them. No one was really hurt, except for one constable who wound up with a black eye. This particular officer played euchre with the picketers at the Franklin Street gate, "and took a lot of teasing the next day when he resumed his post and his place at the card game."

The now famous two-day blockade in November 1945 was organized with the intention of averting violence. Ordered by Premier George Drew, the OPP and the RCMP had arrived in Windsor and rumours were flying that they were to launch an assault. The feds were also preparing to send in armoured tank units from Camp Borden. The union acted pre-emptively, setting out to block every possible avenue and entry point onto the company's property. Fifteen-hundred to 2,000 automobiles swarmed Drouillard, and stretched all the way through the viaduct and both east and west along Riverside Drive, then called Sandwich Street. A mammoth bottleneck.

The infamous blockade of the Ford Strike, taken November 6, 1945. This shot shows union members' cars and seized private automobiles jammed onto Drouillard Road, shown here from the viaduct on Wyandotte Street.

After three days, City Council finally demanded removal of the blockade. It achieved its main objective: the police and military did not intervene. And Ford workers caught the attention of the country and the sympathies of autoworkers elsewhere. Chrysler employees walked out in solidarity to join the pickets.

The Speed Graphic was the tool to document this moment in Ford City. If you look at the history of that camera, it's clear it was the choice of early-day photojournalists. Joe Rosenthal's image of Marines raising the American flag on Iwo Jima in 1945 was taken with a Speed Graphic. The last Pulitzer Prize winning photograph taken with this camera was composed by Yasushi Nagao in 1961, showing Inejiro Asanuma being assassinated on stage. In my first days of working at the *Windsor Star,* I recall seeing those cumbersome cameras on shelves near the old darkroom. Young reporters would pick them up and wonder out loud how the photographers survived hauling these around. They weighed a ton, and they were limited to less than a dozen shots. Our photographers relied upon these bulky cameras to cover

*Windsor Star* photographer Jack Dalgleish with his Speed Graphic, c. 1945.

the strike. I knew three of them who documented that legendary moment in labour history. They were the flamboyant Jack Dalgleish, Bert Johnson, and Cec Southward. Typical of them, whenever they spoke about those heady days of 1945, it wasn't tinged with a one-sided opinion. It was storytelling. All three had been photographers during the war with the RCAF. Cec was the quietest, always flashing that mischievous smile. In the darkroom at the old *Star* at Pitt and Ferry, there was always a bottle stashed away. It didn't take much to get Cec to talk.

But his photographs, and those of the other two, spoke volumes of what happened on the street here. The intersection of Drouillard and old Sandwich Street was their territory. They roamed it like attack dogs, poking their way through the blockade to capture the moment in its immediacy.

In the piece by Rosemary Donegan from the Ford City exhibit, we learn how the pictures these *Star* photographers captured showed "the predominance of young men and the portrayal of their militancy and strength of commitment." She wrote:

> Many… had only recently left the armed forces for civilian life. As veterans, they knew their rights—their need to make a decent living and their right to strike… the photographs capture the emotion and the discipline of the union membership especially the almost military organization of the picket lines, the auto blockade, and the women's auxiliary that fed the strikers.

Southward climbed the roof of the former Ford City Town Hall at Wyandotte and Drouillard to view and capture the bedlam on the street below. His aerial shots tell the whole story. Donegan said "his images of the viaduct use dramatic angles and architectural forms as frameworks… Their strong graphic compositions are energetic and deserved their front-page placement…"

But Southward pushed his way with his Speed Graphic along the street too, and went elbow to elbow with the men who had gathered there. He was familiar with many of them from the war.

It's difficult to imagine that time, to feel the anger, anxiety, to witness the frayed edges of a debate taken to the street, to these extremes. Ordinary people caught up in a cause. No one is ever conscious of seeing themselves as part of history, or conjuring the future to see themselves as part of a chapter describing how they inevitably changed the course of labour relations forever in this country. It happened right here, right where I'm standing as I continue walking south, away from the river.

This shot of workers trying to organize the blockade on November 5, 1945, was taken by a *Windsor Star* staff photographer, and may be one of Cec Southward's shots taken from the Ford City Town Hall.

here photographing these boxers, travelling with them to Ohio, through Michigan, Niagara Falls, and spent nearly a month in Iraq with Josh Canty, André Gorges, and the Olympic Iraqi boxing team. The club also sponsored a fundraiser match in which I boxed—and survived. I had to train in the club for about three weeks, but I could never get the skipping down to a comfortable level. I gave up, switching to shadowboxing. During the fight, which took place at Riverside High School, I lost my hearing in my left ear, but managed to get a good right hook to

## Richmond and Drouillard

At this juncture, or just before it, there are three places that I know well. One is the Border City Boxing Club (1072 Drouillard Road)—home for so many champion boxers. Margaret Sidoroff, Jeannine Garside, Josh Cameron, and Samir El-Mais have all had careers here, along with a host of others. I spent a year and a half

Border City Boxing Club, the home base for many notable local boxers, is located at 1072 Drouillard Road.

make my opponent stumble. Jeannine Garside and André Gorges were in my corner.

The afternoons at this club were a delight. I watched Canty's daughter, Miranda, grow up here. She trotted around in diapers among the sweaty boxers, all of whom were careful not to knock her over. As she grew older, I'd spy some hulking six-foot boxer resting beside her on the floor—he had been assigned to babysit her—and his hands were wrapped. I'd see him sharing a make-believe cup of tea with Miranda. They were playing "house."

There was another fellow, a bruiser who was straight out of the *Rocky* movies. He carried rolls of cash with him. Like Rocky, his job was breaking legs or arms to collect from the deadbeats who owed his clients' money. This big man, whose name I'll keep anonymous, earned victories in the ring, but he was more of a street fighter. He couldn't shake it from his style. Yet, there was also a soft side that blossomed in a big toothy grin. Years later, I'd spot him at Tim Hortons with two delicate little daughters, buying them donuts and lemonade. He once told me that while attending high school, he was hired by a group of prostitutes to stay at their house and watch over them. If needed, he'd toss an unruly customer out a window. In return, the girls helped him get his Grade 12, spending long hours at the kitchen table, coaching him through his homework. "I couldn't have done it without them, really!" he said. It's a story that's stuck with me.

Boxing has always had a presence on Drouillard. At one point, it was done in the basement of Holy Rosary Church. Former welterweight boxer and union activist Mickey Warner trained boxers there before moving downtown. I interviewed him in 2004 when he was 72. He was still keeping in shape, running every day along the riverfront. He remained feisty and served as president of Local 82 of the Canadian Union of Public Employees—whose clashes with the city are legendary. But most remember him for his boxing days on Drouillard. At 21, he was Canada's featherweight champion and the Michigan Golden Gloves champion. In that church basement, he trained the likes of Johnny Kubinec, Stan Renaud, Phil Parent, and others, and led them to win the Golden Gloves in Michigan in 1958.

The story about Mickey that I loved best, however, was from the 1960s in Chicago, when he noticed a lanky kid with long arms and lightning speed battering his opponents with ease. Mickey was there with his own team, but was asked to help out "in the corner" for this black boxer. "I wasn't doing anything special—just giving water and that sort of thing."

Then he saw the fighter move into the ring, and marvelled at his grace.

Years later, he tuned in to the television and watched this same fighter take on the Heavyweight Champion of the World—Sonny Liston. And saw Liston go down in defeat. That fighter, whose corner he had worked, was Cassius Clay, later named Muhammad Ali. Many years later, when Mickey's granddaughter gave birth to a son, she called him Cassius.

My last memory from this boxing club is one early Sunday morning getting a telephone call from Josh Canty asking if I could come down and take a few photographs of a young boxer. The youngster he was referring to was Justin Trudeau. I was taken aback by this, and gathered up my gear, and headed out. Trudeau was just starting his run for the leadership, or actually, considering it. He had been in town for a fundraiser, and wanted to work out. Border City gladly accommodated him. Trudeau arrived carrying a gym bag. Already a small crowd—mostly women—were there to greet him.

He moved into the room, slowly, but decisively making the rounds to speak to everyone —those blue eyes fixing upon each and every soul there. All the while, the lean future Prime Minister started stripping down, unbuttoning his shirt, then undoing his belt, and soon was down to his shorts, and began pulling on boxing gear, and suiting up. Never once losing eye contact. Never hesitating in mid-sentence. Ever aware of the watchful eyes of these women following his every gesture. Soon enough, Trudeau was dancing in the ring with Josh Cameron, a former Amateur Canadian Boxing Champion, and they began sparring. It wasn't long before Pierre Trudeau's son was tagged a few times, though he pushed the lean and lanky Cameron away and fought back courageously. All in fun. And I caught this wonderful photograph of him. I posted it on Facebook the night Trudeau won the election in 2015, remarking that while in the photo, he was taking a beating, tonight, the night of the election, he was in command.

Next door to the boxing club is Atelier Virginianne (1078 Drouillard Road)—the home base for the production of the student documentary on Ford City, as mentioned earlier. The place has since become a cultural hub for writers, artists and actors. Sho Gallery now uses the space for performances.

Future Prime Minister Justin Trudeau getting tagged by former Amateur Canadian Boxing Champion Josh Cameron on September 9th, 2012.

Just before I cross Richmond, there is the yellow-brick St. John the Divine Orthodox Church (1094 Drouillard Road), designed by John R. Boyde. It went up in 1916, but was rebuilt after a fire destroyed it in 1946.

The roots of the church are with a collection of Orthodox Eastern Europeans—mostly Russians, Carpathians, Serbians, and Romanians, who crossed the river from Detroit to attend Our Lady of the Lake. Occasionally, the priest would invite an Orthodox clergyman to attend to their spiritual needs. By 1915, this handful of believers decided to organize their own community church. They raised the money to buy two lots right here at this corner, and threw up a clapboard building in the summer of 1916. The church thrived, and soon outgrew itself. Most of that growth took place in 1924 right after the Communist Revolution when Windsor saw an influx of refugees coming from Russia. Soon, the parish was organizing dances, banquets and concerts, and began the formation of a library of Russian books. It wasn't until 1929 that the church built its own church hall in the basement—the only part of the original structure still used today.

Soon, other Orthodox churches began to spring up in Windsor, some just south down Drouillard. That's why St. John the Divine is considered the "Mother Church of Orthodoxy" in Windsor.

As I pass by the place, I recall attending a Sunday service here, and being invited to return and take part in its Easter celebration, and to photograph the event. I was joined by local photographer Ted Kloske. We remained

Above: St. John the Divine Orthodox Church has been a landmark on Drouillard Road, since 1916. This church building was rebuilt in the 1940s after a fire.

Right: a candlelight Easter mass at St. John the Divine Orthodox Church, which I attended in April 2016.

at the service till 3:00 a.m. It was one of the most beautiful candlelit services with clouds of incense filling the pockets of darkness. I spent a good amount of time talking also to its older parishioners who told me of how the church nearly shut down for good. In 2004, when its congregation faced making necessary repairs to the building, but couldn't raise the funds, it shut its doors. Three years later, however, efforts were made to reopen. In 2015, the community celebrated its 100th anniversary. The church is also on the city's registry as a designated heritage building. If you stop in there for a morning service and trundle down to the basement for coffee, you will hear the stories and meet the people who maintain and continue the Orthodox tradition on this street. And though there is the veneer of rigid liturgical ritual in its mass, there is also a flicker of informality, borne out of down-to-earth values and an intimacy among the faithful.

Across Richmond, there is Drouillard Place (1102 Drouillard Road). Its staff is made up of an army of volunteers, and these individuals offer counselling, support programs, after-school and summer youth programs, neighbourhood renewal projects and assistance with affordable housing. All of this is done with the support of the United Way, private donations, and corporate sponsorships.

Two doors down from Drouillard Place, at 1118 Drouillard Road, is Brown's Breaktime Lounge. On the south-facing wall is a mural of Fred Lazurek with his camera.

Directly across from it is a tiny shop that has a *For Rent* sign tucked in the window.

This was the Corner Lunch Bar for years. The borsch soup there was legendary. Sadly, the place closed, like much else. This street is a veritable graveyard of past businesses. In the 1940s and 1950s, you could live in the neighbourhood, and never have to leave. Looking along the street, you would find Royal Bakery and Morris Dry Goods and Downtown Café.

Farther south on Drouillard is the Gino and Liz Marcus Community Complex (1168 Drouillard Road). Before that, it was Holy Rosary School. My brother, Paul Gervais, was its principal.

Below: Drouillard Road, pictured in its heyday in the 1950s, and today, at left.

A postcard from 1929 of Holy Rosary Separate School. The building was demolished in 1971 and a community centre now occupies this spot.

## Ontario

Just a few feet away is Ontario Street. I thought of covering more ground along Drouillard, but I'm now headed to Walkerville. Farther up Drouillard, there are a few places that have some meaning for me. One is Our Lady of the Lake cemetery; another is a small white wartime house at 1671 with a picket fence, and this is where my uncle Gilbert, a union organizer, lived. As I mentioned earlier, Gil's son was David, whose days were spent in and out of prison. His brother, Gil, Jr., was a Toronto cop.

There's also the strip bar where the *Windsor Star* sent me undercover to live for a week, but I didn't comply once I discovered that there were no doors on the bedrooms. I later read a piece online from someone who lived on Drouillard, and as a boy he claimed that he and his friends would poke their noses into the strip bar, take a few cautious steps inside and then race out of there as fast as they could. He would boast to his buddies how he spied on all these beautiful naked women. Of course, he never saw anything, having gone from stark daylight to smoky darkness; his eyes never having time to adjust.

It didn't occur to me until years later when I returned to Drouillard Road with the students that this street is one of extremes. At the north end, an evangelical church. At the south end, a strip bar. With both, there is that desire of making a living, surviving, making a life. The only judgement comes from outside this collection of streets that at one time was vibrant and alive. Within its boundaries, people function, and carry on.

Now I am on Ontario Street heading west. Right at the corner is a sprawling mural about the rumrunning days (1207 Drouillard Road). It bears a quote from me. I remember the artist Donna Mayne calling me about this, and wondering if I could send her something that would sum up the prohibition period for her wall painting. I complied. All these years later, I am surprised at how these murals have been respected, left free from graffiti.

My walk takes me over to St. Luke. This was the neighbourhood my father lived in when he first came to Windsor. Once after my mother died, I took a tour of the streets, driving my car, and listening to my aging father recount what life was like in the plants, what he remembered. Like so many others, when the time came to flee Ford City, my father did. First, he made his way south to George Avenue, where he built his own house from gigantic crates reclaimed from the plants. My grandfather did the same a few houses down from him. From George Avenue, he moved to Riverside. But when my father lived here on Albert Road, he walked to work. Everyone did. Few could afford a car, or, for that matter, needed one. Life was here. You lived and worked in the neighbourhood. It was like an army hitting the street and filing along to stream through the plant gates. My father never left the Canadian Motor Lamp on Seminole. Worked his way up the ladder, and during the Second World War, was superintendent of the female workers that were employed to manufacture shell casings. Much later, he was asked to manage a branch plant in Bracebridge and Parry Sound, Ontario.

As I toured the streets of Ford City that day with my father, I could tell that he possessed a particular nostalgic affection for the area just from the way he spoke about it, his voice shaky and emotional. As we drove along Albert and Drouillard, he strained to make sense of its geography, desperately trying to figure out where the old grocery stores were, where the sprawling Studebaker plant once existed on the edge of Ford City, or even the fish and chip joint that he'd stop at on a Catholic "meatless Friday." As a kid, I remember him coming through the screen door with the fish and chips wrapped in newspaper, and he'd dump it onto the tablecloth in the kitchen for us to fill our plates.

For residents here, Ford City is maybe one of the most misunderstood of the five towns. It was really the engine for the Border Cities. As Maria Clemens' rebuttal editorial to the *Star* indicated, Ford City was not "an island of misfit toys." She had a point. The Ford City Redevelopment Committee has worked tirelessly to transform that stereotypical image, and to that end, has made strong links with the Ford City BIA, neighbourhood residents, the City of Windsor parks department, area councillors, Windsor Police Services, area churches, and the community-university partnership through the University of Windsor School of Social Work. This led to the launch in July 2010 of the Ford City Renewal Project funded by the United Way and East Windsor Cogeneration Inc. It also led to a new splash pad opening where over 300 families, seniors, children, and youth gathered at the park to celebrate, play, share stories, and at dusk enjoy a family outdoor movie.

Clemens argued that the picture of the people was "incomplete." She notes the stories of "hard-working, middle-class residents; seniors who are the backbone of the area; businesses which have been here for 40 years; newer residents who see the neighbourhood's potential; churches that have opened up in the last 10 years; our not-for-profit housing complex..." and much more. Ford City seems forever trying to set the record straight. And yet, we all have ties to this neighbourhood in one way or another. We know someone there, or we did. Or we lived there at one time, or someone in our family grew up there. We are linked to its history and culture. It is part of our blood, our identity, and that's what overwhelms me as I pause in the cold street just before venturing on to the next leg, to Walkerville.

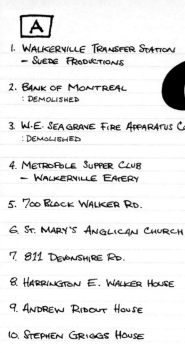

# Walkerville

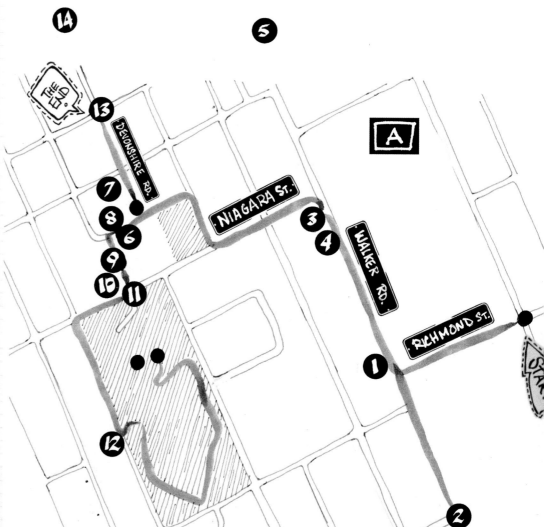

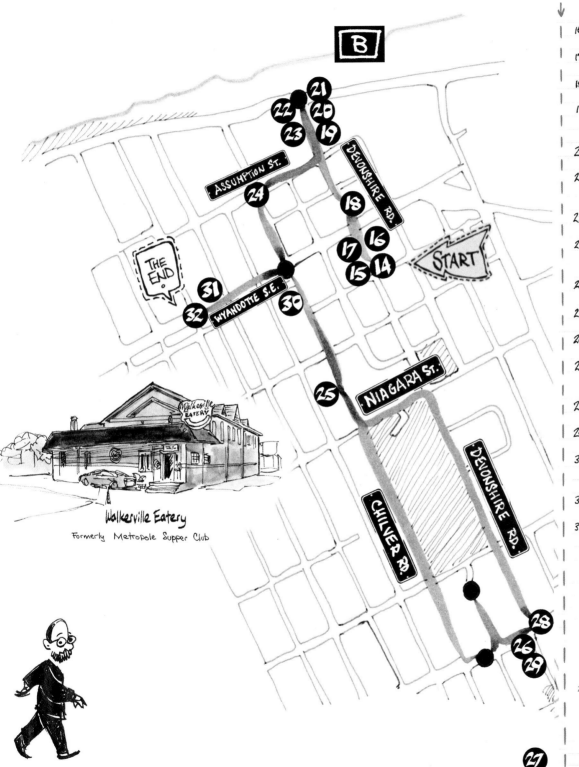

START

THE END

ASSUMPTION ST.

DEVONSHIRE RD.

WYANDOTTE S.E.

NIAGARA ST.

CHILVER RD.

DEVONSHIRE RD.

Walkerville Eatery
Formerly Metropole Supper Club

Gourmet Emporium
Formerly Bank of Montreal

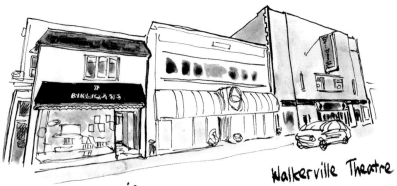

Biblioasis

Walkerville Theatre

Willistead Manor

Taloola Café
Formerly The Crow Inn

Low-Martin House

Victoria Tavern c. 1930

St. Mary's Anglican Church

Strathcona Block

# WALKERVILLE
*February 21, 2016*
*4.5 km*

It is February 21. The sun is beaming. It is supposed to go to a high of 11 degrees Celsius. Two days ago, temperatures reached a high of 14.4 degrees, breaking the record from 1994. I'm wearing a light jacket. I take St. Luke over to Richmond, and walk west towards Walker Road. I can spot the fire station at the corner where my son worked until the city replaced it with a new station. I am entering Walkerville, the jewel of the Border Cities.

### Ottawa and Walker Road

I approach Walker Road and in, adjacent to the old fire hall, at 1057 Walker Road, is Suede Street Productions, a trendy film and media company. It is housed in the redbrick Walkerville Transfer Substation that was built in 1914. Now I head south on Walker to Ottawa Street. There on the northwest corner was the Bank of Montreal, long gone now, since it was torn down in 2008 so as not to obscure the plaza behind it. The building was erected in 1919; it was never on Windsor's heritage list. It caused a bit of stir in the community because the city had already overlooked the razing of the former heritage-listed Seagrave fire truck factory nearby.

As for the Bank of Montreal building, Greg Heil, chair of the heritage committee in 2008, told the *Windsor Star* back then that he never knew why it was not on the inventory list. He said it met "all the criteria for heritage preservation." City officials, however, reported there was no legal justification for denying the demolition permit.

The Walkerville Transfer Substation, built in 1914, now houses Suede Productions. It is located at 1057 Walker Road.

The Bank of Montreal at the northwest corner of Walker Road and Ottawa Street sits empty in this *Windsor Star* photograph, taken shortly before it was demolished in 2008. This branch was said to have been robbed by the infamous Red Ryan in the 1920s.

Chris Holt, of ScaleDown Windsor, and now on City Council, launched a campaign against the demolition of the bank building, saying, "It's the gateway to Old Walkerville… These old buildings are the reason people live in Old Walkerville. We are losing the fabric and want to see it stopped."

Windsor's heritage planner John Calhoun told Frances Willick of the *Windsor Star* that the municipality's perspective was "tilted in favour of architecture," when determining heritage designation. He argued that memory plays into the decision to preserve. Calhoun rightly says, "The power is not so much the architecture, but the stories…"

The old Bank of Montreal bore witness to some great tales—the most wild being when it was robbed by the infamous Norman "Red" Ryan, the Depression-era gangster about whom movies and books have been made. This was a man whose whole life was crime.

At 17, he was sent to Kingston Penitentiary. By the 1920s, Ryan was robbing banks like they were going out of style. At one point, when he was incarcerated in Kingston, he escaped with a gang of inmates and went on a crime spree across Ontario. It was during this period that he robbed the Bank of Montreal on Ottawa Street. Although he went on to become a model prisoner and even caught the attention of Prime Minister R.B. Bennett, who urged his release in 1935, he turned back to crime, and was gunned down during a robbery in Sarnia. Morley Callaghan, the Canadian novelist and short story writer, penned the novel, *More Joy in Heaven,* about Ryan.

## Niagara and Walker Road

I turn around, and head north past Ontario and Richmond; the next westbound street is Niagara. But just before you get to a rather nondescript building at 911 Walker Road, now called Walkerville Eatery (formerly Big Tony's), there was not so long ago a two-storey brick building that hugged the street. According to Carl Morgan, former editor of the *Windsor Star* and author of *Pioneering the Auto Age,* few would have taken notice of this lean-looking building as they passed it. It looked like any other derelict structure. "You have probably seen it without really seeing it—or, more importantly, without knowing that it was home of the first company to produce a motorized fire engine in Canada."

The factory, that made equipment for firefighting, was owned by Warren E. Seagrave, head of W.E. Seagrave Fire Apparatus Company of Ohio. That business was established in 1881 in the United States by his father, Frederic S. Seagrave, who died in 1923, and incidentally, is buried in Windsor Grove Cemetery on Giles Boulevard at Howard Avenue.

Warren's company on Walker Road was the first Canadian factory to produce fire apparatus. The exact date that the building was constructed is not clear. Carl Morgan estimates, from his research, that it was erected between 1895 and 1904, but the Town of Walkerville's assessment rolls reveal that a row of six private homes were located on that stretch of Walker Road as late as 1904. Regardless, in 1905, the registry indicates that the lots were owned by W.E. Seagrave. The company delivered the first three motor fire engines to Vancouver in 1907. Warren died in 1953 and is buried in Port Huron, Michigan, where he had lived for many years running an awning business after the fire equipment company failed. The Walker Road plant shut down in 1923.

What is interesting to note, according to Walt McCall, former public relations executive at Chrysler Canada and a leading authority on fire apparatus equipment and companies, is that when Seagrave moved into a 13,000-square-foot factory in 1904, it was also the same year that the Ford Motor Company began its operation in McGregor's wagon works assembly operation. Six years later, in 1910, Windsor bought its first aerial ladder truck. It was a

Windsor firemen pose on the department's first aerial ladder truck, purchased in 1910 from Seagrave in Walkerville.

horse-drawn, 85-foot spring-raised Seagrave. Four years later, the city purchased a Seagrave motor powered pumper.

According to Morgan, Seagrave was manufacturing hundreds of fire engines for fire departments throughout the country, transforming the company into the nation's most trusted manufacturer. Morgan writes: "When the Seagrave combination truck purchased by the City of London was heavily damaged in a train collision in 1913, the fire department thought so highly of the vehicle that, instead of scrapping it, the truck was sent back to Walkerville to be rebuilt."

It is ironic that in April 2008, without anyone really noticing, the city issued a demolition

Pictured above in 1913, the W.E. Seagrave Co. factory manufactured fire apparatus and was located on the west side of Walker Road, just south of Niagara, until it was demolished in 2008.

permit to remove this historic building from Windsor's landscape. Ironic because as Morgan had noted, although the building appeared "to be down-at-the-heels," its historical importance overrode its physical condition. He writes:

It is one of the last known industrial buildings still standing in Walkerville that can trace its roots back to the early years of the 20th century (despite the fact that in its heyday, Walkerville was the site of dozens of different industrial companies)," wrote Morgan. "What fate awaits this nearly 100-year-old building is uncertain. In larger urban centres, it would probably be snapped up for converting into fashionable condos, studios, boutiques or a combination thereof.

But not so in Windsor. Instead, we sent in wrecking crews. We're good at that. In *The Mayor of Monmouth* blog on April 9, 2008, when this redbrick historic building came crashing down, the writer said:

Same old City of Windsor. If it's old and historic, it's got to be razed… Nobody who witnessed the event today could believe it either. No advance warning at all. It was obviously done on the hush. […] Rick Gruber who is the area building inspector rushed out today to halt the demolition because even though there was a permit to raze the building, there was no permit to close Walker Road. In fact, the sidewalk is the only thing that separates the building from Walker Road. Witnesses said that a man riding a bike almost got clocked by falling bricks. Four thirty rolled around. Quittin' time for city employees and Jones [Demolition Company] fired up the beast and started tearing the old girl down. Right in the middle of rush hour… Within two hours the building was really history.

And that is what is so sad about our urban landscape. History lies just below the surface. If someone doesn't write about it, or tell stories about it, then it vanishes as if nothing ever existed here. The neighbourhood fills with new families or new businesses, unaware of the foundation they are building upon.

Left: The Metropole Supper Club, owned and operated by the colourful Nick Drakich in the 1940s to mid-1970s, is now home to the Walkerville Eatery, pictured below.

At the southwest corner of Walker and Niagara, Walkerville Eatery (911 Walker Road) is just a few steps away from the ghostly remains of Seagrave. I remember this sprawling edifice as The Metropole Supper Club. I knew its owner, Nick Drakich, the broad-shouldered tavern owner who sported a handlebar moustache and had a heart of gold. His brother, Mike, owned the high-flying Top Hat downtown.

Nick and his supper club were the stuff of legend. Before it was christened The Metropole by Drakich, it was a drinking establishment called The Farmer's Roost. Dating back to the late 19th century, it was frequented by area farmers who ended their day here for a cold brew after hauling grain to Hiram Walker's.

The farmers would lounge on the broad porch that faced Walker Road.

One particular event that stands out in this bar's history was during Queen Victoria's Jubilee in 1897 when Hiram Walker & Sons presented the Jubilee fountain to the town.

There was a lengthy parade that started on Sandwich Street (now Riverside Drive) and went up Walker Road, then east on Tuscarora and north on Devonshire Road. A telegram from Buckingham Palace was read, and Mrs. E.C. Walker was asked in the name of the Queen to lay the corner stone for the fountain, which now sits in Willistead Park. Where the old Metropole figures into this event is after the children sang "Rule Britannia"—the volunteers, who had helped in the celebration, repaired to the tavern for drinks.

By the time Drakich bought the hotel in 1942 and renamed it The Metropole, the building stood in a bustling industrial zone. Down the street was Canadian Bridge Company at 1219 Walker Road. It was here that the massive Detroit–Windsor tunnel tubes were made in the late 1920s. Also a stone's throw away was the Gotfredson Truck Company. It was a busy factory district, right on the edge of sprawling Walkerville residences. Yet, this was typical of Windsor, where the backyard view from one's home was an industrial landscape of silhouetted smokestacks. All evidence of these two Walker Road buildings has been erased. You would never guess at how hectic a place this street was in the 1950s, allowing Drakich to turn his business into a going concern.

His nightclub was the first of its kind in Windsor, and introduced the city to the smorgasbord-style dinner. It was a welcome relief to Nick after working in the iron mines in Northern Ontario as a new immigrant. At one point in toiling in Sudbury's mines, Nick inadvertently used a Serbian word "*Dvoboj!*" when threatening another man to a fight. But the word also carried the meaning—duel. This caught the attention of newspaper writers who reported the challenge, saying it could mean three years imprisonment. Nick pleaded that he only meant for the challenge to be a "fight," not a duel to the death. As it turned out, both men backed down from it and saved themselves the grief of a prison sentence.

When Nick finally had the chance to leave the north, he returned to the more refined life of running a restaurant, the kind of business he had abandoned in Europe. Nick was a showman, and successfully persuaded entertainers from all over the United States to come to Windsor. He often advertised that if you watched Ed Sullivan on television—and liked what you saw and heard—come down to The Metropole, because the same showbiz people were there. Indeed, the supper club with its white linen tablecloths and sprawling dance hall floor, lured the likes of the Diamonds, Sid Caesar, Della Reese, Frankie Laine, and Patti Page. Nick's daughter, Lepa, usually opened most of the shows at the supper club, and it was not uncommon to see Berry Gordie, the founder of Motown, sitting in the shadows watching the shows, on the lookout for talent.

Nick was also a shrewd business owner. He once challenged the magician Kreskin to find his paycheque at the end of nine days of playing at the club. Nick crowed that if Kreskin couldn't find the cheque, he'd have to leave Windsor broke. Of course, the entertainer found it. The wily test drew a throng of people to the club to catch the razzle-dazzle slight-of-hand illusionist.

Chuck Thurston, a columnist with the *Detroit Free Press*, wrote fondly of Drakich in August 1971:

Drakich's moustache is older than any its size in this part of the world. He has been known to play poker on occasion. A couple of attempts to rob the Metropole have ended disastrously for the thieves. Comics usually say he teaches broken English at the university, and you hardly ever hear a bad word from people who have worked for him.

Nick Drakich was 68 when he died in September 1974. Some might say characters like Nick are not to be found anymore, or that the old-fashioned supper clubs of that time are no longer in vogue. The glory of that period has long since passed. Nick complained, as I recall, that people didn't "dress" for dinner like they used to. They would show up in shorts and running shoes. There wasn't the same respect for tradition.

Interior of the Metropole Supper Club, June 1961.

Above: These semi-detached homes from 785–715 Walker Road were built for distillery workers at Hiram Walker & Sons.

Below: St. Mary's Cemetery, in 1907, looking southwest from St. Mary's Gate and Argyle Road. Willistead Manor can be seen in the distance, at left. The cemetery, as it looks today, is pictured at right.

Farther along Walker, heading towards Wyandotte, there are 10 homes in a row, semi-detached—from 785–715. All are on the Municipal Register, but seven with heritage designations. These were built by the Walker family for the workers at the distillery. Many of them are now owned by lawyers and architects. In the 1980s, these homes sold for approximately $15,000. They were not regarded as terribly valuable.

I leave Walker Road, turning onto Niagara going west, into the lushness of Walkerville—stately, moneyed homes. On the north side is St. Mary's Cemetery. This will be my final resting place, an

Anglican cemetery for a Roman Catholic. These are the wishes of my wife, Donna, who grew up in this church. Both her mom and her dad are buried here. My wife plants flowers every year on their graves, where our ashes will be sprinkled one day. Wandering the cemetery lot is fascinating, like a yearbook of those who built this community. And as I begin to pace the neighbourhood, I imagine the life of Hiram Walker and his family, and ponder the effect they had on this town he built. Aptly put by Ronald G. Hoskins in the *Dictionary of Canadian Biography*, this is the description of the community that Walker created when he founded his company in 1858:

By the early 1880s, the village had a population of 600 people, who lived in homes built and owned by Hiram Walker. They worked in Walker-owned industries, drank water pumped through pipes laid by him, received police and fire protection at his expense, and could attend the church built by him (named St. Mary's in memory of his wife, who had died in 1872). In the absence of a commercial bank, Walker's

Hiram Walker's first house in Walkerville, called "The Cottage," is pictured here in 1900. The distillery's main offices are also visible. E.C. Walker and his wife Mary also lived here for a short time.

employees could deposit their savings in the private Walker bank. Walkerville had become a typical company town ruled over by a benevolent founder and his sons and relatives.

But let me take a step back, and digress. Walkerville, of course, was founded by the American entrepreneur, Hiram Walker, in 1858. He was from New England, and arrived in Detroit in 1838. But in coming here and buying up two French farms on the south shore to open up a distillery, he established and maintained what soon became a "company town" where he controlled every facet of its life.

The properties he bought were owned by Eugene Hall and John and Luc Montreuil, but originally were settled by the Labadies. Indeed, Walker himself lived in a home that had belonged to Louis Labadie—one of the sons of the original landowner. It was built around 1839. It is now gone, of course. The Walkers nicknamed it "The Cottage." It can be seen in photographs of the early days of the company. The home was removed in about 1906 when Hiram Walker & Sons decided to expand. Hiram Walker, however, maintained a residence in Detroit, and crossed the river on the ferry to his Walkerville office.

For seven decades, the Walker family developed the town, shaping it according to their own design, and reaped huge profits from it. The Walkerville Land and Building Company (W.L. & B. Co.) was started in 1890 by Hiram's oldest son, Edward Chandler, who presided over it. The company benefited in those early years when Walkerville town council passed a bylaw providing tax exemptions to those attracting new industries, but also building new homes in the town.

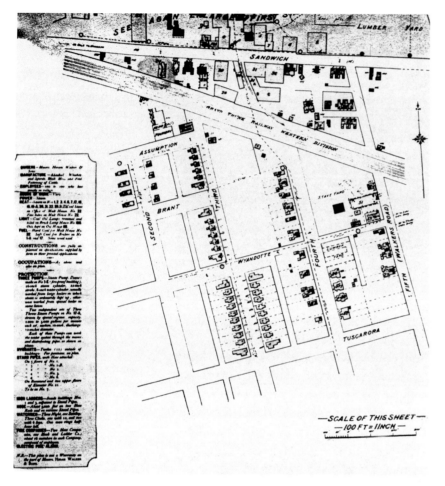

This architectural survey of Walkerville from 1884 shows the early layout of the town, and includes original streets names before they were changed under the directive of Mrs. Walker.

Walkerville, unlike the other border towns, followed a meticulous design. According to a brief history by the Windsor's Architectural Conservation Advisory Committee (WACAC). the W.L. & B. Co. moved swiftly to scoop up land, and hire architects and contractors to build rental housing for the distillery's employees. Soon, "modest frame cottages lined the blocks as far as Tuscarora Street, the original southerly boundary… Five

north-south streets were laid out and later renamed, at Mrs. Walker's urging, to lend a more refined tone to the town's image." She supervised the changes, making First Street become Kildare Road, Second renamed Devonshire, Third altered to Argyle, Fourth designated Monmouth, and Fifth Street christened Walker Road.

Most of the east-west streets carried names of Aboriginal peoples: Wyandotte, Huron, Cataraqui, Dakotah, and Ottawa. Walker also became the provider of a fire brigade and police, streetlights, sewers, paved roads, sidewalks, parks, a music hall, a school, library, and church. "This benevolent dictator thought of everything," says WACAC.

Ronald Hoskins, in his 1964 thesis *Life and Times of Hiram Walker,* wrote that Walker "reigned undisputed monarch of all under his surveillance… he would tolerate no interference from other sources, but would accept nothing less than complete control over the enterprise." The town that he had built, says Hoskins, was "a progressive, self-sustaining, model town…"

Hiram Walker's youngest son, James Harrington Walker, was the one who had the greatest influence on the way Walkerville developed. An aspiring architect, he demonstrated a keen awareness of how the town should be laid out with respect to residence and industry. It became clear in the late 19th century that Walker Road would be relegated to industry, while to the west would be where Walker employees would live. Hence the line-up of modest brick semi-detached residences along Monmouth and Argyle. I can see them to the east, behind me, as I leave the cemetery and walk west along Niagara. Argyle's homes were a little more up-scale. This was reflected in the higher status of its original inhabitants. The families, who lived here, held higher positions in the company. They were rewarded thus.

I reach Devonshire Road. This was really the main avenue, and the architecture here was mostly Romanesque Revival semis for management and clergy. Later development would have greater architectural flexibility as Walkerville embraced the 20th century, and homes started appearing on Kildare. St. Mary's Anglican Church, or at least the second church structure with that name, was also built in the early 1900s. It was Edward, and his wife Mary Griffin Walker, who took over the development of Walkerville's second phase, which is informally marked as beginning with Hiram's death in 1899. Within two years, the family sold its railway holdings (Lake Erie & Detroit River Railway to Père Marquette Railways) so they could expand their holdings between Wyandotte and Richmond Streets. According to WACAC, "the interrupted street pattern reduced the traffic, keeping the park-like setting quiet, and the Walkers used this feature to promote a fine residential neighbourhood focused around St. Mary's Church and Willistead."

Walkerville's lots were sold only to those who could build homes of at least 3,500 square feet. Albert Kahn's signature dominates. He subscribed to the Arts and Crafts Movement in architectural design, a philosophy with its roots in mid-19th century England. The

This 1913 postcard shows the red-brick rowhouses on the 700 block of Monmouth Road. These semi-detached homes were designed by Mason & Rice and housed distillery employees.

emphasis of this movement was on a return to handmade craftsmanship, often featuring "cottage styles" that harmonized with the natural environment—as opposed to the cold, industrial factory.

According to the WACAC pamphlet:

Every home Albert Kahn designed shows Arts and Crafts influence. Kahn believed that historic period styles were best suited to homes and public institutions, while factories should be utilitarian, brightly illuminated, and devoid of ornament. By the 1920s, many architects believed that the simplicity of factories should be models for all types of construction. It is ironic that a man so lauded for his innovations in factory design should maintain a philosophy contrary to the direction taken by modern residential architecture, particularly when his contemporary, Frank Lloyd Wright, was receiving wide acclaim. Except for some changes since the amalgamation, most of this Walker-built town still survives. If conservation persists, this planned, century old, self-sufficient town will be a cultural treasure for Windsor and North America.

Pictured here c. 1900, the original St. Mary's Anglican Church was built on Sandwich Street (now Riverside Drive) and Devonshire Road in 1870.

## St. Mary's Anglican Church

Coming to Kildare Road, I head north and round the corner, heading east to stand in front of St. Mary's Church at 1983 St. Mary's Gate Street.

This beautiful English-style church that rises before me is not the first St. Mary's. The original church stood on the south side of Sandwich Street (Riverside Drive) and Devonshire. In old photographs, it looks odd, out of place on an empty road, and fields beyond. The first St. Mary's, built in 1870 by Hiram Walker, was torn down in 1904 when the new church, built by his sons, opened at St. Mary's Gate. The new church was named in honour of Mary Abigail, Hiram's wife. The original that Hiram Walker supported financially was a Methodist denomination, and remained so for two years from 1870 to 1872, when it reopened as an Anglican denomination in 1874. It was the only place, other than Lincoln Avenue Methodist, where one could worship in Walkerville. The original church sat directly across from Walker's home, "The Cottage." It was a red-brick structure, and had a basement that was used for Sunday School, but also for a day school until a new school was built. For many years, a photograph of the original St. Mary's hung in the vestry at the church at St. Mary's Gate. It was a simple design, and had a steeple with a bell.

It is interesting, too, to discover why Walker turned his back on the Methodists. When he first opened St. Mary's, he was housing two or three young men who were studying for the ministry. They also conducted the services. But when Walker found out that one of the men had done a sermon on the evils of liquor, he quickly discontinued the Methodist services. That's when he sought priests from the Church of England. After all, they served communion wine. At first, however, Walker faced some opposition from the Anglican bishop. The resistance was not over "drink," but concerning uncertain expenses of a new parish. Walker, on the other hand, spurned the whole notion of having the Methodists back, and promised he would take care of whatever deficit might amount. New services with the Anglican persuasion began in 1874.

By 1885, the congregation really began to grow. The Sunday School also doubled in that time—a reflection of the community itself. The church building faced extensive repairs. In July 1885, the floor was carpeted and a steam heating boiler was installed in the basement, thereby ridding the sanctuary of stoves and stovepipes. This brought more parishioners to St. Mary's. Still problems persisted. The congregation increasingly became annoyed at the frequent interruptions caused by the rumbling nearby Grand Trunk and Wabash railway trains. There was still a need for a larger Sunday School space, and no accommodations were made for a meeting of the Ladies Aid Society that numbered 60 members.

Shortly after Hiram Walker passed away, his son Edward Chandler Walker, sent a letter on April 7, 1902, offering to build a new church, a schoolroom, and a rectory to replace

Mary A. Walker, wife of Hiram, is shown here c. 1856. St. Mary's Anglican Church was named after her by her sons.

St. Mary's. Of course, the congregation was delighted, or at least that's what was conveyed in a message sent by Rev. W. A. Battersby to the Walkers. In fact, squabbling abounded among church members over what the Walkers were expecting from the church community. Some were enormously suspicious, thinking maybe the family was hoping for financial support from the congregation.

The original St. Mary's on Sandwich Street was torn down, and many of its fixtures were distributed throughout the deanery. Its foundation was used to build Walkerville's Town Hall in 1904, back then situated on Sandwich Street (Riverside Drive). In 1995, in an effort to save this historic building from demolition, it was moved to its present location at 350 Devonshire. Kahn was its architect. The Walkers had originally thought of hiring Mason & Rice, a firm that had been Hiram Walker's choice, but his sons decided the assignment would be given to Kahn, who was at

The second St. Mary's Anglican Church under construction in 1904.

that point, still an up-and-comer from Detroit. The builder the family chose was Victor Williamson, one of the most esteemed builders and contractors in the area.

The new St. Mary's was all part of that grand plan, purposely situated like an island in the midst of this ever-growing municipality, resting on a land parcel bordered by Argyle on the east, Kildare on the west, St. Mary's Gate on the north and Niagara on the south. Kahn, though having refused the job as primary architect, acted as a supervisor, working alongside Ralph Adams Cram and Ernest Wilby. Construction costs exceeded the original estimate of $50,000—the price tag tallied up at $64,000. That may have been because the Walkers dithered over whether the church should be brick or stone. Finally, the Walkers requisitioned limestone for the exterior walls conveyed from Amherstburg. The interior

panelling was done by the Globe Furniture Company in Windsor.

Cram's first architectural partner was Bertram Grosvenor Goodhue, and according to some in this field, he was the better architect. His artistry is evident to this day at St. Mary's. Elaine Weeks and Chris Edwards in their book, *Walkerville: Whisky Town Extraordinaire,* noted that the general scheme for all of the leaded-glass windows was planned by him. Bertram's brother, Harry Goodhue, prepared all the sketches and watercolours for these windows. A library bookplate for the St. Mary's Library—still present in the church—bears Goodhue's initials.

Weeks and Edwards quote Cram's own observations of Goodhue: "As a master of decorative detail of every sort he had no rival then… I remember him best in two aspects: sitting hunched up over a drawing-board, his lips writhing nervously around innumerable drooping cigarettes, shifting his pen from one hand to another (he was ambidextrous) as he wrought out some inimitable study in dazzling black and white."

The cornerstone for the church was laid May 25, 1903, and Windsor's the *Evening Record* covered the consecration of the new church on April 11, 1904.

Wilby was the on-site architect who worked with Kahn and visited the construction site all through its various stages to ensure that what was transpiring met the wishes of the whisky family, who imagined this new town as reflecting a bountiful community in England. Wilby concluded that the church was "a bit of 16th century transplanted to North America." He wrote: "Here is reproduced the English scene of church, churchyard and rectory, and nearby is Willistead taking the place of the English manor house. Combined, these buildings make a picture of peace and beauty found in England."

Step into St. Mary's and you will marvel at the stunning leaded windows, but you might never know the hidden story behind these. University of Windsor alum Cameron Macdonell, in an intriguing new book, *Ghost Storeys*, says one of the windows depicts the Sermon on the Mount, but shows a man afflicted with leprosy. No such image is associated with that New Testament account. But its portrayal here in the ornate window, Macdonnell believes, relates to a bizarre Walker family secret—that Edward Chandler Walker was dying of syphilis. Hiram Walker's son, apparently, believed that if he built this church, it might lead to God's forgiveness, and ultimately a cure. Ralph Adams Cram dutifully, encrypted Edward's confession in the architecture, and no one seems to have been the wiser, until now.

When we focus on St. Mary's, it's always about the Walker family and their legacy. But another name surfaces in its history, and it's one of great importance. Canon Paul Chidwick, former rector of this Anglican Church, is a name pretty well forgotten, but if it weren't for him, the growth and development of Hospice in Canada might not be what it is. Chidwick was an intellectual who appreciated philosophy and poetry. In 1979, after having witnessed the

work of hospices in England and how they had adopted an approach of managing pain of patients, not just physical pain, but emotional, spiritual, and psychological, Chidwick led the way to founding hospice here in Windsor, which proved the first step in establishing the movement in Canada.

I spoke with Chidwick about two weeks before he died, and nowhere in the conversation did he acknowledge his own poor health, and his own pending mortality. His sole objective was to speak about hospice, its roots in Windsor and his view on its longevity. It was such a shock to learn a few weeks later that he was dying of cancer, the very disease that he had witnessed in others, and what started him on the odyssey to found hospice in these parts.

Dated from 1924, this postcard exemplifies how St. Mary's was designed to evoke the English countryside.

### Kildare, Devonshire, St. Mary's Gate

Nearby St. Mary's and Willistead Manor there are a few houses of note, including 811 Devonshire, a sprawling four-storey mock Tudor design home, also conceived by Kahn, and commissioned by the Walker family. Their intention was that it would accommodate Clayton Ambery, secretary and director of Hiram Walker & Sons. The actual property deed, however, remained with W.L. & B. Co. The house, situated at Cataraqui Street, boasts of 118 windows and dates to 1906.

Kahn fashioned it to imitate a British countryside "cottage" style, hence the half-timber second and third storeys trimmed with cypress wood. The Ambery family moved into the abode with his family at Christmas 1907. It was an easy move since all the furniture—also designed by Kahn—was already there. Ambery died at an early age, and the property was acquired by a former office boy, William Isaacs, in 1915. By that time, Isaacs had become Assistant Treasurer of the firm and, shortly thereafter, a director.

The name of the house came to be known as "Foxley," because the name itself is carved over the entrance. Besides giving it a regal air, it was done mostly to provide the postman back in those days with a means of determining the mail's destination at a time before street numbers. Kahn's Tudoresque architecture of the house received national attention in 1910 in *The American Architect & Building News*.

When the Hatch family bought Hiram Walker & Sons in 1926, the deed for the Devonshire property was transferred to Mary Isaacs, William's spouse. She lived there until 1964. When she died, she left it to the Children's Aid Society, but it was resold to another family, who in turn, eventually sold it to a local developer.

Right across from St. Mary's Church, two prime lots had been set aside for Hiram Walker's grandsons, Harrington E. Walker and Hiram H. Walker, both of whom had Kahn design their grand homes. Only Harrington's house at 1948 St. Mary's Gate

Pictured here in 1913, "Foxley," or the C.C. Ambery House, is still located at 811 Devonshire Road.

remains. He had wished for a plainer look, and his was constructed in 1911. According to WACAC, this house was done "in Flemish bondbrick with a wide, low facade… dormer windows in the hipped roof, and a prominent entrance with a shallow entablature." There was also a detached garage with chauffeur's apartment facing Kildare. The original windows of this house were louvred wooden shutters. The contractor was Victor Williamson.

The Hiram H. Walker house, built in 1906, that once stood on Devonshire Road on the northeast corner at St. Mary's Gate, was built of stone, blending Tudor and Jacobean styles. According to WACAC, this three-storey mansion had "two massive chimneys, several projecting bays and a flat-roofed entrance porch. Its carriage house survives on Argyle Road."

Around the corner on Kildare is the three-storey Albert Kahn designed house at 871 Kildare, built for Andrew Ridout who served as manager of the Canadian Bank of Commerce on Devonshire. This stately home was built in 1906.

Next door there is also the four-bedroom Griggs House (889 Kildare Road), built in 1905, situated at the gates of Willistead Manor at the corner of Niagara and Kildare. Designed in the Arts and Crafts style, it was made to resemble an English country estate. For more than 45 years, it was Dr. Walter Percival's home. He bought it in 1952. The house, however, is named after its first owner, Stephen Griggs, who was vice president of the Walkerville Brewery Company.

The Stephen A. Griggs House, pictured here in 1913, still stands at 889 Kildare.

The home of Harrington E. Walker, pictured left, which still stands at 1948 St. Mary's Gate, is seen here in 1913. His brother Hiram H. Walker's house, long since demolished, is pictured below, c. 1910.

## Willistead Manor, 1899 Niagara

I make my way to Niagara and stand facing Willistead Manor. Everyone should pause at the gates to Willistead, just to take in how this was all part of the design. The leading lines to the manor, taking in the gatehouse, coach house, and the stretch of 15 acres of parkland. Magical. Symmetrical. Reflecting the vision of a community, and maybe the era. In my hand, I carry a copy of the Brownie photograph of this grey, limestone building, fashioned after a 16th-century style 36-room English manor house. It was Hiram's third son, Edward Chandler Walker, who built it. Upon completion in 1906, he assigned it the name of his deceased older brother, Willis, who was a lawyer in Detroit. The photograph, which dates back to 1929, was taken from inside the gates and looks north to

St. Mary's Church. Little has changed. I swing around to replicate that view. The photograph shows a wintry day, maybe late in the afternoon, and a gloomy sky, but the gates, light snow falling, and the tower of St. Mary's, conjure a peaceful scene. It is a gorgeous photograph, and the choice of putting Willistead there is now understood from this perspective. This was planned. This was Edward's wish: to see the church, named after his mother, and the symbol of his pennce, looming just beyond.

The pathway to Willistead, just as you enter the property, arches slightly to the right, then to the left. I pass the gatehouse, now occupied by the Cultural Affairs Office of the City of Windsor. It's unthinkable to ponder that some on city council plotted to usher in the bulldozers to remove this architectural gem and replace it with a condominum, but it's

The Brownie photograph of the gates of Willistead Manor, looking towards St. Mary's Anglican Church, c. 1929.

116

true. In 1978, it was saved from demolition. The big worry among some city fathers was the repair bills, what it would cost to keep the Albert Kahn-designed Willistead from further deterioration. Bert Weeks, Windsor's mayor at the time, led the way to keep the manor from the wrecking ball. He supported the preservationists, eventually leading to a major restoration. This was also the first big victory for the WACAC, which had been founded in 1975. It may have been partly fuelled, too, by the backlash to the demolition of St. Mary's Academy in April 1977 in South Windsor.

Willistead was briefly closed, but reopened in 1981.

In some ways, I wished I had been there in 1904 when the Scottish stonemasons crossed the ocean and rolled in and set up their tools on the nearly 16-acre grounds to begin cutting the grey limestone to build the exterior of this mansion for the E.C. Walker family. The rock had been trucked in from the quarries in Amherstburg. The interior is elegant with marble fireplaces, dark wood panelling, and sumptuous hand carvings.

According to the Heritage Resource Centre from the University of Waterloo, the manor is "the epitome of Edwardian elegance" with inventive work by Kahn including pressure tanks and heating systems that were "the first of its kind in Walkerville residences." The very first "warming oven" used in Canada was introduced here.

Edward Walker spent $125,000 building Willistead, but only lived in the manor for nine years. He died in 1915. Mary Walker remained

alone in the mansion, but when she failed to convince her sister to move from the United States to join her, she departed Walkerville and deeded the property over to the town in 1921. For a time, it served as the meeting place for Town Council, while the coach house became Walkerville's Police Station with the old stables being transformed into jail cells.

Mary Walker, wife of Edward, is one individual who fascinates me. When I was at the *Windsor Star*, I wrote a story about those heritage-minded citizens, The Friends of Willistead, banding together to arrange for a flat grave marker for Mary in front of her husband's massive memorial. This was 2006. She had died in 1937. It had been Mary's wishes to be interred with her husband at St. Mary's Church cemetery yard, and she was, but it took nearly 70 years to arrange for a grave marker to be put in place.

This postcard shows Willistead Manor in 1912, one of the nine years that Edward and Mary Walker resided in the grand house together.

It's clear this was not merely an oversight, according to Kayla Dettinger, in her paper, "Mary: The Life and Times of Mrs. Edward C. Walker of Willistead Manor." Mary's relationship with the Walker family after Edward's death was punctuated by constant mistrust, private misgivings, and internal squabbling with the heirs to the estate. Dettinger describes a woman who struggled being a Walker. It wasn't always like that for Mary Emma Griffin, who was born September 18, 1855, the daughter of the wealthy and influential car maker, Thomas Griffin. She likely met Edward through her father because the two men were deeply involved in the founding of the Detroit Institute of Arts. In 1896, Edward proposed and married Mary at a private wedding held at Hiram Walker's house on Jefferson Avenue in Detroit. This was probably the result of the two being from differing denominations. Mary, unlike Edward, was Catholic, and she continued to be long after the marriage. In 1906, she donated the largest church bell to the newly opened Our Lady of the Lake Church.

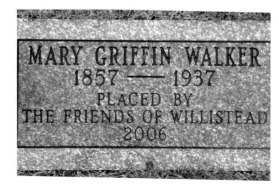

A commemorative grave marker for Mary Walker was erected in 2006 by The Friends of Willistead in St. Mary's Cemetery.

MARY GRIFFIN WALKER
1857 —— 1937
PLACED BY
THE FRIENDS OF WILLISTEAD
2006

"Before building and moving into Willistead," says Dettinger, "the couple lived in the 'Cottage' adjacent to the distillery headquarters." It is clear that the planning of Willistead included Mary's own vision of what this estate would look like. As a matter of fact, Dettinger notes that a personal letter survives that shows a sketch that Mary had done of the landscaping surrounding Willistead Manor. She was also responsible for selecting the furniture for the mansion when she travelled to London in 1906.

Mary was "the quintessential Edwardian socialite" and philanthropist, yet she was devoted to being "active in causes that benefited women in some way." For example, she was involved in The Women's Exchange in Detroit which aided women who had "fallen on hard times" to have a place to sell their handmade goods.

After Edward's death in March 1915, Mary's life as a Walker dramatically changed. Her husband's will made it clear that she could live out her life at Willistead, and that all bills would be paid for by a trust company handling the estate. However, if she decided to depart the manor, she faced two choices: give up all rights to the house and furniture, and receive a lump sum to procure another home for herself, or give up her right to the house and premises, but use some furniture to move into an apartment which would still be governed by the trust company. Mary would also receive $30,000 to purchase another residence, and an annuity of $25,000, along with another $200,000 to be invested on her behalf in lieu of dower rights.

Willistead Park in 1932. Mary Walker likely designed the landscaping of the estate.

The balance of the estate was divided among several family members and friends, and to Edward's two brothers who were given supervision of the will.

According to Dettinger, a collection of five surviving letters shows "seeming friction." In one letter to her caretaker's wife, Mrs. Fox, sent from a hotel in Maine, Mary warns the woman to seek counsel of her Walkerville lawyers about certain individuals trespassing on Willistead. She writes that "the grounds are not open to anyone until I give them up—they must not let them in. They can say I am returning... They might make trouble for me if they let any of them in." Dettinger suspects the reference here is to Harrington Edward Walker, son of James Harrington Walker. It is also clear from other letters that her decision finally to leave Willistead was "hasty." She was not on good relations with the surviving heirs to Hiram Walker's business. Dettinger's view is that her decision to leave Willistead was "potential loneliness... or perhaps a discord between her and the Walkers." Willistead was transferred to the Town of Walkerville in 1921.

After her husband's death, Mary travelled widely, but lived mostly in the United States. She lived a long life, dying at 80. "Her desire to be buried in Walkerville," says Dettinger, "indicates that she must have still felt a strong attachment to the town and its inhabitants with whom she had been so involved in the effort to forge a Walkerville identity."

The Willistead Art Gallery, housed on the second floor of Willistead Manor, in 1960.

I was lucky enough to experience a little of the richness of the place one night in November 2015 when, as the city's Poet Laureate, I organized "Poetry at the Manor." I sat in the dining room with Poets Laureate from around the country. I leaned back in my chair to imbibe the width and breadth of this great room, and imagined being transported back to the early part of the 20th century. It was an exquisite moment, full of enchantment.

It wasn't the first time I had been there, of course. I recall that moment in 1968 when I arrived in Windsor. It was September, and hot, and I took a bus from downtown to Walkerville, and strolled up Devonshire to St. Mary's and rounded the church yard to pause at these gates, before making my way through the massive front door that was hand carved by an Austrian craftsman, Joachim Jungwirth. Before me, when I stepped into the room, was the Windsor Public Library. The perfect spot for book reading. This space hosted a public library from the mid 1920s until 1973. After exploring the rich decor of this library, I climbed the six-foot-wide staircase which I learned later was a copy of a staircase in England's Hatfield House designed by Robert Lyninge. Now upstairs in this grand Tudor-Jacobean style building, I was standing in the Willistead Art Gallery. This exhibition space remained here from 1943 to 1975. It was under the wise direction of the curator and artist Kenneth Saltmarche. It wasn't until the late 1960s that the gallery began to run into a problem with space. In 1970, the suggestion was made that it move to the old Carling Brewery warehouse on the riverfront downtown. That did not happen until 1975 when the gallery finally converted this former Prohibition fixture into the Art Gallery of Windsor.

I met Saltmarche that fall in 1968 at the gallery. I had just turned 22. I was a brash upstart of a poet. I found him disarming, standoffish, but, curiously, entirely generous. Much later in 1971, after I was married and I returned to Windsor, I walked into Willistead one day, and stood in awe of an exhibit that Saltmarche brought there. It was the "Enigma" work by the legendary artist Harold Town. I was so intrigued with these haunting creatures, half human, half animal, that I was resolved to meet the artist. I didn't realize it at the time that Saltmarche had, like Town, graduated from the Ontario College of Art in Toronto. The two were good friends.

As it turned out, I never got the chance to meet Town, but Saltmarche gave him a chapbook of my poetry as a gift. I had read these poems at a reading at Peter K. Ryan's shop with poets Eugene McNamara, Dorothy Farmiloe, and Len Gasparini. I am not sure whether Town ever read my work, but he did roll up a poster for me, signed it, and dispatched it to me with words referencing one of the poems. I was taken by this gift, and have cherished it ever since.

It was maybe a little more than ironic that Saltmarche would set up a gallery at Willistead, because when Edward Chandler Walker lived there, it was a showpiece for art. He was a collector, and someone whose fascination with art led him to become a founding member of the Detroit Institute of Arts. The drawing room in Willistead, for example, once held Impressionist paintings by Claude Monet and Auguste Renoir.

The last time I saw Saltmarche was at his home at 995 Chilver Road across the road from Willistead. I was doing an interview for the *Windsor Star.* He took me down to the basement where there were stacks and stacks of paintings, and we talked about Willistead, the gallery downtown, and the future of art, books, and poetry. It was a peaceful morning spent at the house wandering the hallways, looking at art.

Sadly, Ken Saltmarche is forgotten, or at least, I believe he is. It's hard to believe, seeing as he was the engine of the arts scene in this city. He mentored so many young artists. Yet when I mention his name to artists and writers today, they shrug—they don't know him. But

he, and his wife Judy, were devoted to art, and evidence of this became clear when the family sold the house on Chilver and moved Ken to Toronto. Part of what was hauled away from the house in that final move were the paintings the couple had bought over four decades of marriage. Gifts to one another.

"They didn't buy flowers and chocolates... but paintings," his son, David Saltmarche said. Scrawled on the backs of these were poignant notes to one other.

I sat with Ken Saltmarche's sons in the family home when the movers were there. The empty rooms in that house across from Willistead seemed to accentuate the wallpapered walls, discoloured from years of smoke and marked by dozens of rectangular shapes

Eugene McNamara does a poetry reading at Peter K. Ryan's shop in October 1968. I am seated in the foreground, to the right, with my hand on my face.

Above: Ken Saltmarche, artist and long-time curator of the Willistead/Windsor Art Gallery, sits amid more than 600 pieces in the gallery's storage, c. 1972.

Right: The former Saltmarche home at 995 Chilver Road.

where paintings once hung—paintings that had been placed there carefully by Judy and Ken. These were works by artists who Saltmarche had supported and provided exhibition space.

I only just learned that my brother, Bud, when he was barely 10 years old, used to come to Willistead for drawing lessons. Saltmarche had a studio set up for classes. My father used to drop off Bud, along with our older brother, Paul, on Saturday mornings. Saltmarche was being paid to teach only one of my brothers, but Paul, who was supposed to watch over his younger brother, was handed paper and pencils, and the two boys under the tutelage of this artist, learned to draw.

In speaking of Saltmarche, there is one unsung hero from the past who gave him the freedom and latitude to blossom. People will speak highly of the artist and art gallery director; but it was a spinster, a farmer's daughter, who hailed from Campbellford, near Kingston, who had the initial vision. It was she who gave Saltmarche the permission to dream and transform the gallery into something of importance on the Canadian scene. This was Anne Hume.

I knew nothing about her until I spoke to Eleanor Wickett and Dr. Tom Robson, both of whom were deeply involved with the development of the Art Gallery of Windsor (AGW). Robson, a former president of the gallery board and Wickett, who once headed the volunteer committee, knew Hume well.

"Anne was a dynamo," recalled Wickett. "She gave the gallery and Ken Saltmarche the impetus to make it into something."

The Queen's University graduate and a former teacher, who had also finished a course in library science, was barely in her twenties when she landed in Windsor to take over the Walkerville Library. She wasted no time in putting forth her ideas for a "picture gallery and museum" as part of the library, once it was decided the library should move to the town-owned Willistead Manor.

In her 1921 report, Hume wrote, "The Willistead Library should be the rallying point for all forces that make the artistic and intellectual betterment of a town."

Wickett contends that Hume "realized that Windsor was nothing, that it was an ordinary little town… She realized we had the capacity to make itself more important." Robson added, "Anne Hume was really the first women's libber, long before that was even thought of."

In the summer of 1921, Hume wrote to the Royal Ontario Museum (ROM) asking if it would loan an exhibit to the library. The reply came in a terse note saying under no conditions would it send anything to Windsor. An undaunted and perturbed Hume refused to take "no" for an answer and hopped on a train at Walkerville bound for Toronto. Once there, she barged past all protocol to confront ROM's director, C. T. Currelly, and wound up spending a pleasant day with him and viewing his collection of Egyptian, Roman, and Chinese artifacts. By the end of the day, she had secured a deal for a small exhibit shipped to Walkerville, as long as the town paid the expense. It was the first time the museum would send a sampling of its collection out of Toronto.

Anne Hume, at far left, tries out one of the new benches in the children's department at the grand opening of the Seminole branch of the Windsor Public Library in October 1953.

Hume also contacted the National Gallery in Ottawa and within a couple of years of being in Walkerville, had secured a loan of pictures by Canadian artists. These were sent in March 1923, thus giving birth to the library's picture gallery—albeit a modest one. It amounted to 10 paintings, including one by the Group of Seven artist, J.E.H. MacDonald.

Over the next decade, more pictures, including some by Emily Carr, were transported to Windsor. By 1936, the Windsor Art Association, a precursor to the Art Gallery of Windsor board, became a reality. In 1943, the Willistead Art Gallery came into being in its own right. By then, Hume was put in charge of the entire Windsor Public Library system. Windsor had assumed control over the operation of the Willistead Public Library in 1935 at the time of amalgamation, but the branch continued to be referred to as Willistead Library. And it was at this old Walker mansion that the vision for the gallery took shape.

By 1946, Hume hired Saltmarche as gallery curator. Her genius, both Robson and Wickett contend, was in recognizing that Saltmarche required the latitude and freedom to make something of this modest gallery. Robson said the sad thing is that for the most part, Hume today is a "forgotten figure."

I'm not sure if it's still there today, but in the main branch of the Windsor Public Library's board room, a picture of Hume used to be there, but few in this town realize that she was the mover and shaker behind this dream of a permanent picture gallery for Windsor. On the other hand, when Hume died in 1966, the *Windsor Star* said that she had contributed "more than any other individual to the cultural life of this community." Sadly, from my point of view, both Saltmarche and Hume are forgotten figures in the arts scene today in Windsor.

The former home of poet Leila "Danny" Pepper, at the southwest corner of Devonshire Road and Tuscarora Street.

## Devonshire and Tuscarora Street

Today I'd like to wander through Willistead Manor, but the massive doors are shut. Instead, I return to St. Mary's Gate and go north on Devonshire towards Wyandotte. At the corner of Tuscarora, there is a yellow-brick home on the southwest side. This was the home of Leila "Danny" Pepper, a poet and old friend. She died on New Year's Eve in 2009 at the age of 96. Poet Judith Fitzgerald in the *Globe and Mail* wrote:

Danny's unforgettable. From the instant I first met her in person during the year I wrote in residence at the university, I remember our meetings at her home. I remember our discussions, our back-and-forthing, our joy, excitement and, oddly, her exquisite tablecloths, hand-stitched, old-fangled, incredibly poignant, reminding me of my own elegant and informally formal yet touchingly correct mother. Danny stood on ceremony; but, yes, it looked so good on her and felt so right for each of us. We are truly blessed. We knew and shall never forget an amazing woman and terrific poet...

As publisher of Black Moss Press, I released three of her books and spent many hours working with her on the poems, offering advice and guidance.

From an early age, Danny was writing. At 18, she had published a story in the prestigious *Liberty* magazine—a weekly publication that, at one time, was said to be "the second greatest magazine in America" after *The Saturday Evening Post.* But Danny's career was put on hold to marry and raise a family. Still, she never stopped writing. It was always there. All through the Second World War, she kept a diary. But it wasn't until Danny was in her mid-60s that she started in earnest to pursue her career as a writer. She met the celebrated novelist W.O. Mitchell, author of *Who Has Seen the Wind,* while he was the writer-in-residence at the University of Windsor. Mitchell saw in Danny a writer of enormous talent. He offered to help, mostly to encourage her and to light a fire under her. From there, her work blossomed, and she started publishing again.

In 1997, Danny received the Mayor's Award for her book, *Love Poems for Several Men,* and made the headlines in her remark to then Mayor Mike Hurst. The mayor, in mentioning that title, had remarked playfully, "I guess I'll have to read that!" Danny, in typical spunky style, shot back, "Why don't you buy a copy!" Her words stole the show.

A moment I will never forget is a month before she died when I went to see her with three University of Windsor students—Sarah St. Pierre, Marie Jeannette, and Kellie Chouinard. It was with the intention of doing a performance of her work for her. In a small way, it was to honour her, to celebrate her writing.

At the time, Danny was living at Central Park Lodge, and the students sat in wonder before this feisty woman. And when they read from her books, they caught Danny

shutting her eyes and moving her lips, silently mouthing the words of her poems. In that moment, they had made a connection with her. It was something they will never forget. It's that connection that is so familiar to all those who knew Danny Pepper. She had a way of getting into your heart. I think these three students may have expected someone feeble, someone whose mind had slipped, but instead they encountered a woman of wisdom, quick wit, charm, and spunk. And when they clambered into my car afterwards, they couldn't stop talking about Danny. One finally remarked, "I want to be just like her when I'm 96."

As always, as I pass by Leila Pepper's house, I think of those conversations, the poems, the opinions, her gentle and optimistic way. The yellow-brick home sings of her memory.

Poet Leila "Danny" Pepper listens to one of her poems, read to her by Marie Jeanette, during a visit in 2009.

## Devonshire and Wyandotte

I cross Wyandotte and on the west side of the street, there is a two-storey commercial building with timber-framed oriel windows and decorative gables. This is the Strathcona, also known as the Walker Block. It was built in 1907 and was occupied by druggist F.J. Miller and R.A. Holland who opened up a dry goods store. To digress a little, it was Miller who wrote out a $1,000 cheque to Gordon McGregor in 1904 to invest in the Ford Motor Company. When McGregor failed to pick it up, Miller tore the cheque

up. That's when the Stodgells jumped in with their money. That was not surprising since the Stodgell family was one of influence. John and Emma Stodgell operated three businesses in Walkerville, and John's brother, Charlie, was the mayor of Walkerville for three years.

In the old Strathcona, there was also a hardware store on the first floor, and the Walkerville Library for a time—at least until 1922—stretched out over the second floor. That's when it moved to Willistead.

I continue north on Devonshire, entering a neighbourhood abundant with heritage buildings. At 546–548, sits one of the first homes commissioned for management level employees at Hiram Walker & Sons in 1890. There were three of these massive semi-detached homes built by the Walkers. But this one in particular had a direct connection to the whisky family. Harrington E. Walker, Hiram's grandson, took up residence here while waiting for his house to be completed at St. Mary's Gate. Like so many buildings that the Walker family touched, this one, too, was designed by Mason & Rice of Detroit. It represents an architectural style that is 'Richardson' Romanesque. My wife, Donna, remembers visiting this place when she was a young girl. She would go there to visit her Uncle Syd Butcher who resided there. The Butcher family owned Butcher Engineering in the nearby Peabody Building.

The uniqueness of this Devonshire home, according to writers of *Canada's Historic Places,* is how this structure—with its rounded

The intersection of Wyandotte Street and Devonshire Road, looking west, c. 1910. The Strathcona Block is located on the right.

entryways, square windows and hipped roof—creates "the illusion of a single building while in actuality creating semi-detached units." Apparently, few alterations have been undertaken to the original exterior.

Across the street is 547 Devonshire. This is the John Bott House, designed by James Grey McLean of Windsor. McLean had a tremendous effect on the area, having also designed Windsor's Patterson Collegiate and the Teachers Training School on Mill Street. Both of these buildings have vanished from the landscape. The John Bott House's turret-like dormers and the massive stair landing window on the north facade are what make this 1894 house distinctive. One-time mayor of Walkerville, Bott managed the Walkerville Brewing Company, and was well known for garnering the top prize for malt at the Chicago World's Fair in 1893. Bott, incidentally, sat on the first town council with his friend and neighbour, Thomas Reid, who lived next door at 511 Devonshire.

Thomas Reid was a Quebec-born distiller who worked for Hiram Walker and was active in the community. He actually ran for political office before coming to Walkerville in 1862 to work for the Walker family. In 10 years, he was in charge of the distillery operation. 511 Devonshire was built for him, and completed in 1892. It was designed by Mason & Rice. The house long ago shed itself of the original ornamental flourishes. Also gone are the slate roof with balustrade and the decorated chimneys, but we should be thankful. It's still standing, still occupied.

Above: 546–548 Devonshire Road, a semi-detached home built in 1894, was one of three residences built for managers at Hiram Walker & Sons.

Left: the John Bott House was built in 1894.

A postcard of the Walker- ville Post Office, c. 1920.

## Devonshire and Brant

Farther north on the east side at Brant is the two-storey former Walkerville Post Office (420 Devonshire), a beaux art style brick building that went up in 1914 on property bought by the federal government from the Walkerville Land and Building Company. Again, it was all part of a plan to provide a community with a church, a school, homes, and of course, a post office. What distinguishes it from the neighbourhood—and this was purposely done—is its "buff brick and cast concrete." The preference among the Walkers was red brick and limestone.

## Devonshire and Assumption

Still on the east side, crossing over Assumption, there is a handsome red-brick building at 378– 396 Devonshire. The corner shop is occupied by Taloola Café, now a popular spot with delicious wholesome foods, and sometimes music and poetry readings. This was once the Crown Inn, Walkerville's first hotel. The W.L. & B. Co., hiring their go-to architects, Mason & Rice, started on this four-storey Queen Anne and Romanesque Revival style structure in 1892. The 32-room hotel opened for business a year later. The place—directly across from the railway depot (long ago demolished)—served

The old Crown Inn, pictured here in 1964. When it opened in 1892, it was the first public hotel in Walkerville, conveniently located on Devonshire, the town's main street.

out-of-town visitors. The Crown Inn shut its doors in 1921 at the start of Prohibition, but soon was transformed into an apartment building with shops on the ground floor. Its exterior hasn't changed much from the 19<sup>th</sup> century building that it was. It still has the hipped roof projecting over the bay windows. The edifice also still boasts the original dormers on the fourth storey with triangular hoods, broad-arched first floor windows with glazed transoms and radiating brick voussoirs, and a central balconette on the third floor of the facade.

Next door to this at 350 Devonshire is the Barclay Building, or what was once Walkerville Town Hall. Its name hails from James Barclay and Co. Ltd., a Division of Walker Distillery, which occupied it for a time. It was saved from the wrecking ball, but only after Hiram Walker & Sons got local preservationists to provide their blessing for the demolition of

Left: The Barclay Building in 1912, when it was primarily a post office and was located on Sandwich Street (Riverside Drive), built on the foundation of the first St. Mary's Anglican Church. It is pictured at right in its present location, at 350 Devonshire Road.

the Flat Iron building that sat next to it on the southeast corner of Riverside Drive and Devonshire Road.

The Barclay Building, designed by Kahn and built in 1904, was purchased by the "Preserve Old Walkerville Committee" who moved the building to Devonshire Road from Riverside Drive in 1995. Ironically, the renowned Detroit architect had originally wanted to place the 2,300 square-foot town hall and post office near the present-day location, but instead opted to place it on the foundations of the original St. Mary's Church, east of Hiram Walker & Sons head office. Victor Williamson was contracted to build it. When the municipal offices relocated to Willistead Manor in 1921, the Barclay Building served briefly as a train station. The

building, with its dormer windows on the roof, was restored in 1996 after it was sold to a private firm.

As for the long, brick Flat Iron building, also designed by Mason & Rice, nothing remains except for its bricks that were sold off to individuals. As a matter of fact, a brick sidewalk in my backyard was made from what was salvaged from the wreckage. The whisky company was intent on demolishing the Flat Iron, and battled away with the community activists to make that happen. The compromise was the Barclay Building. If Hiram Walker & Sons had had its way, both buildings would have been removed. The comment in the newspapers from the preservationists was "better one [being saved] than none." Regrettable. As for the reasons given by Hiram

Walker & Sons? Who knows. The company's intentions were shrouded in vagueness.

One of the major merchants in the original Flat Iron Building was John Stodgell, a hard-working immigrant from Somerset, England. As mentioned, he had been one of the 20 original investors in Ford of Canada. His businesses included Walkerville Tea Room, Stodgell's Confectionery Store, and Stodgell's Telegraph office. He and his brother, Charlie, who operated a wine and spirits shop next door, had amassed quite a lot of wealth in bottling Hiram Walker's Canadian Club whisky for sale in the United States. That money was funnelled into Ford Motor Company of Canada in 1904. McGregor convinced them this was an easy way to profit. Camilla Stodgell-Wigle, his daughter, worked in the Flat Iron Building. She kept a copy of that first dividend cheque her father received from Ford. The envelope it was sent in bore only his name and a one-cent King George stamp. Neither his name, nor his house number was written on it. But it got to him.

John Stodgell also wound up owning the first car to come off the assembly line in Ford City.

This postcard shows Sandwich Street (Riverside Drive), looking east from Devonshire Road, c. 1908. The Flat Iron building is located on the right.

The interior of the old Walker Power Building.

An S.W. & A. streetcar travels on the Peabody Bridge, c. 1926. The Peabody Building is at right, in the foreground, with the Walker Power Building behind it.

## Devonshire and Riverside Drive

Across the street from the Barclay Building at the end of Devonshire, there's an ivy-covered building from 1911. Called the Walker Power Building (325 Devonshire Road), it once stood next to the Peabody Building. To this day, it is often mistakenly called the Peabody Building. This 60,000 square-foot structure, designed by Albert Kahn, was used to power the sprawling Hiram Walker distillery. Up until a few years ago, the building provided space for artists until the Windsor Fire Department expelled them because it was deemed a fire hazard.

The beloved Peabody Building was also designed by Kahn. It stood adjacent to the Peabody Bridge, often comically cited as "the only hill" in Windsor. It housed many smaller companies, including Butcher Engineering started by two brothers, Les and Bill Butcher. The company still exists today and is still in the hands of the Butcher family, but it moved out of the Peabody Building long before it was torn down more than 30 years ago.

A strange story surrounding the bridge, and its demolition in 1992, is how archeologists halted the removal of the structure because they convinced Windsor City Council that approximately 56 Norwegian immigrants who died of cholera in the summer of 1854 may have been buried on these grounds near the waterfront. Trenches were dug between the rail line that ran near the building and Devonshire Road in an effort to locate the gravesites.

As the story goes, these immigrants were en route to settlements in Wisconsin and

Minnesota, and were travelling from Quebec to Windsor with the plan of crossing over to Detroit. Joan Magee in her book, *A Scandinavian Heritage: 200 Years of Scandinavian Presence in the Windsor-Detroit Border Region,* says there was serious "overcrowding" on the train, and the Norwegians, unlike the first-class passengers, were crammed into freight cars without windows. When the train was halted because rails had to be replaced at Baptiste Creek, near Chatham, the passengers disembarked because in the oppressive summer heat, the rail cars became hot boxes. While first-class passengers were accomodated on another train, the immigrants were forced to spend two days at Baptiste Creek without food, water, or proper shelter. By the time their train could resume travel, one Norwegian was dead and 33 others had collapsed on the platform. It was reported that many had resorted to drinking the contaminated water in the creek. Upon arrival in Windsor—which then had a population of 750—there was no hospital, and only one doctor to accommodate them. Dr. Alfred Dawson set up a cholera hospital in a warehouse provided by the Great Western Railway on Moy and Sandwich Street. He rallied some volunteers, but he couldn't save them. Some 56 died from cholera.

The railway, at first, promised to assume the expense of the coffins, but in the end, refused. The incident of where these immigrants were buried continues to be a mystery. Former Windsor Community Museum Curator Alan Douglas told the *Windsor Star* that homeowners in the Moy and Hall Avenue neighbourhood uncovered human skeletons in the 1970s, and speculated that these might have been the remains of these Norwegians. But this did not prove to be the case. The Peabody bridge was the next suspected burial ground, but only bones of Aboriginals were found.

However, the Peabody Building is perhaps most famous for the attack it endured during the First World War. Its first tenant, the Peabody Leather Label Overall Company, manufactured the famous Peabody overalls and shiny shoulder strap buckles. During the war, however, its factory workers were producing British Army uniforms. That may have been the factor that attracted American-based, German sympathizers in their attempt to blow up the building at 3:00 a.m. on June 21, 1915. A bomb was placed in a hole under the building, next to the old wooden Peabody Bridge. Part of the bridge was destroyed, and the other side was bent. But the force of the bomb blew out every window in the building, including crumbling some of the sashes and sills. The timing device on a second bomb placed at the Windsor Armouries failed, thereby saving the lives of new recruits sleeping inside.

Oddly enough, Windsor Mayor Arthur Jackson hadn't paid any attention to the warning about the attacks that had been issued to him in the form of a letter. Maybe he believed the good pastor Earl R. Rice from Detroit who assured the Windsor Literary and Scientific Society in December 1914 that there was no fear of a German attack on Canada.

The bombing sent fear into the population here, to the degree that sightings of planes

Left: The Walkerville Ferry dock, c. 1910.

Right: A newspaper clipping showing a rare view of the original Tecumseh Boat Club, located just west of the dock, that burned down in 1908.

flying over the area were being called in to the police on a regular basis. In September 1915, according to historian Brandon R. Dimmel in *Engaging the Line: How the Great War Shaped the Canada–US Border,* one man spotted a biplane over the city, and rushed down to the Armouries to report that it was German and that the 21st Regiment ought to run outside and shoot it down. It turned out the plane was owned by a Windsor resident who was on his way to the Michigan State Fair.

The Peabody continued to serve Windsor until 1985, when it was torn down—despite its dramatic history.

At the foot of Devonshire, too, there was the Walkerville Ferry dock. Next to it was the Tecumseh Boat Club. The boathouse itself actually originated in Detroit. It was taken across the river from the foot of Joseph Campeau in 1890 to this spot on the south shore. According to Elaine Weeks and Chris Edwards, it was to repay a debt owed to Hiram Walker. The ornate boathouse burned in 1908.

Now I make way over to Chilver. I follow Devonshire south to Assumption and turn west to Chilver to meet up with the Victoria Tavern, still with its *Ladies & Escorts* sign over the Assumption Street doorway. Chilver Road was named after Charles Lewis Chilver, former mayor of Walkerville, who owned the Chilver Land and Building Company and whose

The famous "Ladies and Escorts" sign still graces the side of the Victoria Tavern, that looks onto Assumption Street.

Left: Frank LaForet's Exchange Hotel, shortly after it was built in 1903 to replace the smaller hotel one lot over. Today, it is the Victoria Tavern, pictured at right.

family farm stretched from the river all the way to Tecumseh Road. Originally, it was called Susan Road, then was renamed Victoria after his grandmother, Victoire. But when amalgamation brought Walkerville into the fold, it was renamed Chilver Road.

Now I am standing outside the Victoria Tavern, sometimes called "The Vic," and for those in the know, "The Exchange." The story is that the deal to create Ford Motor Company in Canada was signed here with McGregor and Henry Ford in August 1904. McGregor had managed to assemble 12 investors to put their money into building cars in Windsor at a time when it was still dominated by the horse and buggy. These shareholders held 51 percent of the new business.

The original Exchange, however, was the building to the south, just one lot over. It was moved from the corner of Chilver and Assumption by the next owner, Frank Laforet, a door-to-door milkman. But even before it was moved, Chilver had already converted

that building into a tavern, and had given it the name "The Walkerville Exchange." In 1903, three years after buying it from Chilver, Laforet opted to build a new tavern on the same spot, but didn't wish to tear down the original. And that's when the building was moved one lot over. If only the Border Cities had more such individuals. In any case, Laforet moved the tavern to 438–442 Chilver and outfitted it as a rooming house. He then spent $10,000 putting up a red-brick building, calling it "The Exchange Hotel." The name Victoria Tavern was adopted in 1930.

In its earliest days, the Exchange was an overnight place for visitors getting off the train at the Walkerville Train Station. In 1906, the Laforets spent more money building a third storey with a balcony and awnings. The place was heated with coal burning units installed at the end of the hallways. The Laforet family owned the Vic until 1982. As a matter of fact, the eccentric Ida Laforet, according to Weeks and

Charles Chilver crosses Chilver Road on his horse, c. 1905.

The corner of Wyandotte Street and Chilver Road, 1959. Peerless Dairy, the Bank of Montreal, Walkerville Bakery, and Brown's Optical are all visible. The Chilver family farmhouse (not pictured) is located directly behind the bank.

Edwards, lived upstairs for years, but "never came down to the Tavern for 14 years."

Before I make my way back south along Chilver, across the street from the alehouse, is a small, one-storey house that you wouldn't know was a former stable that served the Chilver family. There's a fascinating photo, in fact, of C.L. Chilver riding a horse in Walkerville. He probably kept that horse in that tiny house.

I am now passing Wyandotte. Chilver owned buildings at this intersection, including one at the corner of Chilver where Peerless Ice Cream (1801 Wyandotte Street East) was situated. The family farmhouse—still on Chilver—stood across the street on the southwest corner, what eventually became the Bank of Montreal, now operating as the Gourmet Emporium. The farmhouse had to be moved back to make way for the bank. A parking lot now separates it from the former bank building. Next door to the bank back in the 1950s was the Walkerville Bakery, long gone now. If you turned back the clock to the 1940s, moving east along Wyandotte at this corner you would run into the popular Lustre Café where you could buy a large bowl of chop suey. Next door was Martin's Shoe Repair. Today, the Twisted Apron restaurant has sprawled out over this red-brick building.

I'm headed towards King Edward School (853 Chilver Road), built in 1906. When the Walkers first proposed its construction, this whole area was flat open fields. The vision was to create a community. Of course, the school was a significant part of this grand plan. The first school serving the town was an eight-room Walkerville Public School on Wyandotte. Walter D. Kelly Funeral Home (1969 Wyandotte Street East) now occupies the property. It closed in 1905. The new school— King Edward—was designed by Kahn, who was commissioned to provide a 14-classroom facility. Both St. Mary's and Willistead were already finished. This was the next step. It cost $50,000 to build. The school's history gives an interesting description:

Essentially, the school was all by its lonesome in an open oat field. Students spent many a year trudging through the mud to get to school. Over the decades, as the neighbourhood matured around the school, very few structural changes were made to the original building. Hugh Beaton served as principal until 1917. Succeeding him was Oliver Stonehouse, whose 28-year run as principal makes him King Edward's longest serving administrator.

Stories surrounding this school are legion. Weeks and Edwards, who collected some of these, recount Miss Mary MacRae from 1919, whose "beautifully long fingernails [squeezed] the skin of our necks as she walked up the aisle..." or Miss Mary Wetmore, the school nurse from 1929, who visited three schools every day in her black electric car. Or Miss Jennie K. Nesbitt, who on her way to teach at the school in 1906, would hit a golf ball the entire way from Ouellette and Wyandotte to Chilver.

Unfortunately, the school that one sees on this site isn't the original. No big surprise, is it? In the 1990s, the brain trust serving the Windsor Greater Essex County School Board determined that rescuing this building from the wrecking ball wasn't worth it. Students were already being bussed to other nearby schools. The school board's website proudly related the account of how "under the guidance of J.P. Thomson & Associates, the new building rose from the ground." In a salute

Above: King Edward School in 1906, surrounded by a corn field. The present-day King Edward School is pictured at left, with its front entrance facade salvaged from the original building.

to the past, and to Kahn in particular, the school, as the website contends, "bears a resemblance to Kahn's masterpiece from 1906." Saved from demolition is the original stone facade. Also preserved is the original school bell, the one that was used in the eight-room schoolhouse at Walkerville Public in 1886. It's in the foyer.

I now decide to keep south, heading away from the school. I pass Richmond, and now return to Ontario and turn east, and the first house that I spot is on the right, a familiar place. A stone cottage.

The former home of Pat Sturn at 1875 Ontario.

A portrait of Pat Sturn by Yousuf Karsh, 1951—the photograph I prevented Pat from tossing out.

## Kildare and Ontario

Pat Sturn, the renowned Windsor photographer, lived in this quaint cottage at this corner at 1875 Ontario Street. It was built in 1942. She bought it in the 1950s. When I first met Pat Sturn, she had just turned 91. Those who are new to this city, or those who are young, may not remember her. Pity. Pat Sturn was a jewel. The original bohemian. So fiercely independent. Candid in her talk, yet someone who leapt beyond the cliché boundaries in her conversations. She was someone for whom every word was weighted, every sentence poised. There was no such thing as small talk with her.

Pat Sturn was the preeminent portrait photographer in the city. She was friends with the legendary Yousuf Karsh. Indeed, a proof of a portrait of her was made when Karsh was in Windsor photographing the Ford Motor Company. I caught Pat throwing out that photograph one afternoon, and saved it. It now belongs to the Windsor Community Museum.

Pat charged a fortune for her own work, but people sought her out. She was an artist. She was meticulous, demanding, and challenging. For her, the work wasn't about money or making people feel better about themselves—it was about perfection. One woman told me how upset she was in being subjected to a photograph when she was a young girl. She was maybe 9 or 10, and Pat had her remove her dress, and wear only a white slip. It embarrassed the girl, but as a photographer Pat saw an angelic side, and the combination of light, the purity of the slip, the slope of the neck and the young face, all combined for the most engaging photograph. But Pat wasn't about explaining any of that. Her vision was private. She worked to convey it. The photograph itself jumps off the page.

That first afternoon, I sat across from her in a tiny room in this little stone cottage. A home so small that visitors used to laugh when they looked at the car she used to drive. It seemed so much larger than the house. An afternoon of stories, talk about poetry, photography, about finding the "soul" in one's art, about the way things used to be in this city, about old friends.

She told me of the struggles when she first moved to Canada in the 1930s. She had to work on a farm, even though she had been a photographer in Romania, until she migrated to Windsor where she started working behind the camera again. She said she had no regrets.

The studio in the basement of the Canada Building was her life. The studio with its rose-peach walls—once described by a reporter here as being "a self-contained Greenwich Village"—consumed her days and nights.

The studio was also a meeting place of writers and artists and musicians. Time meant nothing there. It evaporated in talk. She loved to listen—to indulge herself in the stories of these people. And not only the rich and famous. She photographed ordinary souls—the kids, the moms, and the many who couldn't afford the luxury of a portrait. Pat would let them pay when they could. She'd send them home with a gift. When she retired at age 71, she told the newspaper: "You had to drag me

away from my work at times. I could never get married and become a mother because photography was my first love."

She lived a quiet life at 1875 Ontario, surrounded with paintings, tapestries, photographs of friends, sculptures and for each and every object, there was a story. She lived for those stories.

Over the years, I went there more frequently, and when she fell and broke her hip in the hallway of her house, I was drafted to help and contracted nurses to care for her around the clock, from December through to March 2013, when she died. She recited Goethe's poetry in German, and translated the lines for them. My own afternoons were spent reading poetry to her.

Outside her bedroom was a painting by Ken Saltmarche. It was a portrait of his wife, Judy. It always intrigued me, and one day, Pat told me how she had snatched it from him in

A photograph by Pat Sturn which I have in my personal collection.

his studio. He had been fiddling with it, but Pat wanted him to stop. She told Saltmarche it was finished. He disagreed, and so she swept past him, and removed it from the easel, sharply warning him to keep his paws off it for fear of ruining it. For years, it hung in her hallway. Unfinished. Exquisite.

My advice is for people in Windsor to go through the dresser drawers or the places where families keep the albums, and see if you can find a black and white picture she made of a grandfather or an aunt. You won't mistake the distinctive screen-textured quality of it. Treasure it. It's the work of an artist.

## Ontario and Kildare

At the corner of Pat Sturn's cottage, I turn north and head along Kildare, and I don't have to go far—three houses—before I come to a set of large, red-brick gates and a smallish gatehouse. Back in the 1980s, a faded wooden sign was attached to one of the brick posts, and it read "Cooper Court." The house to the right, or the south, had belonged to Jim Cooper's daughter. Unfortunately, in writing *The Rumrunners* at a time when people still didn't want to go

A rare existing view of Cooper Court.

public with their stories, she did not wish to be interviewed. Almost this entire block—bordered on the west side by Kildare, the north by Richmond, the east by Devonshire and south by Ontario—was the estate of Jim Cooper. The man was a Prohibition-era liquor entrepreneur who made millions shipping booze made at Hiram Walker & Sons Ltd. to the United States. He had the most palatial three-storey home on this spot, built in 1925, only four years after a massive windfall from the whiskey trade. This $200,000 40-room mansion was the jewel of Walkerville, far outshining any other.

Cooper Court, with its elegant conservatory in one wing, also featured a terrazzo-tiled swimming pool that included an all-glass enclosure with a domed roof. A large bedroom dominated the top floor. There was also a ballroom, complete with a cedar-lined storage closet for his furs at one end; an exercise room with massage tables; and a billiard room that also served as a schoolroom for the Cooper children who were taught by the nuns who called on the family each day.

The solarium that once was part of Cooper Court was moved to Huron Church Road in 1940. Stephen and Olga Kuzyk opened Stephen's Flower Mart and Greenhouses there, but when their business closed in 1988, it was torn down to make way for a hotel and parking lot.

What else remains of that mansion is the massive pipe organ. In the fall of 2013, a well-known local organist, Ron Dossenbach told me that he had restored the famous Cooper Court Aeolian Duo-Art player that was purchased in 1926 by Cooper for $50,000. That colossal organ could pipe music to every room in the mansion, and played music rolls like a player piano but with complete fidelity of natural tone. It has been at Morris Sutton Funeral Home since 1946. It's one of only 1,070 built in North America in the 1920s. Dossenbach actually put on a demonstration at Morris Sutton: "Every pipe is still present, and works." He claims the Windsor instrument may be the only one in the world "with full functionality."

Jim Cooper died in 1931; a mysterious death on a transatlantic crossing. It is said he was being pursued by gangsters, and was fleeing Canada for Switzerland. It was shortly after his death that the mansion was torn down. All that remains of the estate are the red-brick pillars that face both Kildare and Devonshire, and a gatehouse.

## Ontario and Devonshire

I step back on Ontario, and continue east to the former 2 ½-storey Harry Low mansion at 2021 Ontario Street. Indeed, in the heyday of Prohibition, it was called "Devonshire Lodge." It was built in 1928 with rumrunning money. Low spent more than $130,000 to fulfill a dream of a sprawling Cotswold cottage design that feted both the rich and the famous, including visits from Al Capone of Chicago.

Constructed of rusticated stone and limestone trim, Low wanted the rollover thatched roof to be "like the waves of the sea," and to

that end, commissioned wooden shingles to be imported from England. He also situated his house on a diagonal to face the corner of Ontario and Devonshire. As Gary May says in a June 2014 *Globe and* Mail article, the house "stands like a baronial country manor, the convex facade consisting of several bays with gables, a recessed balconette over the arched recessed entrance and leaded glass windows."

This Walkerville home is steeped in a rich and colourful history. Low, who bought the property in the 1920s from the Walkerville Building Company for $18,750, was the epitome of extravagance and eccentricity. He didn't live there long. He saw his financial empire, including a piece of Carling Brewery, dramatically shrink as the federal government sued him for back taxes in 1928. The hapless Low was also linked to the gangland murder of one of his employees who was found bludgeoned and shot through the skull just over the Michigan state line in Toledo, Ohio. After his death in 1956, Low—whose empire had also included a towering office building in Montreal, ships, distilleries, oil well and machine shops—was described in the *Windsor Star* as "a shabby outcast."

Paul Martin picked up his 4,800-square-foot mansion at a cost of $22,000 in 1960. Gary May says this may be the only spot in Windsor's history that can lay claim to hosting both the most notorious gangster of all time, as well as both two Canadian prime ministers, Lester Pearson and Pierre Trudeau. On top of that, it was also home to Paul Martin, Jr., who would later become

Paul and Nell Martin stroll the grounds of the Low-Martin House in 1979, upon Paul's retirement from public service.

prime minister of Canada. The younger Martin was quoted as saying "That's quite a rogue's gallery," as he reminisced about the house his parents bought while he attended university. "That's where I came home to."

I interviewed the younger Martin—then Federal Finance Minister—in May 1997 when the house was up for sale. He spoke about his memories there, and how they still tug at the heart. Whenever he is back in Windsor, he makes a point of driving past the house. "I went by it, and you know, the only thing missing is a sign for Shaughnessy Cohen," says the ever-political younger Martin. "My mother's probably pretty steamed about this in heaven right now wondering where it is."

Martin's memory of his mother Nell, and his elder statesman father, revolve around a small, plain-looking room off the kitchen. "That's where they lived," he told me on the

Harry Low's 1929 mansion, then called Devonshire Lodge, stands at 2021 Ontario Street.

phone from his LaSalle-Emard riding office. "That back room is the size of a clothes closet... It had no particular decoration... That's where my parents lived. They'd sit back there and watch TV. "I always said to them, `You don't need a big house—you need a clothes closet.'"

Martin also recalled how proud his father was of the home's rumrunner history. "My dad used to tell everybody this was Harry Low's house, and my mother would say, 'stop telling everyone!'"

The house, now owned by Vern Myslichuk, a Windsor cabinetmaker, who has done a remarkable job at restoring this grand place to its original glory, is a place I visited often when Paul Martin Sr. lived there. I used to go there on late summer evenings—prompted to visit because Martin would telephone me to come over. And we would sit at the back of the house, and I'd listen to his stories about Mackenzie King, or Louis St. Laurent, or the close relationship he had with John Diefenbaker, even though this former prime minister was a Conservative. I recall one summer evening when I confessed to Martin that my grandfather, who had helped in Martin's first run for political office, had voted for Dief, like so many others in 1958. Martin at first ignored my statement, but suddenly mid-sentence in talking about something completely irrelevant, said, "I don't believe that. I knew your grandfather well, and he never would have voted for a Conservative. You are wrong. He was a Liberal to his very fingertips. You are mistaken." I wasn't—my grandfather did vote for Dief, the first and only time he ever veered from the Liberals. I wasn't about to argue this. I let it go.

## 1219 Devonshire

Across the street from the Low-Martin house at 1219 Devonshire is the yellow-brick home with a sloping brick sidewalk and a red door. That was the residence of Russell Farrow, former mayor of Walkerville, who vehemently opposed amalgamation, and sought whatever legal loopholes that he could find to stop it. A curious detail about this place is the tale of the young Ken Saltmarche approaching Farrow

The former home of Russell Farrow at 1219 Devonshire Road.

Walkerville Town Council in 1934. Mayor Russell Farrow is front and centre. Other council members are: Stephen A. Griggs, Albert Long, John F. Martin, Bruce H. Chick, A.E. Cock, Cyril Cooper, and A.W. MacMillan.

with a request for financial support for his art. The politician—and a man who had made a fortune in the brokerage business, and whose family carries it on to this day—commissioned Saltmarche to paint a mural on an upstairs bedroom wall. The mural is still there, but sadly, is covered over.

Farrow is a significant figure in the history of Walkerville. The Ottawa-born politician and businessman settled here in 1910. At first, he worked for Dominion Customs Appraiser, but in 1911, left to set up his own customs brokerage place in downtown Windsor. He saw an opportunity in the bustling commercial ferry traffic between Detroit and Windsor. He was one of the first in Canada with a fleet of delivery vehicles to smooth the way for the conveyance of goods, offering both brokerage and transportation. It was during the 1930s that Farrow also became actively involved in politics. He worked as an organizer for the Liberal Party, and became the last mayor of Walkerville in 1934.

After the Province of Ontario announced it was forcing the four towns—East Windsor (Ford City), Walkerville, Windsor and Sandwich—to join together, Farrow campaigned vigorously against any such move. But the Royal Commission, appointed to facilitate this amalgamation, flatly told Farrow there was no turning back—it was a done deal. The reason for forcing the Border Cities together was because three of the four—Windsor, Sandwich and East Windsor—were virtually bankrupt. Walkerville's hesitancy was understandable; it was the only one of the four that fared well during the Great Depression.

Farrow finally relented, but he really had no other choice. The reaction in Walkerville was one of shock. At the corner of Kildare and Tecumseh Road, someone erected a sign that announced that Walkerville, founded in 1858, incorporated in 1890, was now "Crucified" in 1935.

Farrow, for all his stiff obstruction wound up serving on Windsor's first City Council. He died in 1949. He was 58. His wife, Alice, took control of the company. Two sons, Robinson R. Farrow and Huntley J. Farrow, both worked at growing the company's local operations. Huntley, like his father, was lured into the political arena, first serving on Riverside's town council, then Windsor's city council after annexation.

## Wyandotte and Chilver

Back north on Devonshire, turning west on Niagara to Chilver, then north again, and I am making my way towards Wyandotte. My visit to Walkerville is nearly complete. Back at the corner of Chilver and Wyandotte, I didn't mention earlier that this former Bank of Montreal building was the victim of a bank robbery in June 1959. Two hooded men, later identified as Nicholas Hamilton and Kenneth Irwin, walked into the bank in mid-afternoon. One of the gunmen stuck a gun into Adele Paré's back when she approached a teller. He said, "This is a stickup. Do as we say, or you'll get it, and we mean it." She complied, and the gunmen forced her into the vault along with 15 bank employees.

By then, however, Norman Wingrover, the chief clerk, had tripped the alarm and police were rushing to the scene. Constable Brian Pickup was the first to arrive from Windsor Police. He spotted a woman with her hand high above her head, and a man with a gun in one hand, a bag in the other. (By this point, Hamilton and Irwin were attempting to make their getaway.) Pickup hesitated in drawing his pistol, fearing potential gun fire might wind up injuring people in the crowd that had gathered outside the bank. As Pickup got closer, he lunged at Hamilton, and managed to toss him over his shoulder and throw him to the ground. He then put his knee on the gunman's chest to hold him down. Pickup didn't realize another robber, Kenneth Irwin, was still inside the building. That's when Pickup was shot in the back. A gun battle followed as two other officers arrived on the scene. Irwin surrendered. Despite being shot in the back, Pickup had somehow managed to keep Hamilton pinned down. The bullet had gone through his back, his stomach and

The robbery scene outside of the Bank of Montreal at the corner of Chilver and Wyandotte streets, June 1959.

lodged in his knee. Pickup survived the incident, was awarded the British Empire Medal for bravery, and retired from the police force in 1988.

### Lincoln and Gladstone

I continue west on Wyandotte towards the former Walkerville Theatre, situated between Lincoln and Gladstone. One might not realize this building, now revived, was designed by C. Howard Crane, who designed the Fox Theatre in Detroit. When it opened in 1918, it was a vaudeville theatre, but soon was showing motion pictures and its name was changed to The Tivoli. From that point on, the theatre underwent numerous changes, being used for live theatre and music in the late 1950s by Windsor Light Opera, then reverting back to being a movie theatre, then transforming to a bingo hall and later as a dance studio. New owners rent it out for live theatre and literary events.

What some might not realize is that right down the middle of centre stage of this theatre was the town line that divided Windsor and Walkerville.

A few doors down is Biblioasis, owned by Dan Wells—both a bookstore and a publishing company. There is so much more to see of Walkerville, but I am heading to Windsor.

It occurs to me that walking in Walkerville is different. It tastes of old world charm and tradition. As I crossed over Walker Road—having come from Ford City with the grim remnants of a factory landscape in one's backyard—it was like stepping into a family friend's living room that's never been sat in or used—the kind that is perfectly preserved only for unexpected guests, special occasions. There is that odd sensation in my beating heart that this is more a promenade than a walk, and it clearly betrays traces of the once-dominant Protestant Ontario. Gazing behind me, there is Riverside with its collection of wartime houses, of Roman Catholic blue-collar families, and nearby Ford City with its residential streets huddling desperately along a harsh and decrepit perimeter of a bygone era. I may have felt more at home in those first two towns, something of my roots being there. In Walkerville, there was a sensation that I was a tourist, a guest, just passing through. My eyes feasted on a neighbourhood that beneath its surface had orderly vision, that rigidly followed a tidy blueprint. It's a place that feels walkable, no need for parking lot mania, a place where history still breathes and thrives. That, too, may be changing.

And so I leave Walkerville, a place struggling to regain its old glory. Before me lies the boundary to old Windsor. I am expecting something haphazard, sloppy, opportunistic, inconsistent; streets where the past, present and future are blurred, where neglect appears to be a way to describe its regard for history. And still, my memories soar in anticipation. Adventure too, awaits.

Pictured here is Wyandotte Street, looking east, in 1950. Below, is Wyandotte Street, looking east today.

# Windsor

Medical Arts Building

Assumption Church
c. 1928
as seen from Ambassador Bridge,
under construction

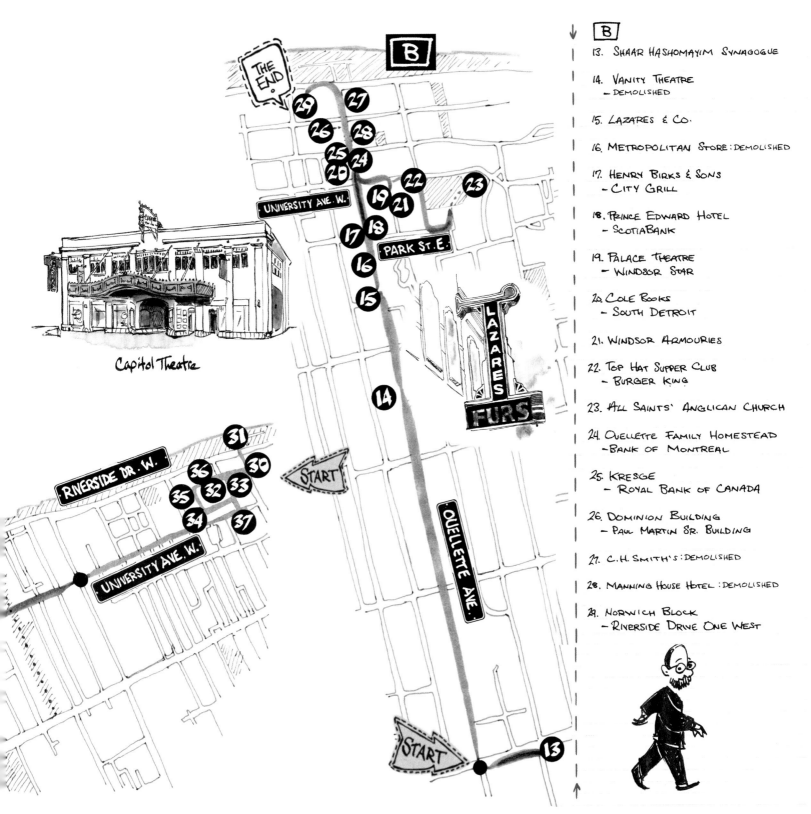

THE END

Capitol Theatre

UNIVERSITY AVE. W.

PARK ST. E.

LAZARES FURS

RIVERSIDE DR. W.

UNIVERSITY AVE. W.

OUELLETTE AVE.

START

START

B

13. SHAAR HASHOMAYIM SYNAGOGUE

14. VANITY THEATRE
 – DEMOLISHED

15. LAZARES & CO.

16. METROPOLITAN STORE: DEMOLISHED

17. HENRY BIRKS & SONS
 – CITY GRILL

18. PRINCE EDWARD HOTEL
 – SCOTIABANK

19. PALACE THEATRE
 – WINDSOR STAR

20. COLE BOOKS
 – SOUTH DETROIT

21. WINDSOR ARMOURIES

22. TOP HAT SUPPER CLUB
 – BURGER KING

23. ALL SAINTS' ANGLICAN CHURCH

24. OUELLETTE FAMILY HOMESTEAD
 – BANK OF MONTREAL

25. KRESGE
 – ROYAL BANK OF CANADA

26. DOMINION BUILDING
 – PAUL MARTIN SR. BUILDING

27. C.H. SMITH'S: DEMOLISHED

28. MANNING HOUSE HOTEL: DEMOLISHED

29. NORWICH BLOCK
 – RIVERSIDE DRIVE ONE WEST

Central United

former HMCS Hunter

School of Social Work
Formerly
Windsor Star

The Barn [WINDSOR ARENA]

Shaar Hashomayim Synagogue

Windsor Armouries

# WINDSOR
*March 14, 2016*
*4.8 km*

Today, skies are still cloudy, and though the streets still betray evidence of rain, the storms of last night have abated. Wyandotte Street East spreads before me as a collection of shops, the more gentrified ones east of Lincoln to Walker Road. Starting at Gladstone, I head west away from Walkerville, passing businesses that interest me more—many of them Middle Eastern. Yet, as with other neighbourhoods, *For Rent* and *For Sale* signs punctuate the walk. It isn't a pleasant sight. The city is at a low point, with some 73,000 in Windsor-Essex living in poverty—19,000 of them children and youth according to Pathway to Potential. It's a grim picture. It's not the future that was envisioned for the Border Cities after amalgamation in 1935. There were those who wanted to set down some order, a defined plan that would transform the landscape of the city.

At the end of the Second World War, Windsor's movers and shakers turned to an expert in urban planning, E.G. Faludi, to plot out what Windsor would become over the next three decades. The city that he found—then made up of Sandwich, Windsor, Walkerville and Ford City—wasn't a pretty sight. Commercial, industrial, and residential areas were intermingled, and in some cases indistinguishable from one another. A reporter for *Time Magazine* in 1946, who came to the city to cover Faludi's report, described Windsor at the time as "a completely disorganized chaos of everything a human being can build… bad streets, slums, blighted areas, factories alongside of houses, no place for children to play;" a city of "dreary wastelands [...] sliced through the middle by three railways clustered with factories." In some ways, that has not changed.

Faludi's plan was unveiled to the public in 1946, in a exhibit held at the C.H. Smith Department Store downtown. He set out to remake the city, attacking what he called "the blighted areas" by city land acquisition. His blueprint shows a waterfront that stretches like a band of green. He didn't dismiss the notion of high-rise apartments along the waterfront, but discouraged commercial development, urging the removal of empty warehouses and the vast network of railway tracks. He also envisioned a Pitt Street Mall with the intention of retaining retail development within the core. Faludi said the former Border

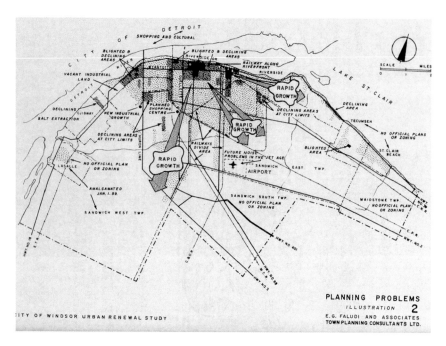

PLANNING PROBLEMS
ILLUSTRATION 2
E.G. FALUDI AND ASSOCIATES
TOWN PLANNING CONSULTANTS LTD.

CITY OF WINDSOR URBAN RENEWAL STUDY

Above: E.G. Faludi's blueprint for Windsor, 1946. He identifies "planning problems," highlighting areas of rapid growth and urban blight.

Right: Sketches of Faludi's proposed downtown mall on Pitt Street.

PROPOSED SHOPPING MALL — PITT STREET
ILLUSTRATION 52
E.G. FALUDI AND ASSOCIATES
TOWN PLANNING CONSULTANTS LTD.
CITY OF WINDSOR URBAN RENEWAL STUDY

Cities suffered from being "as dissimilar organisms, each with its own ends, standards and regulations… highly independent" despite making up one City of Windsor.

Faludi's plan may have followed through in some ways, but the rehabilitation of the core has lagged behind for years, despite efforts from various city administrations. While the blight along the riverfront disappeared over time, the city continues to suffer the ravages of flight from the downtown core, or the "run to the suburbs" as Faludi called it. He warned, "The pattern of outward growth is disorderly and haphazard, but the inward decline is continuous and uniform." True enough. Empty stores abound. The downtown mall that Faludi dreamed up sadly never materialized. The old department stores, lunch counters, shoe stores, and dress shops were all taken over by the nighttime bar trade.

I near Ouellette, Windsor's unofficial main street and the heart of the core, on my walk on Wyandotte. But before I get there, the first stop on today's journey stands just southeast of downtown: the Barn, maybe a symbol of all that old glory.

## Wyandotte & McDougall

The Barn. The Windsor Arena stands on the corner at 572 McDougall Street. For years, people have wanted to see this place torn down to make way for a new arena. Mayor Eddie Francis delivered the WFCU Centre as a replacement facility, but it is located on the far eastern edges

McDougall Street, looking south to Wyandotte Street, 1960. Windsor Arena, affectionately known as the Barn, is at left. Months after my walk, the fate of the Barn was decided: the old Arena is slated for demolition and a new Catholic Central High School will be built on this site.

of the city, far from the core. Meanwhile, the Barn continues to evade the wrecking ball. Calls for its demise go back as far as the 1980s. Chief among them was *Windsor Star* sports columnist Lloyd McLachlan, who in March 1990, called it "a skaters' sewer, a hockey hellhole, a monument to mawkishness." He wrote:

> If there's a wrecking ball out there with that dump's name on it, I say let 'er swing. Let 'er swing till those wretched walls come crumbling down. Here is how she stands, ladies and gentlemen. Windsor Arena is the slagheap of sports. Visiting athletes and officials forced to enter by the rotten luck of scheduling take one look at the interior and gag.

Politicians, retail owners, developers, and even writers, have fuelled this point of view for decades. Tear it down. Build anew. So, I'm content to see the Barn still standing, maybe confronted with an uncertain future, but still there—for now.

The Barn is among the oldest of its type in North America. I haven't been inside it since its last game in 2008, but my memories of it are rich. The halls were adorned with pictures of teams gone by, of former greats, and the hanging banners saluted such heroes as Adam Graves and Mickey Renaud.

According to *Building Stories,* a private home originally sat on this site at McDougall and Wyandotte. A group of 12 Windsor businessmen in 1924 formed the Border Cities Arena Ltd., and planned on opening the arena for the 1925 hockey season. Ernest Clarke Limited built it at a cost of about $200,000. By fall 1925, Border Cities Arena was finished, and the papers of the day deemed it the most advanced of its kind in Ontario. On opening night, November 25, 7,200 turned out to watch the former Stanley Cup champion Victoria Cougars face the New York Americans of the NHL. The following year, the Cougars moved its franchise to Detroit, but because the Olympia was not yet finished, the team—later renamed The Red Wings—played the entire 1926–27 NHL season here. The ice rink in those early days hosted other NHL teams, including the Toronto St. Patricks and the Pittsburgh Pirates.

In 1941, the arena changed its name to 'Windsor Arena' when six of the original owners reorganized the company. Five years later, Bill and Les Butcher of Butcher Engineering acquired the arena. Under the Butchers, the Windsor Bulldogs, a Senior A hockey team, thrived as a team in the Ontario Hockey Association. In 1961, the brothers decided to sell the arena, after trying to turn it into a curling club. Lou Bendo, captain of the Bulldogs

and a real estate agent, stepped forward with a group of six businessmen to save hockey at the Barn. They bought the Windsor Arena for $300,000. From their newly saved home ice, Bendo and the Bulldogs set out on their most successful season ever.

In November 1962, the arena was packed to the rafters as the Bulldogs sailed to a 9-2 victory over the visiting Soviet National team. This same Soviet squad would go on to win Gold at the 1963 World Hockey Championships. Meanwhile, the Bulldogs—the only team to beat the Soviets on their North American tour—would win the Allan Cup that year.

The financially strapped Bulldogs, however, had to cease operations one season later. This soon gave rise to the resurrection of the Windsor Spitfires in the early 1970s. By 1975,

The Windsor Bulldogs pose with their hardware after winning the Allan Cup in the 1962–63 season. Captain Lou Bendo is sitting front and centre.

Donna Mayne's mural of local hockey greats and arena legends that graces the wall of Windsor Arena, facing Wyandotte Street.

the team became part of the Ontario Major Junior Hockey League (OHL). This meant renovations, including lengthening the ice surface, and building luxury boxes and concession booths. Plexiglass also replaced chain-link fence dividers.

Bendo's group poured millions into the arena, and in 1979, acquired some 1000 seats from the Detroit Olympia before it was demolished. These were placed in the Windsor Arena. Years later, when these were being torn out and replaced by newer stadium seats, I bought one. I use it to sit in and watch playoff games. By 1990, the syndicate that owned the arena sold it to the city for $750,000.

My memories of The Barn are endless. I watched my son, Stéphane, play with the Windsor Spitfires, alongside Jason Spezza and Steve Ott in the 2001–02 season for Tom Webster. My other son, Gabe, played in the final days of the arena for the University of Windsor Lancers.

When you stand on Wyandotte and face the arena you will see a mural that was the concept and design of Windsor artist Donna Mayne— also responsible for many of the Drouillard Road murals. I helped choose the featured portraits of fourteen arena personalities: William 'Skeets' Harrison, Dave Oksanen, Jack Costello, Lou Bendo, Siro Martinello, Bill & Les Butcher, Jack Dulmage, Eleanor Freeman, Don Allen, Jennifer Robinson, Miro Martinello, Lloyd Pollock, and Charlie Stewart.

I continue along Wyandotte. Directly across the street from the arena was a neat diner called Frank's, owned by the loquacious

Right: This Methodist Church, c. 1892, stood at Windsor Avenue and Chatham Street until burned in 1904. It was replaced by Central Methodist (now United) Church on Ouellette Avenue, pictured below c. 1910, two years later.

Frank Leventis. He served pancakes the size truck hubcaps. Ham and eggs on heavy china plates. I would sail in there in the still-dark early morning, and Frank was always working behind the counter slinging breakfast after breakfast, talking a mile-a-minute. He had to shut down the restaurant after the city decided to widen McDougall. This was 1998. I miss the place. Great food. Best conversation. Gone.

Now west to Ouellette.

## Ouellette & Wyandotte

At the corner, I turn south, and there is the dignified Central United Church at 628 Ouellette Avenue. This august-looking building, designed by Detroit's Kastler & Hunter Architects, was officially opened in 1906 as Central Methodist Church. Methodism in this area actually dates back to August 15, 1804, when Nathan Bangs rode through here. He was a "saddle-bag preacher" dispatched to this area to evangelize for the American Methodists in the New York Conference. His influence led to the first Methodist church in Windsor, pastored by Rev. Alfred Brown, located on Windsor Avenue and Chatham Street. After that building was destroyed by fire in 1904, this church on Ouellette Avenue was built to replace it. The cornerstone from the original church is at the south entrance, while a new cornerstone was laid by the north door.

It's hard to believe when you see this imposing building smack dab in the downtown core that church members in those early days complained bitterly over the move to this spot. They argued that it was "inaccessible" and "too far out of town." Still, the church managed to get everyone on board after it held a 10-day preaching mission in 1906, and won the hearts of 1,200 who signed up as new members. This was the work of the famous Crossley and Hunter team of evangelists who were sent in to propagate the new faith.

These two men—Hugh Crossley and John E. Hunter—were renowned for their tours of small towns, but especially for an event that allegedly brought about the conversion of Canada's first prime minister. As the story goes, Sir John A. Macdonald was in attendance at a revival meeting in the winter of 1888 when Crossley and Hunter were preaching. According to the *Methodist Christian Guardian* at that time, "when the well-known form of the Honourable Premier rose in the centre of the church, many strong men bowed their heads and wept for joy."

The church follows the classical Victorian Methodist preaching design with its double entrance doors, domed roof, and the pulpit and half-circle of pews spreading out on the main floor. It wasn't until 1980 that church members discovered a "hidden memorial." It was uncovered when workmen were renovating the sanctuary. The main flooring was taken up, and found below it were the "charred timbers" of the former Windsor Avenue Methodist Church. This was evidently used in the construction of Central United in 1906. As one writer at the time said, "When you walk the floor of the sanctuary, then you are literally walking 'where the saints have trod'—on the very boards where the early Methodists in Windsor met to pray and worship."

## Ouellette Avenue & Elliott Street

From Ouellette, I turn east on Elliott Street and walk over to Goyeau Street. The Windsor Fire & Rescue headquarters is at the corner on the west side (815 Goyeau Street). Across the street is yet another parking lot, this one serving customers for the grocery chain, Food Basics. On this spot was the first high school that served Windsor. Opened in 1871, it was called Windsor Collegiate Institute (880 Goyeau Street), then was renamed Patterson Collegiate in 1929 after a Windsor lawyer and politician. But even before it was a high school, it was a grammar school, dating back to 1854.

Patterson closed its doors in 1973, and was demolished in 1979. All that's left of it are a collection of bricks that form a memorial for the school. It sits at the intersection in one corner of the parking lot. It's across the street from the Beer Store, and occasionally is defaced.

My memory of the school was sitting in its amazing theatre space with the renowned playwright James Reaney, watching *Baldoon*, a play that we wrote together, performed by Toronto's NDWT Theatre. Others might remember that Patterson spawned the likes of Abdullah the Butcher, a 400-pound wrestling icon who was the terror of the fight world. His real name, however, was Larry Shreve. For nearly 50 years,

the kid—who grew up on McDougall Avenue in Windsor—battered and bloodied the likes of such icons as Hulk Hogan, André the Giant, Bobo Brazil, The Sheik, and Ric Flair.

It was at Patterson that he learned the basics of wrestling, but Olympic style. At 18, he started his career in Detroit. He was surprised when he was inducted into the WWE Hall of Fame in 2011 because he considered himself one of "the bad boys" of the sport.

I make my way back to Ouellette and walk south, just past Elliott, to the Windsor Public Library. In 1971, the property was purchased to construct the existing Central Branch at 850 Ouellette Avenue. The 101,467 sq. ft. facility opened in 1973 to much acclaim. It cost in excess of $3 million to build. It has been a refuge for writers. Hailed children's writer Christopher Paul Curtis, originally from Flint, Michigan, wrote a novel, *Bud, Not Buddy,* here that would later lead him to a long list of international prizes including the Newberry Honor, Publisher's Weekly, *New York Times* best books, and the Coretta Scott King Award. Curtis credited the library as being his home, the place where he'd go to write. I know it to be a place for others, too, including myself. I spent an enormous amount of time here researching *People of Faith,* the history of Hôtel-Dieu. I'd also run into Patrick Brode, who was working on yet another historical book. We'd sit facing the cumbersome microfilm machines and occasionally share remarks about our work.

The library's history is an interesting one. Windsor has always had a library downtown,

Above: This postcard, marked 1910, shows Windsor Collegiate Institute, which was renamed J.C. Patterson Collegiate Institute in 1929.

Right: All that remains of Patterson Collegiate is this memorial, erected by alumni in 1973 after the school was demolished.

or rather, at least since the late 19th century. In 1855, James Lambie built a small frame building on Ferry Street. This ramshackle edifice doubled both as Windsor's first Congregational Church and a general store. By 1876, James decided to pack up and take his store to 32 Sandwich Street West. The empty storefront provided the opportunity to open a lending library, and with the lack of a name, it was simply called "Lambie's Hall." It opened in 1894. It was a free public library—though patrons paid five cents a year for a library card. This allowed them to borrow from a collection of some 5,254 books and 60 periodicals. By the turn of the century, it was time to move on. Lambie's Hall was torn down in 1914, and this gave rise to the *Windsor Star* building, a site now occupied by the University of Windsor's School of Social Work.

The new library to grace Windsor was Carnegie Library. In 1901, city officials figured they had nothing to lose in sending in a request to Andrew Carnegie, the American philanthropist, to see if they could get some financial support. The response was positive, with the foundation offering $20,000 to build a new facility. Lambie's Hall had become inadequate, and when word came that a grant was forthcoming, a site was selected at the corner of Park and Victoria streets to build this new Carnegie Library. It opened in October, 1903. An addition was built in 1957 and the library served the public until the early 1970s, when it was demolished, and replaced by the Central Branch on Ouellette. I remember the Carnegie

Left: The Central Branch of the Windsor Public Library, designed by Johnson and McWhinnie and opened in 1973.

Below: Windsor's Carnegie Public Library opened at the corner of Park and Victoria in 1903 and was demolished in 1974.

building, running up its steps, and sitting for hours at the sprawling wooden tables to write poetry. I miss the place, and somehow wished that the city had kept it. In its place is yet another commonplace apartment building of no particular architectural interest.

Erie Street, c. 1937. The Martin Marketorium is the white building, at right.

## Ouellette & Erie

The next stop is the two-storey 90,000-square-foot HMCS 'Hunter' (900 Ouellette Avenue). My brother, Paul, would take me to Christmas parties here in the late 1950s when he was a navy cadet. What I didn't realize until just a few years ago was that this structure was built in 1929 by Fred W. Martin, the man behind the construction of the Detroit-Windsor Tunnel. Martin hired R.J. Davies, President of the Toronto Building Company, to create a market space surrounded by retail shops. It was initially dubbed Martin Marketorium. The idea may have been a solid one, but with the start of the Great Depression, it failed miserably. For a long time, the building was used as a badminton club.

Martin always had a knack for fundraising. After joining the Salvation Army at 18, the smooth-talking, charming Martin quickly rose in the ranks to staff captain, and served across Ontario. He was responsible for the financing and building of 101 Salvation Army buildings across Canada. Windsor's former Grace Hospital was born out of Martin haggling with the owner of the Ellis House, a mansion at Crawford Avenue and University Avenue, to hand over the property so he could build a hospital. That was 1922. Grace Hospital closed in January 2004 after 82 years.

But his dream was the Detroit-Windsor Tunnel. Few took Martin's plan of an underground tunnel seriously. Still, this former Sally Ann captain started acquiring properties in 1926 that he believed would be needed for terminals and customs facilities on both sides of the border. His critics suspected that he didn't know what he was doing, and that he was nothing more than a real estate speculator.

For six weeks, Martin sat at the docks, counting the number of people using the ferry. He wanted to be certain that there would be enough traffic for such a tunnel. Martin learned what many naysayers hadn't—that there existed a growing movement of Windsorites crossing the border each day to get to work. For one, in the late 1920s, as historian Holly Marie Karibo noted in *Ambassadors of Pleasure: Illicit Economies in the Detroit–Windsor Borderland, 1945–1960* some 15,000 of 25,334 employed residents of the Border Cities were "commuters who worked in Detroit, a situation unparalleled in any other large Canadian community." That's why Martin wasn't at all dismayed at the building of the Ambassador Bridge—there was more than enough traffic to share.

After bartering with government officials for months, Martin finally received formal approval to build the tunnel. Now it meant finding investors. He knew he couldn't get any support locally, so he rode the train to New York, where he managed to convince an architectural and engineering firm to take on the job. This firm was Parsons, Klapp, Brinckerhoff and Douglas—the same ones who built the Hudson River tunnel linking New York with Jersey City. Martin also managed to land financial support, totalling $23 million, from Detroit, New York, and Chicago bankers. The Detroit-Windsor Tunnel opened to traffic on November 3, 1930.

The Martin Marketorium limped on long after Martin died in the midst of the Depression. It was in December 1942 that Angus MacDonald, Minister of National Defence for naval services, announced that the Marketorium Building had been purchased for $83,400 to provide permanent headquarters for the Royal Canadian Navy Reserve in Windsor. The military services moved into it the following spring. The HMCS 'Hunter' had been established in March 1940, and first operated out of the Toledo scales building at 2462 Howard Avenue.

The name 'Hunter' has been associated with British warships for more than 300 years. The Windsor division chose it because during the War of 1812, a previous 'Hunter' served on the Great Lakes and took part in battles on Lake Erie. Today, the facility on Ouellette stands empty. A new armoury was commissioned for

Dignitaries mark the official opening of the Detroit-Windsor tunnel on November 3, 1930. Included in this group are Windsor Mayor Cecil E. Jackson, Fred W. Martin (fourth from left), Michigan Governor Wilbur M. Brucker, and Col. Walter L. McGregor.

The intersection of Erie Street and Ouellette Avenue, 1951. The Masonic Temple is at right, with the HMCS Hunter located just north of it.

HMCS Hunter at 90 Mill Street in Windsor on May 3, 2015, coinciding with the Battle of the Atlantic Parade.

Next door to the old Hunter building is the three-storey red-brick Neo-Classical Revival-style Masonic Temple (986 Ouellette Avenue), designed by James Carlisle Pennington, and constructed by Muxlow and Gale Construction Company in 1921–22. According to *Canada's Historic Places*, this handsome building was the first permanent facility for the Masonic Fraternity of the Border Cities. It still functions as a meeting place for Freemasons, as well as hosting banquets, weddings and concerts. Architecturally, Windsor's Masonic Temple displays "characteristic rhythmical symmetry and classical elements" while its main façade has eight fluted stone pilasters with simple capitals. The three wooden front doors are magnificent, with triangular stone pediments.

Every time I pass these two buildings, I'm intrigued. How have they managed to defy our knee-jerk impulses and innermost tendencies to demolish our heritage?

I cross Erie and stroll carefully on to the lawn of Windsor Regional Hospital, the Ouellette campus, that people still call Hôtel-Dieu, fearing my shoes might sink into the still-wet grass. The lawn, situated north of the former chapel, is the place to gather up chestnuts. I discovered this only a few years ago, and each October, I pause here to fill my coat pockets to bursting. Ernest Hemingway collected them from the Luxembourg Gardens in Paris and would carry them in his pockets. He wrote about running his thumb and forefinger over them, yearning for good luck in his writing. I do the same. The rest I offer to other writers, or students, and I tell them that story. As I stand here, I survey the massive assemblage of buildings that make up this hospital. My mother died here. That's what makes this personal. I also spent a number of harrowing nights here battling Crohn's Disease. We have our histories. Our stories. It defines who we are.

It was in 1888 when five nuns arrived on the train from Montreal, invited by James Theodore Wagner, the enterprising pastor at St. Alphonsus, to build a hospital here. Up till then, Windsor area residents had to cross the river for such attention. The nuns, wearing heavy wool garb, stood in the humid September air, right at this corner where I am now, and appraised the prospects of a hospital being built on this site. In a diary she had written of that day, Mother Pâquet—drained and wearied from the train trip—wrote about that first encounter: "While passing on Erie, we saw two blacks who were mowing hay on a large vacant tract of land…" There and then, this dutiful sister, a member of the Religious Hospitallers of St. Joseph, decided that upon this spot, at the edge of town, would be their new home. Mother Pâquet selected six lots, and paid $2,300. The mission of these nuns was to build a hospital, but it meant raising the money to accomplish this. To that end, these French-speaking sisters ventured out each day to knock on doors. They barely spoke English, but still managed to find support, even visiting the racetracks, where they were surprised when someone offered them a racehorse. The sisters promptly accepted the donation, then sold it. Mother Pâquet also started writing letters to influential people, including Hiram Walker. He kindly sent them $500. A year later, she wrote to him again, but this time, he did not reply. On the other hand, he readily agreed to donate three gallons of liquor every three months to be used for medicinal purposes. Hiram's son, Edward Chandler, and Mary both donated years later in 1911.

One cannot recognize the original hospital from what exists today. In October, 1889, a new three-turreted hospital with a Norman-style architecture faced Ouellette Avenue. It was designed by Montreal architect Charles Chausée. A local contractor, Hypolite Reaume, was awarded the job of building the new facility. Brick for it came from Robinet's brickyard

The original Hôtel-Dieu Hospital, c. 1920s.

on Felix Avenue. Ten thousand people turned out for the opening of the new hospital on October 13, 1889.

I cross Ouellette to the southwest corner at 1011 Ouellette Avenue, where there is a seven-storey Art Deco commercial building. According to *Canada's Historic Places,* it was one of the city's first "tall" buildings, built in 1930, "characterized by classical symmetry and graceful lines" and designed by J.R. Sculland of Windsor. The Medical Arts Building has a "finely detailed limestone facade… crowned by an angular parapet and enhanced by three vertical bays and an arched stone entrance sheltered by a bronze and glass canopy."

The Medical Arts Building, built in 1930, pictured here five years after opening.

I recall this place because it housed the offices of Dr. Henri Breault, our pediatrician, where I brought my newly born daughter in 1970. Holding my firstborn, I was struck by the marble and decorative plaster in the lobby, waiting to ascend on the elevator. I didn't realize it then, but part of this building's importance lies in the fact that it was the birthplace of Windsor Medical Services, which was the first prepaid medical plan in Canada—a forerunner of the Ontario Hospital Insurance Plan (OHIP). And there I was—a freelance writer back then—taking advantage of a medical plan that had been worked out by a committee of caring individuals, led by Dr. Freeman A. Brockenshire. This orthopedic surgeon was one of the most renowned surgeons in the country. He moved his offices to the Medical Arts Building in 1937— the same year that his group received a $23,800 grant from the Rockefeller Foundation, allowing them to create Windsor Medical Services and usher in a new era of voluntary medical insurance in Canada.

The Medical Arts Building, unlike so many in this city, has undergone extensive restoration work, and now accommodates medical residents doing a rotation in Windsor hospitals. The *Windsor Star* praised the building's owner and developer, Ray Redekopp, a Calgary-based entrepreneur for restoring this nearly 90-year-old building "to its art deco glory on the outside, with modern amenities like a gym and spa, and beautiful living spaces geared to both singles and families, on the inside."

Farther south at what was once 1077 Ouellette Avenue, there is a parking lot, carved out in 2013 after City Council decided to permit a group of physicians to demolish the old Grayson House—listed on the municipality's heritage registry—for yet another parking lot for a medical practice next door. Good for them.

For former Windsor Symphony violinist Anna Grayson, who lived in that house for 35 years, it was "devastating" to see her former home demolished in favour of a parking lot. City heritage planner John Calhoun in the spring of 2013 vehemently opposed this city council decision, citing the home's unique Tudor-style architecture and its historical connections. The place had been owned in the early 1920s by Frances Baby-Davis, the widow of John Davis who was the city's mayor from 1897–1901. The Graysons inhabited the home in 1949. Anna used this home as her personal studio. Her husband owned Grayson Jewellers. The couple kept the home until 1984.

Calhoun reported to council that the house ought to be "permanently protected" and emphasized that it was situated "in the middle of the last best-kept row of large homes on Ouellette." In an interview with the *Windsor Star,* the city heritage planner said:

> I would hope that we have learned that doesn't gain us a better city. Removal for parking is not a good example of urban form. Generally speaking, when you tear down something that has heritage value, it should be where the property will have significantly greater value than what you are tearing down—especially in terms of visual character.

If you walk farther south on Ouellette, you will come to a collection of homes and apartment buildings as interesting and as valuable as the Grayson house. There's the cobblestone house at 1304 Ouellette, erected in 1922, and next door, the Maple Apartments; the once splendid 1925 Paramount Apartments with its arched windows; the fabulous Art Deco Ambassador Apartments built in 1928; the Spanish Colonial Casa del Mara Apartments,

John Calhoun stands in front of the Grayson House at 1077 Ouellette Avenue, during his campaign to save this heritage home. The city voted in favour of demolition in 2013.

designed by G.B. Colhurst; or the sprawling Windsor Court at 1616 Ouellette, designed in 1927 in Classical Revival by architects Craig & Modill. Some have fallen on hard times. Some will be eyed for future development. The conservationists are watching over them, but "progress" takes precedence. We see it happen time and again.

I'm not going up that way, though if I did, it would take me to Jackson Park that once was the site of The Windsor Jockey Club and the Windsor Race Track from 1883 to 1928. At one time, it was a place of competition, of betting, of hundreds of spectators. There were other tracks in the city—two right across from one another: Devonshire (now the mall) and Kenilworth (now a subdivision).

It was in 1928 that the Jockey Club was purchased by the city, and its 64 acres made it one of the largest public parks at its time. In 1929, it was renamed Jackson Park after Mayor Cecil E. Jackson, who advocated for its acquisition. During the Great Depression, the entrance to the park and the lily pond were

The Windsor Jockey Club, c. 1915, in what is now the site of Jackson Park. The grandstand, seen at left, remained in the park until it burned in 1957.

for $1250. It was transported by barge, and remains one of the 430 Canadian built Lancaster Mark 10s. The Lancaster Bombers were employed throughout World War II bombing campaigns in Europe. It weighed over 25 tonnes, and was refurbished in 1983 and 1991. The plane was also repainted in 1993.

I don't walk this stretch to Tecumseh, stopping on my trek south where Ouellette meets Giles. I'm saving on these shoes. I'm not particularly fond of running shoes. Instead I'm wearing moccasins, slips-ons, and they don't possess the firm support needed for lengthy walks. I'm not in a hurry.

created as make-work projects for the unemployed, sponsored by the federal government.

For a long time, the Jockey Club grandstand stood in place, but both it, along with an elaborate bandshell, were destroyed in a fire in 1957.

One of the most popular attractions in the park is the Lancaster Bomber. The fighter plane was delivered in 1964, having been purchased from the Canadian War Assets Corporation

## Ouellette & Giles Blvd.

At the northeast corner, there is a dusty empty lot that I can only remember as a former Tim Hortons site. The first house next to it, notable for its red-tiled roof, is now a childhood centre (36 Giles Boulevard East). Both this place and the townhouse next door are on the

Left: A postcard from 1965 featuring Jackson Park's most famous attraction: the Lancaster Bomber.

Right: My "walking" shoes: a pair of moccasins and leather boots, pictured here sitting on my front walk, which is made from bricks salvaged from the Flat Iron building in Walkerville.

municipal heritage list. For years, at this corner was the massive cenotaph that stood in the middle of the boulevard, facing Ouellette. It rose to a height of 20 feet and was made from Canadian pink granite designed by Windsor architect George Y. Masson. In 1924, it cost $25,000 to build. Five thousand dollars of that money was raised by the Ladies Auxiliary of the Great War Veterans Association. Lieutenant-General Sir Archibald Cameron Macdonell (1864–1941), a highly decorated soldier of the First World War and the son of Windsor's first mayor, Samuel Smith Macdonell, officially unveiled the monument on Armistice Day 1924. The cenotaph was situated here until 1965 when the 106-tonne structure was disassembled stone by stone—some as hefty as 4,300 pounds—and moved to its present City Hall location. I turn left, and head east on Giles.

## Giles & Goyeau

The Shaar Hashomayim Synagogue (115 Giles Boulevard East), built in 1929, overshadows this corner. The story of Windsor's Jewish community begins in the 18th century with the pioneer merchant Moses David, recognized as Windsor's "first Jewish settler." He married Charlotte Hart, daughter of the first Jewish settler to Canada. David was born in 1767 in Montreal to a wealthy fur-trading family. Like others, he was lured by the opportunities in this part of the country, but his family also pressured him to extend their

The Essex County War Memorial, seen here in 1957, was located at Giles Boulevard and Ouellette Avenue from 1924 to 1965. The cenotaph can now be found in City Hall Square.

The Shaar Hashomayim Synagogue has graced the corner of Giles Boulevard and Goyeau Street since 1929.

business ventures here. Settling in Sandwich in the 1790s, he joined the local militia and rose in the ranks to become a captain. The circumstances of his death in 1814 are still unclear. His wife, Charlotte, buried him in the backyard of their Sandwich home directly across the road from where the Dominion House Tavern is located. Since he was the only Jewish person in the area, his burial site was simply called, "The Jew Cemetery."

The biggest influx of Jews to this area occurred in the late 1800s, nearly a century after David arrived. They fled the pogroms in the Russian Empire in search of security and work, escaping poverty and personal violence. Some two million Jews made their way to Canada and the United Sates.

They were the ones who built the first synagogue at the turn of the century. Morris Gitlin was Windsor's first rabbi, working out of a synagogue (later Shaarey Zedek) on Pitt Street around 1903. This place became the focal point for the Jewish community.

Still, it wasn't a peaceful welcome for the new rabbi, reports Rabbi Jonathan V. Plaut in *The Jews of Windsor:*

Windsor's first synagogue, later called Shaarey Zedek, c. 1906.

Despite the fact that its members all had the same Orthodox background, they were certainly not a homogeneous body. By then, some had become so assimilated that they saw Rabbi Gitlin's very strict rules as a hindrance to their efforts to earn a livelihood...

Nevertheless, the community grew, and by 1911, there were 300 Jews living here. By 1921, their numbers totalled nearly 1,000. The second wave, originating primarily from Russia, landed here in the 1930s. Windsor was the ideal place for Jewish immigrants because of its proximity and access to traditional Jewish observances in the United States. The community grew to more than 2,200, and led to the establishment of a school in the 1920s and the building of the Shaar Hashomayim Synagogue in 1929.

The Shaar Hashomayim really came into its own when Rabbi Samuel Stollman, its Orthodox spiritual leader during the 1950s, oversaw a foundational period of development for the community. For one, the Reform movement was changing the face of Judaism here. Stollman recognized this and fostered openness, while still nurturing the Orthodox traditions. The influence of the Jewish presence on community life in Windsor is evident with prominently respected Jews rising in importance here. These were David Croll and Herb Gray, both members of the Shaar Hashomayim. Moreover, many synagogue members were instrumental in raising money for the Jewish Community Centre, which opened in 1959 at 1641 Ouellette Avenue.

## Ouellette & Tuscarora

I now head back to Ouellette, and turn back towards the river. When people in Windsor provide directions, we say, "Head towards the river…" or "Go away from the river." It's our point of reference, our beginning and end. And so I head towards the river, when I easily could be saying, "I'm going north."

I'm headed to the former Vanity Theatre at 673 Ouellette, just past Tuscarora. You would never know there was a theatre here. The building survives, but it is boarded up, despoiled, an eyesore on the main drag. At one time, it was a glorious 966-seat movie house, designed by A.H. McPhail, a Windsor architect. Today, as Anne Jarvis noted in the *Windsor Star*, this once-great theatre that opened in 1937 is "a crumbling hodgepodge of tile, brick and corrugated siding. It's punctured with holes. Wires dangle. Birds nest in the openings. The inside, dark and cold, is trashed."

After its demise in 1987, the Vanity was re-purposed as a live music venue. As a matter of fact, in 1990, it was sold for $425,000 and turned into the Roxy the Nite Club. Nearly a year and a half ago, it was sold again, this time for $190,000. Its new owner insists he might build a hotel, but nothing is certain. For now, it's an eyesore. At one time, it was the jewel of the city. The front of the Vanity was covered with black Vitrolite, a reinforced, opaque, polished glass. It was a look that was popular in the 1930s. The marquee itself was also unique. The letters were positioned in blocks and stacked on top

of one another. All that remains as I look at it today is remnants of that black Vitrolite. Everything else is gone.

John Laycock, former entertainment editor of the *Windsor Star,* says the Vanity's most glittering moment may have come in 1968 as part of the joint Windsor–Detroit premiere of *The Devil's Brigade,* a Second World War movie with Cliff Robertson attending.

The history of the theatre also includes the once-popular Christian Culture Series, initiated by the Basilian priest, Father Stan

Above: Only weeks after I went on my walk, the Vanity Theatre was demolished. This is the spot where the once-glorious theatre stood since 1937.

Below: The Vanity Theatre's famous marquee can be spotted in this shot of Ouellette Avenue from Tuscarora Street in 1951. Champagne for Caesar was playing.

Murphy. He alternated these public talks, renting downtown locations, and in the winter of 1943, Murphy drove English painter and novelist Wyndham Lewis to the Vanity to give a lecture. As the story goes, Lewis nearly missed the event because a piece of cinder became lodged in his eye. As his biographer Paul O'Keeffe says in *Some Sort of Genius: A Life of Wyndham Lewis,* the painter was "practically hysterical with panic." Murphy quickly took Lewis to Sister St. Desmond, the infirmarian at Assumption, and she swabbed the eye, took the inflammation down, and Lewis was on his way. He had to be led like a blind man by Murphy to the stage of Vanity. Lewis' first remark at the podium was to say: "I cannot seem to make out what I have written here: seems like islands of light and dark." His address that night was "Religion and the Artist."

A 1944 portrait of Bishop Denis O'Connor by Wyndham Lewis—one of many paintings done of the Basilian Fathers from Assumption—during his time in Windsor.

The Windsor engagement, and speaking at the Vanity, are what led Lewis to settle eventually in Windsor. He moved into the Royal Apartments at the corner of Ouellette at 16 Ellis. Today, this is adjacent to the Ouellette office of Windsor-West MP Brian Masse's riding headquarters. Several years ago, when Greg Gatenby, former founder and director of the Harbourfront International Authors Festival, was in Windsor, we went in search of that place. The landlord permitted us to take a peek in the apartment where Lewis had lived in the 1940s.

According to Philip Marchand in *The Medium Is the Messenger*, it was Father Murphy who "rescued Lewis from poverty and isolation in Toronto… by offering him a job at Assumption." Survival was partly accomplished by the painting commissions Lewis received, including numerous portraits of Windsor's Basilian priests. One painting in particular—the one of Father Murphy—was part of Britian's Tate Gallery collection. The others, up until recently when the University of Windsor took over Assumption's buildings, were on display in the school's board room. I am not sure what has befallen these paintings.

But the Vanity? Jarvis may be right, but it's sad to be resigned to the perspective that although there is every intention of planning a major "streetscaping" on that block, "it's too late for the Vanity." Jarvis wrote: "With little of the original Vitrolite left and the funky marquee gone, there's little reason to save it."

So be it.

## Ouellette & Wyandotte

I'm now at Wyandotte. Still a busy corner. At one time, it was even busier. Long before Devonshire Mall, this was the place to be. At the northwest corner in the mid-to-late 1940s was Pond's Drug Store. Next door was Bright's Wines, United Cigar, Mario's Restaurant, and across the street the Radio Tavern beckoned customers with its jazz. Many of these were still in the same locations when I returned to Windsor in 1968. I regularly picked up a bottle of Bright's red wine for $5. Meretsky & Gitlin's Home Furnishing was also across the street. But very noticeable was a gigantic sign at the northeast corner that read: "Tunnel to Detroit." The Prince Edward Hotel could also be seen in the distance, easily dwarfing the urban scene on the east side of Ouellette. All have vanished. So has the hustle and bustle in the downtown core. The landscape has changed. So have the reasons to come here.

## Ouellette & Maiden Lane

You might miss this, mostly because it's always been there. The Lazares Furs sign hangs over the 1928 art deco building (493 Ouellette Avenue) that was designed by architect Albert J. Lothian. In those early days, the site was a real estate agency. It wasn't until 1942 that Lazares occupied this place. The sign was tailor made for the building. *Windsor Star* writer Carolyn Thompson in July 2015 wrote, "The 1940s sign has faded and cracking paint,

Above: The intersection of Ouellette Avenue and Wyandotte Street, looking south, in 1950.

Left: The Lazares Furs' sign, hanging over Maiden Lane, was added to the city's heritage register in 2015.

## Ouellette & Park

A few doors south of Park, on the west side— and there is no evidence of it at all now—was the location of the Metropolitan Store, a dime store. It was also the site of one of the most powerful explosions in the city's history when a natural gas leak rocked the downtown core, killing 10, and injuring 100.

It was October 25, 1960. The blast at 2:10 p.m. blew out the building's rear wall and caved in the second floor, trapping employees and customers. Some had been sitting at the lunch counter enjoying a cup of coffee and having a smoke. Hundreds of rescuers descended upon the rubble to help search for and free the wounded and the dead. A half dozen automobiles in the alley were crushed in the wreckage, while cars out front of the building had their windows blown out, and merchandise—toys, and dolls, and brooms, and clothing—littered the sidewalk. Sirens filled the streets. As one reporter stated: "The scene was quite a gory mess for the firefighters who had to extricate the bodies. Two firefighters were holding on to a young girl who was stuck down in a hole in the floor trapped by her legs. She bled out before they could rescue her and died in their arms."

Lou Hulay was about 100 feet away from the store when the place "blew up like thunder." He said people were "strewn over the street, screaming and covered in blood." He said he could hear the cries for air from the nearby "clouds of suffocating dust." Father Quenneville, a Catholic padre for whom I had

Above: The Metropolitan Store, at 439 Ouellette Avenue, shortly after opening in 1949 (top).

Below: Rescue workers carry victims from the scene of the Metropolitan Store explosion on October 25, 1960.

broken neon tubes that haven't been lit in more than a decade and a rusting bottom where a truck once struck it as it trundled through the narrow alley." That sign itself has been listed by Windsor's heritage experts, acknowledging its place in the downtown cityscape. Windsor heritage planner John Calhoun said, "It would be a decided loss if it were gone. We'd certainly be delighted if the owner were to bring it back to its early glory." Agreed.

been an altar boy at Our Lady of Guadalupe, was on scene, administering last rites. At one point, he emerged, weeping profusely over the loss. He was assisted by Rev. Earl Schilliday, a Protestant clergyman.

*Windsor Star* reporter Brian Cross, in describing the explosion on its 50th anniversary, interviewed Helen Mabbett, who was then 18. She was catapulted 40 or 50 feet out the front window of the dime store. "Every day, I hear a bang behind me, I jump, and then I start shaking," Mabbett told Cross. That fateful day she had stopped at the unemployment office on University Avenue to collect her last cheque. She was ready to begin a new job at Ford, and planned on celebrating with a cherry Coke at the store's lunch counter at the back. Instead, she "tarried to peer in a store window, wait at a traffic light, and amble past the first entrance before entering the second."

This saved her life.

"I went in through the front door and came back out through the front window," she said. She landed on the sidewalk beside a parking meter in a sea of broken glass. "And a cash register hit me in the back."

*Windsor Star* reporter Walter McCall was among the first on the scene. He clambered over shattered furniture and store merchandise deep into the building, and heard screams in the darkened caverns of the store. "For close to two hours. I scratched and dug through the macabre world of 'living and dead," he wrote. As I pass that block today, it is hard to appreciate the full horror of this account. There was no rebuilding the Metropolitan Store; there was nothing to save. Now, it is better to forget.

I continue north on Ouellette and cross over Park. Before me is the City Grill (375 Ouellette Avenue). To those who knew downtown when it was thriving, they will tell you this was the jewellery store, Henry Birks & Sons. It established itself at this location in 1943, and when the company ran into financial difficulties in the early '90s, it sold off its holdings to an Italian company, but was forced to close many of its stores. When employees in Windsor showed up to work in

Henry Birks & Sons jewellery store stood at the corner of Ouellette Avenue and Park Street, pictured at left in the 1950s. Today, the spot is occupied by the City Grill, seen at right.

January 1993, they found the doors to the establishment locked. The twenty workers were let in one by one, and informed that the company was ceasing operations here. Birks, the largest jewellery store chain with 150 stores across Canada, had been in family hands for 105 years and owed $197 million to more than a thousand creditors.

Across the street sits Scotiabank (388 Ouellette Avenue), but on this spot was once the Prince Edward Hotel, considered in its day as "one of the most modern hostelries in Canada." The nine-floor hotel had 250 rooms, was operated by the United Hotels Company, and designed by Buffalo architects Esenwein and Johnson with Windsor's Albert McPhail acting as an associate architect. It opened its doors in 1922, but 45 years later found itself more than a million dollars in debt. In 1967, the hotel was forced to shut its doors. This imposing building, that remained on Ouellette until 1976 when it was demolished, was the pride and joy of Windsor. Matti Holli's Windsor Symphony Orchestra used to play there every New Year's Eve in the grand ballroom. Holli—a

seven-year-old when his family relocated to Windsor from Finland—studied with the Ursulines in the city, and then with the Detroit Conservatory of Music before beginning a radio career as a violin soloist and conductor with CKLW and CBE Windsor. He was 18 then. Holli also led the dance band at the then-famous Bob-Lo amusement park. In 1947, he founded the Windsor Symphony Orchestra, having taken over the Windsor Concert Orchestra, a radio orchestra that had raised funds for the war effort. In the early years, he served in every conceivable capacity: librarian, manager, fundraiser, and conductor. And every New Year's Eve his musicians pushed past the revolving doors to assemble in the ballroom to bring in the new year.

A story few might know about is when the British writer Evelyn Waugh came to Windsor. He had been invited in 1949 by Father Murphy to speak at Walkerville Collegiate for the Christian Culture Series. Waugh had insisted that if he was coming to Windsor, he wanted to stay in "the most expensive hotel." Father Murphy booked him into the Prince Edward. That's where Pat Whelan met the writer. Interviewing

Left: The Prince Edward Hotel stood next to the Canada Building until 1976.

Right: A Scotiabank now occupies the northeast corner of Park Street and Ouellette Avenue.

the celebrated British novelist was this reporter's first assignment at the *Windsor Star*. Knowing nothing of Waugh's books, or his reputation, the novice reporter headed out to meet Waugh in his hotel room. The two spoke for the better part of an hour. Whelan was understandably nervous, and Waugh for his part, cagey, visibly distracted. However, the novelist had no trouble filling the time with opinion after opinion. The resulting article has him speaking about Communism and how Americans didn't take the threat seriously. He told Whelan: "All this business about pumpkins and so on is so laughable that people may begin to think of the Communist menace as merely a joke."

Irony of ironies, after Waugh had gone to great lengths with Father Murphy to book him into the best hotel in the city, he decided, instead, to bunk in with the Basilian priests at Assumption, leaving his wife behind at the hotel.

Next to the Prince Edward is the Canada Building (374 Ouellette Avenue) with its elegant brass doors. This 14-storey art deco office tower built in 1928, is famous for Pat Sturn's photography studio in the basement, a hive of activity, often the hub for social, political and cultural icons.

A few doors down again, same side of the street, was once the Palace Theatre (300 Ouellette Avenue), dating back to 1920 when it screened its first movie, a silent film. In those earliest years, the movie house was called Allen Theatre, and sat adjacent to the Heintzman Building, which sold pianos. In its final incarnation, the movie theatre was bought in 2005 by Chris Woodall and operated as part of the Imagine Cinemas chain. Gina Facca, general manager of Imagine Cinemas, told the *Star* at the time of the closing that the Palace was part of "growing up." She said, "When we were in our twenties, it was the place to go for your Friday night date." The last movie to be screened at the theatre was *Mission Impossible: Ghost Protocol,* on Sunday, January 8, 2012. The Palace was the last full running movie theatre

The intersection of Ouellette and University Avenues looking south, 1961. The old Palace Theatre is on the east side, playing *Atlantis: the Lost Continent* and *Fox Hole in Cairo*. Crossing this intersection in 1968 is where I met my wife, Donna.

Pat Sturn pauses for a photograph on Ouellette Avenue, with the Prince Edward Hotel visible in the background behind her.

Coles bookstore can be seen in this view of Ouellette Avenue from 1973.

in downtown. Now, the *Windsor Star* occupies this space, having renovated the old theatre into a modern newsroom in 2013.

## Ouellette & University

I'm now at University Avenue. This intersection is significant to me personally. This was where I met my wife when I returned to Windsor in 1968. Donna was working at *The Place,* a dress shop on Pelissier. She was on a break and walking north along Ouellette Avenue. I was standing on the northwest corner when I spotted her. She was wearing a mini skirt, and a black wool hat. She looked spectacular. I stopped her in the intersection, and boldly asked her if she would join me for coffee. She accepted. We got along instantly, and that night we went for drinks. The rest is history. We were married two weeks later. In some ways that is not surprising. It was the tempo of the times.

The centre of my world, too, was Coles books that was located where South Detroit (255 Ouellette Avenue) currently sits. This

was when it was truly a bookstore, and it was vibrant, selling New Directions paperbacks of works by the famous "Beat" writers, Ginsberg and Ferlinghetti. In the late 1960s, this was where you could buy good literature. People there cared about books. There was also the Book Centre, a few doors south of the Palace that sold magazines, and would take chapbooks on consignment. I left copies of the first editions of Black Moss magazine there.

From here, I turn and head east on University Avenue and there before me is the massive Windsor Armouries (30 University Avenue) that was built to be the home for the 21st Regiment of Essex County. It's difficult to imagine today that before the Armoury and the Heintzman building (now the *Windsor Star*) next door, Ouellette Square was also a great playing field for baseball. (Another baseball park existed slightly south of Erie, but between Pelissier and Dougall—then called Williams Park after John Williams.) The big stars for Windsor in 1905 and 1906 were George "Rube" Deneau, who would later become a cop, and "Stumpy" Loughlin, their catcher. Another fellow, Urban Shocker, would go on to be a pitcher with the St. Louis Browns, and later the New York Yankees. These men also played at Ouellette Square, and sometimes practised in the Armoury itself in the offseason.

The Armoury took two years to build, starting in 1900, and replaced the wooden military barracks that many years ago crowded City Hall Square. This structure, designed by David Ewart of the Federal Department of Public Works, follows the architectural tradition of Richardson Romanesque and is constructed

The Windsor Armouries, pictured here shortly after its opening in 1904. This view shows the side entrance, facing west, that opened onto a parade ground.

of red brick with a cut stone foundation. A two-storey addition designed and built by Sheppard, Masson, and Trace, was added to the south side in 1935.

What few might realize though is the original front entrance of the building may have been on the west side where the massive oak door was flanked by sets of five, two-storey arched windows. This entrance led to a parade ground on Ouellette. Today this faces a dark alley behind the old Palace complex, or the *Windsor Star*. The oak doors are now gone. Bricked over. The name "Armouries" is engraved over the entrance. Heritage planner John Calhoun disputes this, suggesting there isn't enough evidence to make that declaration.

A story not so well known, too, is that on September 9, 1911, a 70-year-old Sir Wilfrid Laurier was in Windsor with the slogan "Prosperity to All," and hammered home his desire for free trade with the United States in a speech that took place on the Ouellette Square

parade grounds. More than 8,000 Liberal followers, including another 1,000 curious Americans, cheered Laurier, who had made Windsor his last stop in the Ontario campaign. The 21st Regimental band, with the Essex Fusiliers' bandmaster Adolphus Ruthven, escorted the prime minister to the platform where some 100 prominent local Liberals stood applauding their leader. The results locally on Sept. 21, changed nothing, with both a Conservative and a Liberal returning to Parliament.

Across the street is the former Transit Windsor terminal that was built in 1940, and where the Greyhound buses used to pull in. Both the terminal and the Windsor Armouries were purchased by the University of Windsor and are currently being renovated—the latter as the new School of Visual Arts.

Eastward on University brings me to two other places of note: one is the Burger King that stands at the corner of Goyeau and University, where the Top Hat Supper Club reigned

Left: Proprietor Mike Drakich sits in the sidewalk patio of the Top Hat in 1963.

Right: The popular supper club was demolished to make way for a Burger King in 2008.

supreme for years as the place of entertainment in the city; the other is All Saints' Church.

Mike Drakich owned the Top Hat. I knew him well. *Windsor Star* colleague Ted Shaw and I used to stop in Fridays for lunch, and would sit at a corner table and hear Mike rant about the politics of the day, the difficulties of operating an entertainment club. He was the kindest man I knew. Later I used to bring my father there for lunch, and I don't think Mike ever let me pay the bill. He liked my father. The two were of the same fabric. Old Windsor. Respect and tradition.

It was sad to see his once-beloved restaurant and nightclub go downhill and finally close. I went through it one morning with Mike's son, Sam, just after he had made a deal to sell it. He told me not to whisper the name of the buyer to anyone. "I don't want anything to go wrong," Sam said. I complied. Burger King is there now, and a parking lot.

Mike Drakich opened The Top Hat in 1958, leaving his brother Nick to run the Metropole on Walker Road. All through the 1960s and 1970s, this was the place to be.

Business declined in the 1980s and Casino Windsor probably put the last nail in the coffin for the Drakich family. Mike couldn't compete. As Ted Shaw in the *Windsor Star* wrote, "the old shine had worn off."

Upon selling the club in September 2005, Mike's widow, Mary, said, "This is where my family grew up. The Top Hat was Mike Drakich in many ways. But it was us, too."

There are so many fond memories of the place and the stars who played there, like comedian Jackie Kahane and Ricky Nelson. Shaw wrote that Nelson was the clean-cut kid everyone remembered from the Ozzie and Harriet Show, but when he appeared at the Top Hat, he had long hair, and he was caught upstairs smoking pot. My own memories of the place include Mike's great friend, Al Martino, and how I assisted the famous actor and singer, who played Johnny Fontane in *The Godfather* movie, whip up some pasta with chicken in the restaurant's kitchen. It was a favourite pastime of the singer whenever he came to Windsor to perform for the Drakich family. Martino shared with me the secret of infusing a bit of olive oil in the pasta sauce just before mixing it with the spaghetti noodles. Something he picked up from his bricklayer grandfather.

Performing there, too, was the drummer Buddy Rich, who practically caused a riot when he uttered an insult in Yiddish to some Jewish patrons. Lily Tomlin, Frankie Avalon, and so many others played at the Top Hat. Mike nearly had Motown's Supremes, but the group learned they were too young to perform in a licensed club. The police threatened action if he went ahead with this.

Sam was bitter at the end, and said his father's place was "No. 1 in the city," but it couldn't last.

## All Saints' Church, 330 City Hall Square

This lovely church's history dates back to 1852. Joanne and Conrad Reitz, in *Into the New Millennium: All Saints' Anglican Church, Windsor, Ontario, 1852–2002,* said that for years, parishioners gathered in local halls, or wherever they were welcomed until they could build their own sanctuary. Finally, through efforts made by Sandwich's St. John's Anglican, the new church was built and All Saints was dedicated on September 10, 1857. Newspapers described it as "the prettiest church in Canada West." It took until 1875, these historians say, before the north and south transepts and bell tower were added, thus giving the church the look that it has today.

All Saints' Anglican Church was built in 1857 and is still active today.

Originally, All Saints' was located across the street from a military barracks—a compound that also provided housing for fugitives escaping slavery on the Underground Railway. Over the years, municipal, police, and court buildings (and most recently, Casino Windsor) sprang up around the church in an area known as City Hall Square. Rev. E.H. Dewar was All Saints' first rector. He was also rector of St. John's for a time.

Throughout its history, All Saints' has maintained a reputation for its church music and choirs. The well-known Canadian composer Walter MacNutt served as its organist and choirmaster from 1950 to 1953. This musician's compositions spanned a wide variety, from choral works and songs, to pieces for solo organ and orchestra. His work was published by Broadcast Music Incorporated, Frederick Harris Music and the Western Music Company.

MacNutt's most popular work was *Take Me to a Green Isle,* based on a H.E. Foster poem, but he also composed songs based on the works of William Blake. In 1954, MacNutt left to take a job with St. Thomas' Anglican Church.

The other name associated with All Saints' is University of Windsor Professor Emeritus David Palmer. Palmer's reputation precedes him—his work has brought him to do concerts from coast to coast in Canada, as well as recitals in San Francisco, Washington, New York, and in cities in the Midwest. Palmer has also played in Europe, including recitals at Notre-Dame in Paris and Chartres. Despite this globe-trotting, he continues on as All Saints' organist and choir director.

## Ouellette & Chatham

I've gone a bit too far east at All Saints'. It's time to get back to Ouellette Avenue. Like my storytelling, my feet find appeal in the nooks and crannies of the city. I return to Ouellette along University Avenue, and turn north until I am standing in front of the Bank of Montreal on the southeast corner of Ouellette Avenue and Chatham Street. A little secret about this place is the house that sits behind this bank building, masqueraded by development and makeshift renovations. The house—barely visible and facing an alley that runs behind the bank—is now fronted on Chatham as a strip bar. It was once owned by one of the original French families—the Ouellettes.

The street, of course, takes its name from the French family that settled here in the 18th century. The Ouellettes hailed from a village near Paris and arrived in Quebec in the 1600s. From there, the family made their way westward, and arrived in this part of the country in 1793 where the French crown awarded land grants to the settlers. In 1800, the Ouellettes gained property—two lots extending from the Goyeau family farm on the east to what is now Pelissier on the west, originally given to the Domouchelles—when Marguerite Dumouchelle married Charles Ouellette, a Belle River farmer. Charles bought these two

The Bank of Montreal at the corner of Ouellette Avenue and Chatham Street was torn down in 1964 and replaced by the current building, seen at right. Before the bank, Vital Ouellette's second house was located here.

farm lots from his father-in-law and these lands extended from the Detroit River to what is now Tecumseh Road. Today, this stretch is downtown Windsor. For many years, it was the main retail centre for the city.

To Marguerite was born Vital Ouellette on October 10, 1802. Their family homestead was on Pitt, a few steps from Ouellette Avenue. For those who remember the Norwich Block, they will know the site, just west of the Kamin Building. The actual spot of the Ouellette homestead was where Pitt for Pasta once was. Before that—in the 1920s and 1930s—it was the home of Central Hardware.

When Vital grew up, being the oldest of seven children, he inherited the original Dumouchelle farm. These remained farm lots until the arrival of the Great Western Railway in 1854, a line that connected Niagara Falls to Windsor, running a distance of 852 miles. Vital Ouellette proved to be a prescient individual. Unlike his fellow farmers who rushed to sell off properties along the waterfront to the railway, he stood back and refused. He figured that if the railway couldn't buy up his land at the river's edge, it would force the railway to settle for building its station, or terminal, right there at the end of his farm property. That's exactly what happened. The railway station went up at the eastern boundary of his farm. And right at the foot of Ouellette was the ferry dock. This meant his farm would become the thoroughfare for activity, thus giving birth to naming the street after his family. As Dave Connery wrote in the 1920s in *The Border Cities Star*, "It was inevitable that the avenue should become increasingly attractive to merchants as a location for their stores and to

banks and business houses. That was where people were gathered, and that was where a business centre slowly but surely developed."

Vital built himself a new home at the corner of Ouellette and Chatham, where today the Bank of Montreal is situated. The house later may have been moved back one lot after John Curry bought it. The house still exists, but a succession of business owners have altered it beyond recognition. At one point it was The Windsor Club, then the Windsor Castle Restaurant. Much later, it became the Commodore, then Jason's Strip Club. If you stand in the alley behind the bank building, you can still make out the upper windows of the original building. Years ago, going to the bus station that was on the eastern side of the building, I remember gazing up at the upper windows of this old farmhouse, and waving to the smiling, scantily–clad strippers.

Ouellette helped in the development of St. Alphonsus Church that stands next to the Detroit-Windsor Tunnel. Both he and Daniel Goyeau donated lots to the diocese to create the church. He also donated the land to the Sisters

Vital Ouellette's farmhouse can be spotted from the alley behind the Bank of Montreal. The upper windows are just visible below the peak of the roof.

of The Holy Names of Jesus and Mary for the original St. Mary's Academy—where the tunnel stands today. The religious order built this school in 1915, then sold it to the Tunnel Corporation for a million dollars. It was demolished in 1929. That's when the nuns took that money and built a new academy in South Windsor. And that grand, Gothic-style structure was demolished in 1977.

According to Dave Connery, Vital was also a very cautious man, who, though offering the church the lands they needed, didn't feel so inclined to sell to anyone else. As a matter of fact, he leased out his holdings instead of selling them. An amusing tale about him is from the 1870s when John McCrae, an insurance agent, tried to convince Vital about using the telephone, a new invention. McCrae called his own shop from across the street, and when his son, Allan, answered, he spoke to his father, then handed the phone to Vital. Hearing McCrae's voice, Vital remarked, "I hear your voice John. Surely, this is a mechanism of the Devil."

Vital Ouellette died in 1882. He is buried in Assumption Cemetery.

From where I'm standing at the corner of Ouellette and Chatham in front of the Bank of Montreal, across the street on the southwest corner is the RBC Building. This replaced the Kresge Building that ran all the way over to Pelissier. The five-and-dime store was there in 1929. *Windsor Star* columnist Jim Cornett uncovered many of his stories just sitting at the lunch counter. At the time of the store's demise, he wrote retrospectively about accompanying his parents to its creaky wooden floors in the 1930s. Later in the 1940s, Jim and his brother, Sam, rode buses from Riverside to downtown and stopped at Kresge's. It was "a port-of-call for a big hotdog for 10 cents and a giant mug of root beer for a nickel." Jim was dismayed and shocked when an early morning fire December 24, 1945 destroyed most of Kresge's. His uncle Pat who worked on the fire department told him how the firefighters "in extremely cold weather, wound up looking like icicles." The place was soon rebuilt, and Cornett, certainly unaware that it would become his second office many years later when

Kresge's was a downtown destination from 1929 until 1991. The Royal Bank of Canada now occupies this spot on the corner of Chatham Street and Ouellette Avenue.

he was assigned to writing a city column for *The Star*, wrote:

> The Kresge counter was a place to shoot the breeze over coffee at five cents a cup during a three-month period of unemployment in 1954 when I travelled downtown once every two weeks to pick up my pogey. By 1956, I was seeing the place daily, being so close to my new employer, the *Star*. One went there for coffee, for lunch, for gum and chocolate bars, and for general merchandise.

When Jim started writing his *Windsor Star* column, he joined what he called "the unofficial Kresge Coffee Club… composed of a minister, a citizenship court judge, a lawyer, an insurance agent, a travel agent, a business manager, and others totalling a dozen or so…" He'd sidle up to the U-shape counter every day at 10:00 a.m., down a coffee at seven cents a cup, "settle most of the world's problems in 20 to 30 minutes, and then head for other daily tasks." The shape of the counter, Cornett said, made it easy for conversation.

Around the corner on Chatham is a reddish building on the north side (46 Chatham Street West), and during the 1930s, it housed a variety of businesses, including the offices of the architects (in 1934) and the Equity Chambers. Originally, this building was the Grinnell Brothers Company—or piano makers.

Now, the imposing Dominion Public Building, renamed the Paul Martin Building,

The famous Kresge lunch counter, pictured here in 1975.

looms before me. Built in the mid-1930s, it spans a full block, from Chatham to Pitt on the west side. In the 1960s when I first walked into this six-storey masonry edifice, it was the traditional post office with the grated wickets. For years, I had a P.O. box there for Black Moss Press. Offices upstairs housed various government offices such as the Customs Department, Department of Pensions, National Health, Income Tax Department, and for a while even the RCMP. Designed by John Edward Trace of Sheppard, Masson, and Trace and Buller-Colthurst Architects, it was begun in 1932 and completed in 1934. A modernist interpretation of Beaux-Arts inspired the government building. As the heritage experts state, it was designed as "a sculptural whole," and

Windsor's first post office in 1857, where the Paul Martin/Dominion Public building now stands.

The scene in downtown Windsor in the aftermath of the Great Fire of 1871.

this represented a divergent point of view in architecture.

In recent years, it has been the subject of controversy with Stephen Harper's Conservative government, seemingly unwilling to save it from further deterioration. But just prior to calling the 2015 election, the federal government agreed to cover the costs of repairs. It didn't save the seat of the only area Conservative incumbent.

But long before the Dominion-Paul Martin Building was built, there was a small park with a large cannon at the corner of Chatham and Ouellette, and at the far end on northwest corner was the post office, a three-storey brick and partly ivy covered building. You can find these in old postcards, or photographs. Not a trace of it here.

## Ouellette & Pitt

I continue north, now pausing at the intersection of Ouellette Avenue and Pitt Street. In the northeast corner is an unassuming parking lot. This was where the Great Fire took place on October 12, 1871. It started in McGregor's livery stable, and spread quickly to the bank and post office. The Windsor Fire Department made it there within a half hour, but without a proper piping system to pump water into their hoses from their steam engines, it was futile. A message was dispatched to the Detroit Fire Department to send engines and men across the river by ferry. Understandably, that was delayed. By dawn, as Neil Morrison describes in *Garden Gateway to Canada*, there was "a dreadful scene of ruined buildings, blackened fire fighters still struggling with the danger, homeless families, broken hopes." More than 100 buildings were destroyed. The result was that the fire-ravaged community was forced to invest in a proper waterworks system, but still this didn't come about until the municipal politicians put it to a plebiscite.

Before we had the parking lot at that corner, there also existed a department store: C.H. Smith's. In 1871, 10 days after the fire, Cameron and Thorburn, well-known dry goods merchants, hired a Detroit architect to draft plans for a three-storey brick store. Morrison says, "fine, new brick structures replaced many an early, outdated building… This was one advantage of the disaster."

The Smith store was by far the most upscale department store in Windsor. It had entrances on both Ouellette and Pitt and Riverside Drive and was a favourite of W. L. (Lum) Clarke, president of the *Windsor Daily Star*. He used to send Gail Pire, who worked as a reporter in the Women's Department of the editorial offices, to pick out embroidered handkerchiefs for retiring female employees. Part of the rambling building—or an annex of it that fronted Riverside Drive—had once housed the Windsor Opera House, the last 19th-century theatre in the city, and the place that hosted Sir Wilfrid Laurier in the 1900 federal election campaign. When that old opera theatre was demolished, Larry Kulisek and Trevor Price in *Windsor 1892–1992: A*

*Centennial Celebration* said it was removed from the urban landscape "without a murmur of regret after the retailer closed in the early 1970s."

Across the street from that parking lot on the southeast corner of Pitt, there existed the once-glorious Manning House Hotel, a three-storey red-brick building constructed in 1887. Years after that, this historic hotel structure also housed a Royal Bank. Up until 2008, the centre portion of the structure still remained. It was finally removed to make room for a $10-million bank edifice—the TD Canada Trust that stands there today.

C.H. Smith Department Store, which was built to replace Cameron and Thorburn. The facade that faced Riverside Drive was at one time the Windsor Opera House. C.H. Smith remained a downtown landmark until its demolition in the 1970s.

Above: The Manning House Hotel in 1911 was on the southeast corner of Pitt Street and Ouellette Avenue, where a T.D. Canada Trust bank now stands.

## The Norwich Block

Continuing north on Ouellette, you come to the flashy Canderel Building, renamed "Riverside Drive One West." This is the site of the former Norwich Block. Directly across the street from the old post office, on the northwest corner of the block, was the Kamin Building. I remember interviewing Morris Kamin in his upper floor office that overlooked Pitt and Ouellette Ave. The Beans Café was below. Around the corner was the original Slieman's Elias Deli. There was also Wansbrough's Cameras, once owned by former Mayor Frank Wansbrough.

The Norwich Block housed the city's oldest buildings—many of them erected in the late 19th century. All replaced when a group of investors convinced the city that a skyscraper would spawn a new era in business downtown. This new kid on the block was heralded as the new corporate headquarters of Chrysler Canada. But it needed help, and it needed more than the financial backing of

investors. It needed the city's involvement. And money. City Council declared its support, and spent $24-million and ordered tenants in the Norwich Block to pack up and leave, so it could begin the tear down.

Sadly, the promise of the venture fell short. The vision of a 32-floor building with a major car company and retail outlets, residential units, and offices galore never materialized. At least not in the way it was imagined. Chrysler did move in when the Canderel opened in 2002. Eventually, so did other tenants, such as the Keg Restaurant, Investors Group, and National Bank. But what about the 20,000 square feet of retail space on the ground floor? This is the part that faces Pitt Street. When I made my daily run for bacon and eggs at the new Elias Deli after it moved into the CIBC building, I used to spy a security guard resting all alone like a prisoner in a chair in the vast open space.

Meanwhile, the city is still holding the lease for space on the third and fourth floors, which largely remain occupied through subleases. That lease is costing taxpayers $1 million, but it sublets the space for much less, requiring the city to cover the remainder of costs, reported to be around $400,000 annually. Windsor poured another $16 million into the building's attached parking garage.

I miss the Norwich Block. I miss Morris Kamin, and his wonderful stories. Especially the Valentine's Day story about how one day in 1967, he was accompanied by another lawyer on his way back to his office when he spotted his childhood "flame" in a car stopped at a traffic light near the Top Hat. Kamin didn't hesitate—he jumped into the car beside this woman, much to her surprise. They hadn't seen each other in years. They parked in front of St. Alphonsus Church, a block away, and talked for an hour, catching up on their lives, and their youth when they'd been so much in love. Within a year, the couple was married.

When Lila Kamin told me this story, her husband—once a top criminal and divorce lawyer in the city—sucked on his pipe, sending haloes of smoke around his smiling face. The glint in his eyes revealed how much he relished this old-fashioned romantic tale— how zany and how fateful it was. Kamin was then 84, and retired. In their youth, both families had vehemently opposed any notion of Morris—a Jew and the son of a rabbi— marrying Lila, a staunch Roman Catholic. Then, all these years later, they were married in a wedding ceremony at Christ the King Catholic Church.

Kamin's penchant for yarns was legendary. He indulged eager listeners in how he'd been pestered all his life by people wanting him to handle their cases. "I guess it was because my name was in the paper all the time—I'd lost more cases than I'd won. And they just kept seeing my name. They didn't know, or care, what I'd done."

That's only partly true. Kamin, a graduate of Osgoode in 1942, built for himself a reputation as one of the hardest-working criminal and divorce lawyers in the business. He took cases others ignored, cases where he often didn't make a dime. Windsor's prostitutes often wound up at his office, because he wouldn't turn anyone away. In the early '70s, Kamin defended a native woman who'd been charged with murder. Proving her innocence, he won the case and earned $800 from Legal Aid, far less than his costs. "When you're dealing with someone's freedom," Kamin said, "It's not about money. You haven't got a choice... Nothing's more important than freedom—to think, to act, and to speak."

One of the first purchases I made in Windsor was in that Norwich Block. I picked up a portable typewriter. It cost me $49 in the early fall of

The historic Norwich Block, viewed from Riverside Drive, in 1980.

The intersection of Goyeau Street and Pitt Street, looking north, in 1959. The Ritz Hotel can be spotted on the far left in the background, where I lived for a brief time in 1968.

1968. It has remained with me all my life. It still works. It rests on my desk at the University of Windsor; I readily show it to students to remind them that this was how it started. It was this little white machine that set me free.

As I halt here at the corner of Pitt and Ouellette, remembering the Norwich Block, it is difficult to imagine what life was like on this street if you've never experienced it. When I first arrived here, and lived downtown, ever so briefly through the fall months of 1968, I rented a one-room place at the Ritz Hotel. It was located to the east, at the corner of Goyeau and Pitt. A towering building, Le Goyeau Condominiums (111 Riverside Drive East), has replaced it. In the 1960s, the Ritz was a dive. I paid for my room at the bar. I worked midnights at the *Windsor Star,* and so I was absent when the hookers roamed the hallways. I finally had to check out of the place because a fire engulfed it. The rooms were charred right up to mine. When I returned home that morning

from *The Star*—just a few blocks away—a firefighter barred me from entering the building. "I live here," I protested. He finally let me by, and I tiptoed along the scorched hallway to my room. I slept with the window open.

It was in that room that I tapped out poems after poems all through the afternoons. Late in the day, I would also hear the Tigers and St. Louis Cardinals battling it out for the World Series on televisions rented by the winos in the rooms near me. The hookers gathered in those rooms down the hall to take in the games, and curse the umpires and bitch about a bad pitch from the 30-game winner Denny McClain. Years later, I met and interviewed McClain. At the time, he was working in a metro Detroit 7-Eleven slinging Slurpees serving parole on work-release. I'd also spoken to him earlier in his career after baseball when he was a fast-talking morning radio host that consumed a dozen cans of Coke during a show, and hand-crushed, tossed each of them into a pail across the studio.

Back then in 1968, downtown was alive. I patrolled its streets. Saturday nights, I'd walk down to Riverside Drive, to the north-facing side of the Norwich, and climb that long flight of wooden stairs to the Paradise, a Chinese restaurant with high oak booths. I never witnessed the prostitutes offering favours to customers in those large booths, but I watched these women congregate there late at night. They'd pace on the street, smoking and chatting up customers.

In those days, too, there was Lee's Imperial Tavern at the corner of Ferry and Riverside Drive. It was the watering hole haven of *Windsor Star* reporters who would saunter in for a beer after a late shift. The Lee family operated the tavern. They hailed from a man called King Lee (Lee Thung), who became one of the most influential merchants in Windsor. Born in 1877, he left China at age 17 and settled in Vancouver. Two years later, he moved to Brantford, then to Chatham where he opened his first café called the Royale. It was in 1911 that King Lee opened up the Savoy on Sandwich Street West. He briefly left Canada to return to China to marry Lily Wong and bring her back to Windsor. King ran the Savoy for eight years before opening King's Café on Pitt Street. It closed after four years.

At this point, King leased the Lincoln House on Ouellette Avenue, but when the Great Depression hit, he lost everything. Still, he continued to live here, raising his sons and never relaxing his engagement to the community, serving as president of the local Chinese Nationalist Society in 1924

Lee's Imperial Tavern, a favourite watering hole of *Windsor Star* staff, was located on the southeast corner of Riverside Drive and Ferry Street.

The Imperial Hotel, pictured here in 1935, was opened by Lee family patriarch, King Lee, in 1932. The family operated the hotel, and later tavern, at this location until the Norwich Block was demolished in 1999.

and on the executive board of the Border Cities Association in 1925.

It was in 1932 that King Lee finally opened the Imperial Hotel at Riverside Drive and Ferry. As the children grew older, they joined in the daily running of the business. With the advent of the Second World War, King's sons Peter, Edward, and Ben went overseas. When they returned home, they discovered that their father had become ill. He died in November, 1946. The four brothers refused to shut down the business, and stayed to operate it. One son, however, relocated to Boston to open a restaurant. Another became a silent partner and started the Edgewater Marina near Abars in Riverside. Both places have vanished completely.

The Norwich Block also housed the media personality, cartoonist and former high school teacher Bob Monks. He occupied the second floor—both home and studio. He was a good friend. When I met him, he was teaching art at Lowe Technical School. To earn a bit of money, I agreed to pose for his drawing classes. Monks was also a cartoonist for the *Windsor Star* and a humorist on Channel Nine television for many years. His most famous outing was "Wander with Wansy," where Monks and former Windsor mayor Frank Wansbrough canoed along the Grand Marais ditch.

Bob and I chatted for years about him doing a book telling the history of Windsor. And one day—25 years after I had hatched the

The two locations of Elias Deli: the original one in the Norwich Block, at left, and next to the CIBC building, its second home until Louis Slieman retired and closed up shop in 2013.

One of the cartoons from *Bob Monks' History of Windsor*, that explains how the book came to be.

idea—he telephoned to announce that he had finally completed it. Black Moss published it, and the book sold several thousands of copies.

"Anyone who has been in this town for any length of time, knows who Bob Monks was," remarked Bob Steele, former host of CBC's *The Bridge* at the time of Bob's death in February, 2011. "A fixture, iconic, a history of television, very funny guy. I don't think you were anybody in this town until Bob Monks did a caricature of you."

Monks was 83 when he died. It was at the Norwich Block that Monks had found home, the place to root himself in Windsor and grow his reputation. The other place that he called home was Elias Deli, adjacent to the CIBC building on Ouellette Avenue. Bob would enter by the back door, wave to Louie, and meander his way through a maze of tables to a spot along the south wall, sip on a coffee, order toast and peanut butter, and bury his head in the newspaper. He never paid his bill—Louie refused to take his money. I saw Bob almost every morning. This was home to me, too. I'd conduct

interviews for the *Star* here. The staff knew the table I sat at, and when someone would arrive to meet me, they'd point to that table. I launched *My Town* here at the restaurant, and Bob launched his book *Bob Monks' History of Windsor* here. I also used to invite students here and buy them breakfast, and we'd hold our class there with Louie sliding over, wearing his apron and spewing out one hilarious story after another. These two men—Bob Monks and Louie Slieman—were the characters of the street.

You couldn't miss the aproned Louie sitting outside, smoking, and chatting up those passing by on the sidewalk. He gabbed to everyone. I remember once doing an interview with David Burr (but this was in the Norwich Block establishment that faced Ouellette Avenue, near the camera shop). This was when the former mayor had pretty well dropped off the face of the earth, and was working as a dealer at the Casino. Louie spotted him across from me at a table. "Hey, aren't you a former mayor?" Louie shouted. "Weren't you somebody at one time?" Burr nodded and frowned a little. That was the kind

Louie Slieman and I with our Queen's Jubilee Medals.

of exchange you would get at Elias Deli. Down-to-earth, honest, and open. Louie had a heart of gold, and a big moment for him was receiving the Queen's Jubilee Medal. No one deserved it like he did.

Elias, both on the west and east sides of Ouellette, was the grounding place for political decision making. Municipal, provincial and federal politicians, as well as judges, lawyers, and police officers gathered here. They could make connections and hammer out convoluted deals, scrawling out decisions on lumpy napkins before shaking hands. They could be seen here. Louie always hovered nearby with his own opinion. He was the unofficial mayor of the city, forever righting what was wrong. He once introduced a hard-done-by waitress to a lawyer over a silly immigration ruling that might have sent her deported, back across the ocean. In a day or two, it was cleared up. The lawyer did it

pro bono. Mind you, he might've got a smoked meat sandwich plunked down in front of him the next day. And a smile and slap on the back, from Louie.

Elias has vanished. Bob has passed away, and Louie is retired somewhere in the city. The soul of the downtown without these two men hasn't been the same. The personality of the street has changed.

## Ouellette Avenue North

I'm now standing at the foot of Ouellette Avenue. This street didn't always run all the way to the river. It came about in the late 19th century after the Great Fire. Even so, the town fathers were cautious, and slow, about making it happen. The one good consequence about the fire was that it cleared away many of the buildings and permitted the widening of the street. Ouellette's clay surface, back then, was marked by deep mudholes. The surface was also slanted so water drained to open gutters, and into these, people regularly tossed their garbage. The situation was so bad that the *Essex Record* in June, 1874, demanded a closed drainage system to guard citizens from contracting typhoid and cholera. Ouellette possessed broken and ill-repaired board sidewalks. The only street in Windsor that could boast of a decent road in the 1870s was Howard Avenue. It actually had a crushed stone road, which made it far easier to navigate.

Standing at the river's edge and looking south, this was once the gateway to Windsor.

It was the busiest corner in the city. When you stepped off the ferry boat, you were met by row upon row of shops, businesses, ornate street lamps, and rumbling streetcars.

On the northeast corner was the British American Hotel, a large rambling hotel. It was there in the 1960s when I returned to the city. It was a drinking hole, a haven for prostitutes, but oddly enough, it also had a stamp shop. This waterside place was a haven for spies during the Civil War in the United States, who would make their way to the border, and run back and forth across the river to run intelligence operations on the northern armies. The hotel was put up in 1871 right after the Great Fire, or rather was repaired and enlarged upon by its owner E.E. Ingram, who renamed it British American Hotel. Before that it was called Hirons House and run by William Hiron, a wine merchant who operated his business in the 1860s.

I never went into the place. Like so many other people in the city, I also wasn't sad to see it torn down in 1975. I don't even remember it occurring. At this point in my life, I wasn't so invested in the city, and didn't possess that visionary perspective of a green waterfront. Despite my ambivalence, others were fighting to see the nature of our riverfront change. You see, tearing the British American down came about after much discussion to replace it with a modern high-rise. This did not happen—at least not on the same site. The reason lay in the dispute Councillor Bert Weeks had with Frank Wansbrough, then mayor of the city. The latter favoured the proposal pitched to them by Valhalla Inn. Weeks

insisted that nothing be built on the north side of Riverside. His vision was for a waterfront bereft of development. Our parkland, running from the Ambassador Bridge to Hiram Walker & Sons, is the result of that vision. Weeks actually campaigned on that issue against Wansbrough in 1974. The night of the election, the incumbent mayor went to bed believing he had won, but when all the votes were counted, it was Weeks who had triumphed. A year later, the British American was torn down. To this day, the waterfront has been cleared of hotels and other development.

Kitty-corner to the British American was the Toronto Dominion Bank, part of the Norwich Block. It was built in 1909 by renowned architects Carrere and Hastings. It was fashioned in classy beaux-arts design.

Below, the British American Hotel, c. 1890. One of the last commercial holdouts on the riverfront, north of Riverside Drive, the hotel was demolished in 1975 and transformed into green space.

The Toronto Dominion Bank, on the corner of Riverside Drive and Ouellette Avenue, in 1911.

Old postcards show a smart looking, tasteful work of architecture. Just next to it, south on Ouellette, was the International Hotel. It provided the city's first movie house, called The Royal Theatre, in 1907.

Everything at this corner, was demolished in 1999 to make way for the Canderel Building. The Toronto Dominion's facade itself fell victim to such questionable progress—in an effort to "save" it, the marble was put into storage at the sewage treatment plant. Historian and community advocate Elaine Weeks rightly complained that "despite hopes that it would be reused in some capacity along the waterfront or in old Walkerville it continues to remain in bits and pieces at the sewage plant… A sad metaphor for our city's inherent disregard for its past."

From here, I return south on Ouellette Avenue. I'm going to leave the core, on my way to the last town, Sandwich—but there are a few places that I want to visit first.

When you walk Ouellette Avenue at night,

you don't worry about how well-lit it is. It was a different matter in the 19th century. Long before electric lights were available, many cities had gas lamplights. In 1875 and 1876, the Fire, Water and Gas Committees negotiated with several companies to provide street lighting, but to no avail. There was then talk of building a gas plant and laying down pipes beneath the streets. This didn't materialize. Again, town council grumbled bitterly over how it should be done and what it would cost. Of course, the public moaned loudly too.

Finally, a Mr. Shears stepped forward with a solution. He did all the legal work in advance of making his proposal, went ahead and purchased land on the west side of McDougall, just north of Wyandotte East, and built two red-brick structures at a cost of $60,000. One was a roadhouse oven; the other was designed to store equipment. From there, his intention was to lay out pipes and put up lamp posts. But he needed the support of the Windsor Gas Company. Shears then found himself in the middle of another spat, this time among citizens who felt they deserved the street lighting more than others. Neil Morrison explains it this way, saying those "of the more densely populated areas demanded more lamp posts in their sections than in the outlying areas."

The decision was finally made: install 70, with the larger number for the more populated areas. The posts themselves were to be eight feet tall and two and one half feet below the ground, and fitted with a tin lantern at a cost of $15.75. A lamplighter was hired to maintain the lamps. He was paid $12.50 a month. Now, before these lamps were installed, citizens carried candle and coal oil lanterns, so this was a giant leap forward.

As I head back south along Ouellette, I imagine the lamplighter starting his job a half hour after sunset, as it was stipulated. But that was only with the provision that the moon was not in a phase to shed enough light for people to walk around. Morrison wrote, "In case of dark or cloudy nights when the calendar showed that the moon should be shining, he was to consult with the town clerk as to whether the lamps should be lighted."

## Pitt & Ferry Streets

When I reach Pitt Street, I turn and head west. This street in the 1950s, was a haven for prostitution, and was chock full of pool halls and gambling dens. It was also the home of the *Windsor Star*, (167 Ferry Street) which stood at the corner of Pitt and Ferry. I worked there for more than 35 years. It was home. I knew every square inch of the place. I pored over the documents in the "morgue," as we called the library. I read the Last Will and Testament of both W.F. Herman and his wife, Adie Knox. Among the names of those given cash in the settlements after their deaths were people I worked for.

Years later, I wrote a story for the paper about the son of the chauffeur for Mrs. Herman. He told me that he lived above the garage where the newspaper family's mansion once stood on Riverside Drive. Mrs. Herman would be driven to the *Star* in the morning, and she would step into a narrow elevator that was reserved solely for herself and editor Lum Clarke, who was like a son. He had been engaged to their only child, a daughter, and after her sudden death in a car accident, the Hermans invited him to live in the mansion. He continued to reside in that house after the Hermans died.

Few remember the elevator in the former *Star* building. As a matter of fact, it was taken out of service and removed long before I started working there. All that I remember is a locked, elegant oak door visible as one stepped into the lobby of the *Star*. It was on the left. Upstairs was its mate, masquerading as a closet. I noticed how high its ceiling was, and realized I'd discovered that this was the original shaft of the lift used by Adie Knox. She had had this built after her husband died.

The Hermans purchased the weekly *Windsor Record* in 1918. It had been running since 1888. This four-storey brick building was located at 36 Sandwich Street West (Riverside Drive).

The *Windsor Star*, my home away from home, pictured here in 1960. While the building now houses the University of Windsor's School of Social Work, the limestone facade was preserved during the renovations.

Left: Newspaper magnate, W.F. Herman. The Herman family controlled the paper until 1971.

Right: Dick Harrison, the prolific and colourful *Star* columnist, is seen at his trusty typewriter in 1958.

That building was a replacement for a two-storey wooden building that was devoured in the Great Fire when the *Record* printing was done upstairs above a billiard hall. Herman changed its name to the *Border Cities Star*, and in 1927, he built the Pitt and Ferry building in a mix of Palladian and beaux-arts architecture. It became the *Windsor Daily Star* in 1935, following amalgamation, and finally the *Windsor Star* in 1959. After W.F. Herman died in 1938, the paper continued under the direction of his wife, Adie Knox, along with Hugh Graybiel and Clark. The paper was sold to Southam Press in 1971, then to Canwest, and later to Postmedia.

A legendary story from those earliest days concern W.F. Herman at a baseball match in Detroit. He hobnobbed with that city's elite, and being a prominent figure on the border, he was caught by a Detroit newspaper photographer attending a Tigers game. The cutline in the next day's Detroit paper identified the Windsor publisher as taking in an afternoon game with his wife, Adie Knox—except that the woman he was with was his mistress. As I was told by old timers at the *Star*, Herman, upon hearing about the photo from friends across the river, commanded an army of paperboys to get down to the ferry docks to scoop up all the Detroit papers coming into the city. He bought them all, and had them destroyed before his wife might see them.

The *Star* had no end to personalities, oddball creatures who made this a fascinating place to work. There was Dick Harrison, whose life as a columnist spanned four decades from 1925 to 1958. He was described as "untouchable" when it came to being reprimanded or fired. Harrison banged out three columns under different names, and also penned his famous "Now" column, giving his opinion on the day's news, usually skewering some politician or nit-wit cultural icon. It was not uncommon for Harrison to show up to work after midnight. He'd sidle into his office, a cigar dangling from his mouth, and he'd settle under that hanging green-shaded lamp in his office and start pecking away at the Underwood on his desk.

Harrison, once in a righteous rage, tossed his typewriter out of the second-floor office of the *Star*. Another time, he drove his car into a downtown restaurant's front window, casually emerged from the vehicle, strolled up to the counter, and ordered a coffee. Harrison was by far the most colourful columnist we had. But there were other writers of note, too. One, (I won't mention his name), was actually fired, but was so likeable that when he offered to make up for his mistake by working a couple of more weeks without pay, his boss agreed. Instead, the man simply continued to work and hand in stories for weeks on end—never receiving a paycheque. The editors reminded him that he had been fired, and he ought to leave, but the reporter begged for one more week till he got this final story done—and no, the *Star* didn't have to pay him. After a few more weeks, and no sign of him departing, the editors reneged, and put him back on payroll. That reporter went on to work for another 25 years till his retirement.

I loved working there, and from time to time, would make my way down to the press room to hear and watch the thundering presses working their magic. In the third-floor newsroom, there were days when if you were really paying attention, you could feel the building tremble and shudder like a wet dog emerging from an ice cold pond. You didn't need to eye the little red light flickering on in the newsroom to signal that the presses were running. You felt it.

There were crazy moments, too, like the time I was reporting on the United Church of Canada, debating the ordination of gay clergy. My wife was driving me to work one morning, when one of my younger sons piped up: "Dad, why is that on the front of the *Windsor Star*?" That's when I saw the graffiti—"Gervais Is Gay!" and "Marty's a Homo." As a matter of fact, there was more of it along Pitt Street near the post office. My editor, Carl Morgan, was so angry about this, and confronted me in the newsroom, shouting, "Did you see that?

The Crabtree presses in full swing at the *Star*, seen here in the 1950s.

Why?" As if I had engineered this. I stammered, "Carl, I didn't do this. Do you think I want to see this painted all over the building?" He stormed off, grousing, "This is going to be quite a job getting that off, Marty!"

Across from the former *Windsor Star* is a ramshackle building that has been a bar (156 Chatham Street W.) for years, and before that, The Old Fish Market, the Baum & Brody Furniture Store, and the Universal Car Agency. None of that interests me. What does fascinate me is that this was once the site of

This derelict building, at Chatham Street West and Ferry Street, was once the Universal Car Agency, Baum & Brody Furniture Store, the Old Fish Market, and finally the Loop Complex, including the bar the Coach and Horses, as indicated by the sign still hanging above the boarded-up entrance.

the 19th-century home of Alexander Bartlet, Windsor's first town clerk. He was also the town's police magistrate, assigned to cleaning out the jail cells once a month.

The billy-goat bearded Bartlet was a founding member of St. Andrew's Presbyterian Church at the corner of Park and Victoria in 1857, just a stone's throw from where he lived. Every Sunday, he carried a harmonium to the sanctuary, and played it during services. Bartlet—to earn a bit more money—was St. Andrew's janitor, and Sunday School superintendent. The church building, that dates back to 1895, now faces an uncertain future. Its dwindling congregation is trying to stay alive, but that may not happen. The building will likely go up for sale. Another of the mainstay churches being closed.

Bartlet's diaries survive and tell the stories of this man. The one entry that caught my attention is Easter weekend, 1865. It's like a scene out of Charles Dickens. Hearing the paperboys announcing the death of President Lincoln, then reading the paper, he feels saddened, and makes arrangements to join 40,000 mourners in Detroit.

For years, it irked me that after having learned that his house was moved from this corner of Chatham and Ferry, where the Old Fish Market restaurant was, I was never able to find it. I drove all over the neighbourhood, and narrowed it down to a few spots, including one on nearby Victoria and Dougall. I finally figured out where it went—diagonally across the street from St. Andrew's Church at 408 Victoria, next door to the Carnegie Library.

Before the furniture store or bars, Alexander Bartlet, pictured at left, built his home at the corner of Chatham and Ferry streets. The house was moved to Victoria Avenue, next to the Carnegie Library. It is now a parking lot.

It was moved after Bartlet had passed away in 1910. His daughter wound up living there, and then her daughter, Margaret, took possession and donated it to the library. Today, both the Carnegie Library and the Bartlet house are gone. A parking lot now sits where the house once stood.

## Chatham & Dougall

Another place in this neighborhood lies behind the *Windsor Star* to the west, at the southwest corner of Dougall and Chatham. It is directly across the street from the Quality Suites Hotel. I'm speaking about a rambling red-brick building at 309 Chatham Street West, called LaBelle Terrace. It is a commercial property, originally built as a townhouse in 1905. Many years ago, it housed the Wooden Spoon restaurant and bakery. My daughter, Elise, worked there

briefly as a baker, but for me, it was a place of refuge. Daily. I'd sit there and read, do some writing, conduct an interview and always before a Windsor Symphony concert, would meet with Susan Haig, the conductor, and go over the details of the event. Later, Elias Deli became the domicile for such time spent. But while here in this downstairs café, and while working on the bestseller *The Rumrunners*, I discovered this two-storey building's ties to the greatest writers of the 20th century—James Joyce and Ernest Hemingway. In the 1920s, when Hemingway was living and writing in Paris, he searched for ways to send copies of James Joyce's *Ulysses* to friends in the United States. The 265,000-word novel—that was deemed obscene—appeared in 1922 when Sylvia Beach, the philanthropic proprietor of Shakespeare & Company Books in Paris privately published it. It was a heady time. T.S. Eliot's *The Waste Land* also appeared later that year. Anyway, Hemingway—anxious to get his friend's book into the United States where it was banned, dispatched copies to a pal who lived at this Chatham Street West address

La Belle Terrace, on Chatham Street West, pictured here in 1979.

The front entrance of Alvin Apartments, where my parents lived when they were first married.

behind the *Windsor Star*. This man worked for Curtis Publishing in Detroit, and daily took the ferry across the river. Tucked inside his coat, he smuggled copies of *Ulysses* into the United States, and mailed them to Hemingway's friends all over the country. The first copies of this banned book made it into the hands of Americans from this man in Windsor. An old friend of mine who

was a serious book collector was out one day and found a box of books at a Windsor address that contained a first edition of *Ulysses.* Right away, he spotted the tiny trademark signature of Joyce. The book was sitting in a cardboard box along with some dime-store novels. My friend asked the woman how much she wanted for the book. She said, "I know what it's worth! But you have to take the whole box." My friend's heart sank, because he knew its worth, and he couldn't afford to buy this signed first edition. Then the woman said, "Give me $10!" My friend handed her a $20 bill and said, "Keep the change—that's fine."

Back in the 1920s, the parking garage that sits kitty-corner to this building, adjacent to the *Windsor Star,* was nowhere to be seen. There was an orchard there for a time, before buildings started going up. Directly across the street from the garage on Pitt was the Alvin Apartments (286 Pitt Street West). It went up in the Roaring Twenties. My mom and dad lived there for a time. Just before it was torn down in the 1970s, I toured the abandoned interior with its broken doors and shattered windows. It was difficult to imagine that this was a place that was once respectable and homey.

Across Pitt from LaBelle Terrace is the new bus station (300 Chatham Street West) that spans Dougall, Pitt, and Chatham Streets. It replaces the one across from the Windsor Armouries. The terminal sits on a spot that was once the Canadian Tire Store. I can't forget that day when my car—constantly in for servicing with mechanics at this shop—was parked in the lot when a crane fell and crushed the car next to mine. All I could say was, "Why not mine?"

Left: The Canadian Tire on Pitt Street West, in 1968. This spot is now occupied by the Transit Windsor International Terminal, seen at right.

## Pitt Street West

Also across the street from the *Star* building is the François Baby House, part of Museum Windsor. It is tucked away in the shadows of a hotel and St. Clair College Centre for the Arts—a building still called The Cleary, because for so many years it housed the Cleary Auditorium where the Windsor Symphony played.

Having worked across the street, I made many trips to this museum to sift through documents in this place, impatient to find something different, more unique. I confess that often I was tempted to ask if I could drape myself in the Union Jack that had—allegedly—wrapped the body of the dead Tecumseh at the Battle of the Thames during the War of 1812. I was also fascinated with how Brock had spent the night in this house before he led his troops across the river to attack the Americans. Tecumseh had been invited, but instead went among his own. I imagined this great chief pacing in the darkness before the battle, comforting and encouraging his warriors.

In any case, this 19th-century home, once owned by the prominent local politician François Baby, was always called *La Ferme* locally. It sat on a French-Canadian ribbon farm that fronted the Detroit River. Originally, the farm land was granted in November, 1751, by Pierre Celoron, Sieur de Bienville, commandant at French Detroit, to Pierre Reaume. In 1800, however, Suzanne Reaume Bâby sold the farm to her son François for ten shillings plus one grain of pepper. Twelve years later, during the spring and summer, Baby built his house. It was virtually a new residence in July when the War of 1812 began. The Americans, guided by American Brigadier General William Hull, crossed the river and seized the house, making it their headquarters. The Americans built a defensive camp here, with their soldiers occupying the orchard across the street.

The armies didn't stay long. By August, they retreated to Fort Lernoult, directly across the river. Weeks later, Brock was on the scene, and began the bombardment of Detroit. Finally, the Americans surrendered. That was not the only time the Baby house figured in war. During the Patriot War, the Battle of Windsor took place on December 4, 1838; it was fought mostly in the Baby orchard. The battle was a short-lived campaign with a small militia of men that came together in 1837 to seize southwestern Ontario between Detroit and Niagara Falls and make it part of the United States.

The Baby House is pictured here in 1956, right before it was renovated into a museum space.

The house underwent many structural changes and uses. In 1890, the house was made into a double dwelling, and Pitt Street was now the front entrance. Bay windows were added, and during the 1930s, the place was vacant, abandoned. After the Second World War, attempts were made to resuscitate this historic dwelling. These renovations were completed in 1958, and the place was opened to the public as the Hiram Walker Museum. Now, with a new museum opened in the Art Gallery of Windsor building down the street, the Baby House site continues to be a museum, but its focus is mostly on research, providing resources for historians, and those of the general public seeking historical answers.

When I worked at the *Star,* I used to sit along the north side of the editorial office, overlooking Pitt Street. From the third floor, I had a great view of the Detroit skyline. To the east was the Norwich Block, and at the corner, back in the 1960s, was a greasy spoon, Adrian's. But the story I want to tell you is what occurred upstairs on the roof of that northwest corner. Former editor and publisher Bob Pearson, when he was a cub reporter at the paper in the early 1950s, used to stand there, and half-wonder why all these men were scrambling on the roof, carrying wires and equipment. He didn't realize that this biggest race wire operation in North America was taking place on this spot. These were telephone company employees, re-routing calls for people making bets over the telephone. These men would divert calls to actual homes, but just prior to executing these, they would connect with a homeowner and apologize and inform them that their phone would be temporarily taken out of service, but just for a few minutes while they were working on the lines.

The City of Windsor came under extreme pressure from across the river in 1948, when the Detroit police Commissioner Harry Toy claimed that Windsor was a "central wire service" for illegal gambling. He gave testimony of this in 1951 at an organized crime committee hearing in Washington, D.C. He cited Windsor as "the source of illegal race track wire information," feeding Detroit and several other American cities. The FBI also reported that Frank Costello, the powerful New York mob boss, was actually controlling Windsor's bookmaking operation, and had been doing this throughout the 1940s. In *Iced: The Story of Organized Crime in Canada* by Stephen Schneider, we learn that Costello sold the operation to Windsor's Howard Kerr who apparently was described as the "best handicapper" in the business. By the 1960s, organized crime in Ontario, however, was dominated by Vito Giacalone, the new mobster kingpin in Detroit. The Windsor connection was uncovered and resulted in a major provincial inquiry.

Pitt Street was a den of gambling, prostitution, and blind pigs. At the time, a *Windsor Star* columnist called it "a carnival of carnality" led by "populist playboy mayor Art Reaume, that rolled out the fleshy welcome mat for Detroiters eager to sample the sex, booze and gambling attractions of their cross-border neighbour."

Patrick Brode in *Unholy City, Vice in Windsor, 1950,* wrote: "The presence of so many Americans on the city's streets in search of sex was one of the dominating features of downtown Windsor." He quotes one officer as saying, "On the weekends you could hardly walk the beat there were so many people, and so many were Americans [here] to sample the prostitutes. It was a show."

There was one madam, Cecile Lamontagne, who turned 359 Brant Street, near the Windsor Arena, into "one of the most profitable and renowned bordellos in the Mid-West." According to Brode, it was so popular that weekend patrons forked out their money while queuing up outside, waiting on the street. This enraged neighbours because of all the commotion and traffic jams. Pitt Street East back then was nicknamed Windsor's "Bowery," or a neighbourhood that "respectable" women needed to avoid.

A view of Pitt Street looking west from Goyeau Street in the 1950s, when it was notorious for its blind pigs and bawdy houses.

The inquiry forced a drastic overhaul of the police department in Windsor, with the chief being forced to retire. The cleanup started in earnest with the new chief, Carl Farrow. Gord Henderson wrote about Farrow in the *Windsor Star*:

Bit by bit, naughty Windsor was hauled into line. The crackdown, of course, eventually went off the deep end. In 1952, city police raided a reunion of the beloved Essex Scottish Regiment and hauled away a Detroit stripper, triggering a near-riot. Among those present at the downtown Armouries were the city's morality-enforcing Crown attorney, Bruce J.S. Macdonald, and much of the Windsor bar.

I interviewed Chief Farrow after he retired, and he told me that when he took over the Force, he ordered each and every cop to appear at his office. One by one, he told them he didn't care if they had been on the take, that he was

Chief Carl Farrow in 1951, shortly after his arrival to clean up the Windsor Police Force.

"wiping the slate clean." But Farrow warned each of them that he wouldn't hesitate to fire a police officer if he heard even the slightest hint of a rumour. They knew he meant business. The next day the police invaded the streets of Windsor—especially Pitt—with axes and sledgehammers—and started ripping down the gambling dens. The scene changed. The cleanup had begun. Farrow became the worst nightmare for these criminals.

### Victoria & University Avenue

I make my way to Victoria, then head south to University Avenue, and turn east, go past the Phog, a fabulous bar and lively place for entertainment. My destination is 121 University Avenue West, the Capitol Theatre. It seems unbelievable, but there were some who

thought this could have made a great condo or parking lot. The theatre now serves the Windsor Symphony—it's their home. It's also the home of the Windsor International Film Festival (WIFF). Some think the Windsor Symphony's use of the Capitol has only been in recent years, but its involvement actually dates back to 1947, when Matti Holli led the musical group in the symphony's first performance here.

This theatre has been running since New Year's Eve, 1920. It opened after Marcus Loew of Loew's Vaudeville Theatres snapped up the lands on the south side of old London Street (University Avenue) at the corner of Pelissier. He built what opened as Loew's Theatre at a cost of $600,000. The vaudeville house that took only nine months to erect was designed by Thomas White Lamb in his trademark style of Adam-Empire. It had 1,995 seats. Two years after the theatre opened, Simon Meretsky, owner of the Windsor Theatre, Ed Glasgow of the Empire, and Dr. J.O. Reaume joined forces to sign a lease and rename the movie house, the Capitol. In 1923, some of the best vaudeville acts were showing up here. In 1929, Famous Players bought the place for $270,000.

By 1989, the Capitol's fortunes had changed. Then used primarily as a movie house, it shut its doors. Demolition was on the agenda. Not even a year later, the Arts Council Windsor & Region signed a lease, and Theatre Alive put on a production called *Big River*. In 1995, more than $5 million was poured into the interior restoration of the theatre. The facade was restored in 2000. By 2007, however, the old theatre was far

from sustainable and bankruptcy papers were filed. Five years later, the Capitol was given new life, with the city handing over the keys to the Windsor Symphony.

This was a spirited neighbourhood. Around the corner was the Norton Palmer Hotel. This establishment dominated the northwest corner of Park Street and Pelissier Street. It was designed by the architectural firm of Hutton and Souter (Hamilton), and opened December 17th, 1927. The hotel closed in 1974, and was promptly demolished. Victoria Park Place (150 Park Street West), an apartment building, now stands in its place.

This hotel was the part of Detroit hotel magnate Charles Norton's deep desire to widen his hotel reach. He had already had an impact on our neighbour across the river, and given the chance to expand to the south shore, he seized the opportunity to join up with Perry C. Palmer to build the Norton Palmer. It was a 12-storey building—Windsor's tallest when it was built—and boasted 200 rooms. Three years later, another 100 rooms were added. Eleven years after it opened, Charles Norton died. He was 74. Palmer inherited the ownership, but it was the Norton family that continued to run the hotel. Norton's son, Preston, took over, and actually lived in the hotel while operating both the Norton Palmer and the hotels in Detroit.

The hotel was also where the International Hockey League was founded on December 3, 1945 with four cross-border teams from Detroit, Windsor, Sarnia, and Chatham. The league lasted until 2001, but Windsor dropped out early, in 1950.

The Norton Palmer Hotel towered at the corner of Park Street and Pelissier Street from 1927 until 1974.

## Crawford and University Avenue

I'm on my way to Sandwich. I'm taking University Avenue West. In particular, I want to pause at a couple of places. The first is on the southwest side of Crawford where there is expansive open grassland, larger than a football field. Not that long ago, Grace Hospital occupied this corner. This was the Salvation Army Hospital, starting first in a home, the Ellis House, with a capacity for 28 beds, then swelled to a building in 1922 with 122 beds. Renovations and additions resulted in a south wing in 1942 and a north wing in 1945. After the hospital suffered a major fire in June 1960, a new five-storey building was opened in September 1966. All that remained of the original hospital was the front door to the Ellis House. But Grace—a once-thriving medical centre, and later faced major cutbacks by the province—was forced to shut its doors for good in February 2004. The sprawling building sat empty and abandoned for years, until demolition in 2013. You would never know it existed. All that remains, really, other than the original Ellis front door, are graduation photos of nurses who got their training there. These adorn a long upstairs corridor at the former Hôtel-Dieu Hospital on Ouellette Avenue.

A stone's throw away on the north side of the road is a long narrow building that is currently under construction as a restaurant establishment. It is the last remnant of the trolley line that once dominated Windsor streets in the 19th and early 20th centuries. In 1873 and 1874, the city cleared and graded a route that was 100-feet wide through the fields and orchards from Bruce Avenue to Huron Line. It would later be called London Street, then University Avenue. Their objective was to accommodate a six-car trolley line where one could ride the train from "any point in Sandwich" to Our Lady of Assumption Catholic Church for seven cents.

Right: Grace Hospital, now a bare field, served Windsor from 1922 until 2004. It is pictured at left in the 1920s, including the original Ellis House in the forefront.

An additional eight cents would have taken you all the way to Windsor. The line was called the S.W. & A., or Sandwich, Windsor and Amherstburg Railway. Originally, these cars were horse-drawn.

The brick barn that sits facing University Avenue today was the repair terminal for the streetcars. The property, that also housed The Junction before it was closed, is being developed by Van Niforos and George Sofos. In 2015, on a tip from a bus historian Bernie Drouillard, the two entrepreneurs bought an old streetcar, and went to see if it was in good enough shape to be restored and moved to the site.

Niforos was so excited about the adventure that led him to this discovery. He emerged from the back kitchen of the Penalty Box restaurant one afternoon to tell me all about it. He couldn't believe his luck when the 72-year-old Drouillard approached him with news of an old streetcar that might be available. He didn't realize, however, that a house had been constructed and wrapped around the streetcar to transform it into a private residence.

Shorn of its original seats, because it was being used as a residence, the streetcar still possesses some of its original windows and interior art deco wood trim. Drouillard found it by accident one day while driving around Belle River. When he spotted the distinctive nose of the electric-operated trolley jutting out in a car port, he instantly knew what it was. Drouillard said this streetcar, with its special smoking compartment, was built in 1918 in Cincinnati, Ohio, and was first used in New Jersey before being sold to the S.W. & A. in 1926, along with 19 others. When

The S.W. & A. streetcar repair terminal, with its distinctive facade, as it looks today on University Avenue.

the city opted for buses in the 1930s, it sold off these cars for $100, and people who scooped them up converted them into cottages, garages, even chicken coops.

When the 50-foot long, 24,688-pound streetcar was moved from its Lakeshore home to the University Avenue site, backed in on a transport truck into the open doors of the brick barn, it was like a cow returning from the pasture. Niforos wants to restore it and put it on display.

The man responsible for putting horse-drawn streetcars that rumbled along old London Street was William Boomer. Even more obscure is that it was his mentor, J.W. Tringham, who is said to have invented the first electric streetcar—which started its run in Windsor in 1886. Many believe that this was the first electric streetcar system in North America. It all started in a workshop that was situated at the roundabout intersection of Aylmer and Glengarry at Howard Avenue.

Tringham, who worked for a telephone company in Windsor, created the streetcar in this shop, slightly southeast of downtown

The roundabout where J.W. Tringham's workshop was once located, pictured here in 1953.

of the car, and two pulleys that ran along the top of the car connected it to overhead electric wires. He says Tringham never saw how this would revolutionize public transportation. He died two weeks after introducing his invention in 1886.

In that roundabout where Glengarry and Aylmer begin and run north to the river, there is no sign of that shop, no plaque, nothing but houses and apartment buildings.

Windsor. He called this 25-foot long electric car, with seats running down each side, the "Dynamo." Historian Neil Morrison talks about it in *Garden Gateway to Canada*, explaining how the Dynamo sat in the centre

## University Avenue & Huron Church

Let me begin at the ending. Our Lady of Assumption Church (350 Huron Church Road) sits on the south side of University Avenue. It is

The doors of Our Lady of Assumption Catholic Church have been shuttered to the public since 2014.

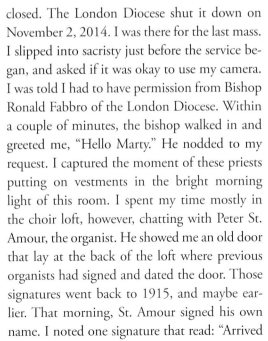

closed. The London Diocese shut it down on November 2, 2014. I was there for the last mass. I slipped into sacristy just before the service began, and asked if it was okay to use my camera. I was told I had to have permission from Bishop Ronald Fabbro of the London Diocese. Within a couple of minutes, the bishop walked in and greeted me, "Hello Marty." He nodded to my request. I captured the moment of these priests putting on vestments in the bright morning light of this room. I spent my time mostly in the choir loft, however, chatting with Peter St. Amour, the organist. He showed me an old door that lay at the back of the loft where previous organists had signed and dated the door. Those signatures went back to 1915, and maybe earlier. That morning, St. Amour signed his own name. I noted one signature that read: "Arrived March 1, 1987 Choir Director Malcolm Johns, Fired or Died. Oct. 1991."

That morning, I photographed the church, the service, and peered down at the congregation that was bidding the place adieu. At the time, some still believed this historic church would reopen. Others doubted it. Most prayed for it. For me, it was yet another example of the excuses we make that often lead to places of beauty being torn down. The day may come for Assumption. Too early to tell at this point. Instead, the diocese is letting it sit shuttered, awaiting a miracle.

It was this church that I frequented at Christmas. At that last Christmas mass in 2013, there in the front pews was the legendary short story writer and novelist Alistair MacLeod. After I turned from communion, I

I photographed the last mass held in Our Lady of Assumption Church on November 2, 2014.

To me, the boundary between Windsor and Sandwich is (unofficially) marked by these two architectural marvels: the Ambassador Bridge and Our Lady of Assumption Catholic Church.

passed by him, paused and shook his hand, and wished him Merry Christmas. A few months later, Alistair died after suffering a stroke.

My fondest memories for Assumption, too, reach back to its history as the oldest, continuous parish in Ontario, dating back to 1765 when many of the French families on the south shore of the Detroit River petitioned to have a parish of their own. The "Gervais" family was part of that first mission. Assumption's first pastor, Fr. Pierre Potier S.J., remained at his post until his death in 1781. The Mission of Assumption, constructed of timbers, or squared logs, stood in front of the present church between what is now University Avenue and Riverside Drive.

The cornerstone for the present building, however, wasn't laid until July, 1842. Three years later in 1845, the beautiful Gothic-Revival church was opened, and four years later, Assumption College was established. London Diocese Bishop, Pierre Adolphe Pinsonneault, opted to move his "see" to Sandwich in 1859, making Assumption church his cathedral. This didn't last. The diocese returned to London in November, 1867.

The Basilians didn't take over Assumption's church and college until 1870, when its first superior, Rev. Dennis O'Connor, and parish priest Fr. Jean Joseph Marie Aboulin arrived. It was O'Connor who added the tower and sanctuary of the present Assumption. In 1893, a new bell tower was added, and three years later, a new brick rectory. The leaded windows in the main part of the church were added in 1882.

I walk down to the river. There across the way, to the east of the Ambassador Bridge, but on the north side is Detroit's Ste. Anne's Church. It was built in 1886, but its history actually predates Assumption. The French settlers on both sides of the river were attached to the original Ste. Anne's that started up as a mission parish after Antoine de la Mothe Cadillac, accompanied by potential colonists, landed on the north shore in 1701. The first building they constructed was a church. Nicolas Constantine del Halle was their first priest. Native Americans, however, burned the church down two years later, and by that time, the settlers had also built Fort Pontchartrain du Détroit, or Fort Detroit. It, too, suffered damage in that fire. The site of the former fort is now within the city of Detroit in an area that sits between Larned Street, Griswold Street, and the Civic Center.

Ste. Anne's church had a rocky early history, being burned again in 1714, partially reconstructed in 1755, rebuilt in 1796, burned down in 1805, re-opened in 1828, and demolished in the 1860s. The present-day church was begun in 1886, designed by Albert E. French and built in the Gothic Revival style with flying buttresses. It sits on the river, like its sister Our Lady of Assumption, on the south shore. Sometimes when the mist envelopes the river at this spot, the steeples of Ste. Anne's are all that you see towering above.

Sandwich awaits me. The Ambassador Bridge looms large. It sits like a wall across this end of town. I must say that when I am crossing from Detroit to Windsor, this aerial view of the university and Assumption Church gives one a different impression than being on foot. As I peer over the rooftops, it looks like Windsor stops right at the edge of this bridge. On foot, it doesn't. I think we have become accustomed to it. It's always been there—at least for most of us. It's part of nature, of the flow of streets, maybe as common as fences in a yard. Yet it has proven to have changed the landscape, altered our perspective, ironically in the subtlest manner. Ironic because there is nothing subtle about this bridge.

As I leave Windsor, I see it as a city driven by the whims of its neighbours. It has always been one of catering to Detroiters, placing its loyalties there. At the same time, it has striven to heed the wishes of those in Walkerville, Ford City, Sandwich, and Riverside. Four communities all vying for attention. As I ready myself to walk into Sandwich, I sense ahead of me is forgotten territory.

# Sandwich

Mackenzie Hall

RUSSELL ST.

THE END

24

Old Towne Bake Shoppe
Former McGregor-Cowan House

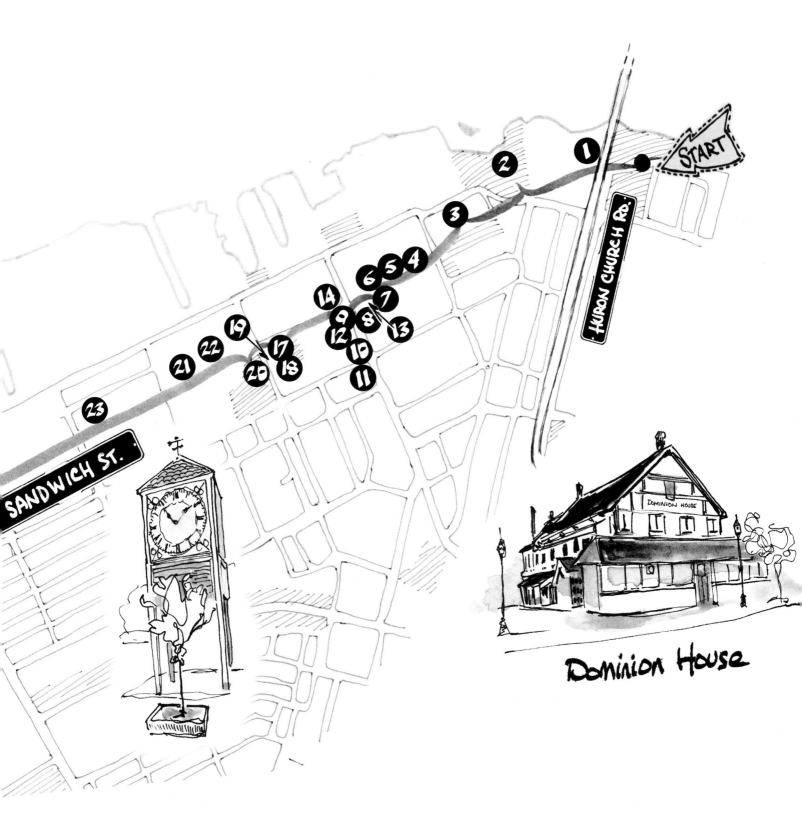

START

1

2

3

4
5
6

14

19

22
21

23

17
18
20

SANDWICH ST.

9
12

8
7

13

10

11

HURON CHURCH RD.

Dominion House

St. John's Anglican Church

Ambassador Bridge

Post Café

FORMERLY SANDWICH TOWNE POST OFFICE

The Chappell House

# SANDWICH
*April 13, 2016*
*4.5 km*

For me, the beginning of Sandwich is the Ambassador Bridge. Partington Street is the official boundary line, thereby making Assumption Church and the former Assumption University, and now the University of Windsor, a part of the original Sandwich. Since my walk through Windsor, I have been away on a holiday in Ireland where preservation of history is second nature—though at times, it may only be a collection of stones that was once a 12th-century castle, ancient church, or graveyard. No one in Ireland dares disturb the past. And in a week that I was gone, I am told the Vanity has now disappeared from downtown Windssor, leaving an empty gap, like a missing front tooth. I have also returned to a debate over tearing down Abars, the last of the former Prohibition roadhouses—the very first stop on my walk through these five towns. Another irony: the owner of Abars, who is seeking the demolition, is Matty Moroun—a magnate who figures darkly in this last town into which I am about to venture: Sandwich.

Matty Moroun's company, the Detroit International Bridge Co., owns the Ambassador Bridge. I stand on Riverside Drive—which becomes Sandwich Street in Sandwich—and

I survey this 7,500-foot bridge with its main pillars held up by steel in a cantilever truss structure. I sense how its uncompromising imposition on the landscape is maddening. The bridge, made up of 19,000 tonnes of steel, and a roadway that is 152 feet in length, is supported by suspension cables. It has walled off Sandwich Town.

When the Ambassador Bridge first opened, it was gloss black, but in 1995 and 2000, it

An aerial view of the Ambassador Bridge from December 1957. To me, the bridge acts as a barrier, separating Sandwich from the other Border Cities.

was stripped and repainted the colour it is today: teal. Its history is also tied to the story of the Great Depression. The official opening took place 21 days after the infamous 1929 Stock Market Crash. Moreover, it faced significant competition from the Detroit-Windsor Tunnel, which opened a year later and had cheaper toll rates. While for the Border Cities, the Depression faded and the Second World War jumpstarted their economies with munitions manufacturing, the Ambassador Bridge faced severely restricted travel and cross-border trade during the war years. Only at the war's

William C. Wyatt, a customs officer, was the first suicide recorded at the Ambassador Bridge, in April 1930. This newspaper clipping uses an arrow to indicate where he jumped. Wyatt's three children are pictured in the foreground.

end, did the bridge enter into an age of stability and prosperity, hitting more than one million travellers in a year in 1945—a first since 1931.

The bridge's history is one of polar opposites. It boasts a long list of stunt seekers that involved planes flying under it, a man parachuting off it, and another individual deliberately walking backwards over it just to say he had done it. In another incident, someone else commandeered a wheelbarrow and crossed the international span pushing a friend. Men would often propose to their girlfriends at the boundary line, in the years when pedestrians and cyclists were allowed to travel across. The Ambassador Bridge, too, has also been a source of tragedy. It wasn't that much longer after its celebrated start nearly 90 years ago that a Canadian immigration official jumped over the rails to his death, the first of several suicides.

I witnessed another one winter when crossing into the United States to go to my son's first Ontario Hockey League game. Traffic had slowed to a halt, and a stranger—a man heading in the opposite direction toward Windsor—pulled alongside our car, calmly opened his car door and trotted to the icy rail. He turned and stared right at me. I wondered for an instant, what was happening, but then witnessed him swivel back to the rails, and begin clambering up, and vaulting to his death. His body was discovered in the spring. I wrote about it in the *Windsor Star*, even though we had a policy of not covering suicides. My story was about an anonymous fellow, where I speculated about what goes through the mind of a troubled man who has the wherewithal to rise in the morning, plot out his actions, then motor to the centre of one of the longest suspension bridges in the world, stare down strangers in the eyes, then plunge to his death. I remember telephoning my editor to report what I saw, and after giving him all the details, his next question was: "Why the hell are you going to the United States?" I confessed that I was skipping out of work and this good editor, "Lefty" Frezell, laughed.

At night, the Ambassador Bridge's shimmering display of lights, the dark rich hues of blue, coupled with the halo of the city beyond, can be so appealing, so summoning. Daytime you gawk at the never-ending procession of cars and trucks. The more you learn about it, the more you come to realize that this bridge, built and opened in 1929, plunged a dagger into the heart of this once-promising town beyond to the west. It continues to do that. As you wander along Sandwich Street from Assumption Church and begin to stroll beyond the bridge, you can't help but think of the war of words that have surrounded the construction of a new bridge to span the Detroit River. Matty Moroun, of the Canadian Transit Company and the Detroit International Bridge Company, single-handedly owns the Ambassador Bridge. He has sparred with the city over his decision to build a twin span to rival the federal government's Gordie Howe International Bridge—even to the point of landing him in jail over an infraction involving ignoring boundaries and building his Duty Free store on state property.

The endless stream of cars on the Ambassador Bridge, pictured here in a postcard from 1956.

Moroun's efforts to build a new span have had a devastating byproduct; he has further transformed this west-end community into what may turn out to be the beginnings of a ghost town. The curmudgeonly billionaire has wolfed down more than 200 homes to the south of Sandwich Street, so that he can start construction and thwart the plans of our federal government and Michigan for their new bridge. These homes—which he now claims as his own—lay boarded up, bare, and forsaken. His appetite for properties and room for expansion is all rather ironic considering that just before the start of the Great Depression, Assumption's Basilian priests offered to sell most of its properties for a song. The religious order was deeply in debt. The priests approached the Ambassador Bridge company with the intention of selling off their lands from the river all the way along Huron Church to where the high school exists today, including making a provision to take care of the relocation of the cemetery. The bridge company declined. An official from the company remarked to me with a smile, "I wish you hadn't told me that."

Despite Moroun's greedy efforts to erect yet another span over the Detroit River, Sandwich's inhabitants refuse to capitulate. As I keep telling people, this bridge—once the longest suspended central span in the world until the George Washington Bridge opened between New York and New Jersey in 1931—has had a tremendously negative impact upon this community west of Windsor. The people here possess pride. They exude a doggedness, a tenacious determination to do better, to soar above events that have undermined their neighbourhood since the Ambassador Bridge opened.

Just before continuing along Sandwich, and leaving the bridge behind, I spot these pale-gray granite blocks all along the riverfront near Assumption Park. I wondered if originally these were the ones set into sand in the Ambassador Bridge ramps' roadbeds on the United States side so that the trucks would have more traction. I know that these were finally removed and replaced with asphalt, but are these huge blocks of stones the same? My queries to the city brought me no closer to their actual identity. The original Ambassador Bridge granite stones that I am referring to came from the Blair Quarry in Fairfield County, South Carolina, and were deemed too valuable to be disposed. Windsor opted to take them for their parks. I believe that what I am seeing along the riverfront pathway are those stones, but there's no marker or plaque to tell me that. For the moment, they serve a modest purpose as resting spots for the fishing gear for local fishermen. And according to a city source, the granite pieces were also used in the building of the new nature centre at Ojibway Park.

I continue along Sandwich, past the bridge, and cross in front of the former Ville Marie on the riverfront, once owned and operated by the Sisters of St. Joseph Hospitallers. My grandfather lived there briefly in the 1960s, when the place was used for assisted living.

I am experimenting with shoes now, trying to find something suitable for such walks. Nothing seems to work. My feet resist so many varieties. Today, I am wearing my L.L. Bean moccasins. They're comfortable. Have a little support. If I were to pick up my pace, these moccasins would soon become annoying. I take my time. I don't worry about heart rate. I'm walking to see. I don't want to miss anything. I scrutinize windows, porches, chimneys, rooflines, all in an endeavour to decipher architectural elements that might betray something older, richer in heritage. After all, this, the last of the Border Cities on my journey, is also the first. Sandwich—originally the township—is the oldest continuous European settlement west of Montreal. It was chosen as the seat of government of the Western District of Upper Canada in 1796. It proved to be the battleground during the War of 1812 between Great Britain and the United States. Windsor, by contrast, was the ugly child of the five. Walkerville, the golden child that felt set apart, better. Ford City was the engine, the driving force of the five. Riverside was the late blooming child, a bit spoiled, naive.

## Sandwich & Chewett

So, into the oldest town, I make my way. I can't help but notice the Tudor Revival house at 3020 Sandwich, sometimes called Casa Grande, with its twin gables, leaded windows, half timbering and carved faces of creatures on the beam-ends. It is out of character on this street that curves to the west. I have always wondered about this dwelling built in 1907 for William Johnson McKee and his wife, Mary Baby.

William was a founding father, philanthropist, and wealthy lumber merchant. He was born and raised in Sandwich, the son of Thomas McKee, Jr., and grandson of Thomas McKee. His wife, Mary, was the granddaughter of James Baby. William's interests were in transportation, and he invested in horse-drawn S.W. & A. streetcars that ran between Sandwich and Windsor. He was a political figure in these parts, representing Essex North as a Liberal in the Legislative Assembly of Ontario from 1894 to 1902. He died in 1929. His wife, Mary, passed away

"Casa Grande," at 3020 Sandwich Street as it looks today. The house was built in 1907 for William McKee.

within a week of his death. The two are buried in St. John's Cemetery, farther west on Sandwich Street.

Casa Grande once boasted 22 rooms: 17 bedrooms and five bathrooms. When the Sisters of St. Joseph bought it in July 1959 for $45,000, and renamed it House of Studies, it was intended to accommodate those attending Assumption University and serve as a base for those nuns employed in nearby elementary schools. In July 1974, the religious order decided to hand over the keys to Rev. Paul Charbonneau of Charity House. He reopened it as Brentwood, a rehabilitation centre for alcoholics, until they moved into the old Elmwood Casino in 1984. Today, Casa Grande is a student residence for the University of Windsor.

Back to the McKee family, whose roots are deeply embedded in Sandwich. William's great grandfather was Alexander McKee, a deputy agent with the Indian Department at Fort Pitt (Pittsburgh) where he traded with and was highly regarded by the tribes north of the Ohio River. The woman who instructed him in the language and customs of First Nations people was his sister-in-law, Chief Tecumseh's mother. McKee's first wife, Sewatha Sarah Strighttail, was a Shawnee. For many years, McKee lived in Pennsylvania on a plantation that entertained George Washington, who in his diary, actually mentions dining at Alexander's eight-room log house called FairView. When he fled the United States, McKee was branded a traitor for siding with the British when the American Revolution broke out, says Judy Jacobson in *Detroit River Connections: Historical and Biographical Sketches of the Eastern Great Lakes Border Region.* Alexander was imprisoned briefly, pardoned, then joined Loyalists

Often mistaken as a portrait of his father Alexander, Thomas McKee is pictured here in his 60th Regiment of the Foot uniform, c. 1790s.

Matthew Elliott and Simon Girty on their flight from Fort Pitt to seek asylum in British-occupied Detroit.

Alexander was welcomed here at the border by the British who needed his skills in dealing with the First Nations people. He was promoted to captain and interpreter by the British, and later appointed a deputy agent, and finally Superintendent of Indian Affairs. Jacobson says, "He stood up for the Indians… to forbid licensing traders who dealt in rum because unethical traders had been using excesses of liquor to defraud." He settled here in Sandwich, but only after the British gave up Detroit. This was when he began his rise to become one of this area's most influential figures. He started to acquire properties. So did his son, Thomas, whose homestead was where the former Sandwich Post Office stands today. Alexander was appointed judge of the Court of Common Pleas. He was also a colonel, at an age well over sixty.

In 1799, Alexander and John Askin were in the middle of promising negotiations to purchase land (part of what would become Sandwich Township) when Alexander died suddenly of lockjaw. The deal-making fell now to his son, Thomas. Having married Askin's daughter, Theresa, and being a captain in the militia, this seemed attainable. By 1800, Thomas took his father's place as Superintendent of Indian Affairs. All of this went awry with the outbreak of the War of 1812, and his family had to flee to Lower Canada with the advancing American armies. The underlying problem, however, was that

Thomas was "a hopeless drunkard," according to Canadian writer Pierre Berton in his history of the War of 1812. Jacobson adds this: "Through the years, his overindulgence with liquor had ruined Thomas McKee and brought about the loss of the estate he had inherited from his father."

By 1815, the McKee family was penniless. One tragic incident after another had shattered the family. One of Thomas' grandsons died in a house fire, another drowned in the Detroit River. That boy, aged 18, was buried at St. John's Cemetery.

Frederick Neal, in his 1909 book, *The Township of Sandwich: Past and Present*, reveals that Thomas's homestead—and not the Casa Grande, owned by his grandson William—was picked up by his more astute daughter Jane McKee. The house apparently was also removed from the corner of Mill, not demolished. Some believe that the structure still stands, and it is situated on nearby Chippewa Street, occasionally mistaken for the Wilkinson Homestead. According to Neal's history, the Wilkinson building itself was constructed in 1818, or shortly after the War of 1812. Apparently John James Hume, the man murdered by the Americans in the Battle of Windsor in December 1838, was a frequent visitor there. Hume's story is an interesting and gruesome one. He was a surgeon with the 32nd Foot, and in the midst of the Battle of Windsor, he was on his way to bring help to the local militia when he encountered the American patriots who promptly killed him with an axe, then fed his severed limbs to local hogs.

This early photograph shows the Wilkinson Homestead on Chippewa, which many believe was originally Thomas McKee's house.

The Wilkinson building, or original McKee homestead, today has fallen on hard times, and is now a rooming house. Its original lines have practically vanished. No one knows whether it is really the McKee homestead, but regardless, it is a surviving product of the 19th century.

## Sandwich & Chewett

A nondescript bluish-grey house—near Chewett at 3066 Sandwich—that almost fades into the background, was where Pierre Marentette lived. It was built in 1856. You would almost miss this English cottage style home if it was not for the retained "nun's coif" gable at the front. Marentette was the town's blacksmith, but he also shackled the prisoners at the County Jail. In 1858, Marentette was among those who sat on the town's first council. Around Sandwich, he was better known for distinguishing himself in the Battle of Windsor, while serving under Col. Prince in the rebellion of 1837–38. The story goes that Pierre Marentette shot the man carrying the rebel flag, and apparently, James

The Marentette house, at 3066 Sandwich Street, was built in 1856 and is still occupied today.

Dougall had offered $25 in gold to the soldier who could manage that feat. After the conflict, Dougall set out for Sandwich to hand over the reward to the solider, but Marentette declined it: "I am not fighting for money, I am fighting for my country."

The family that lived in this tiny house was also known widely for their musical talents. Marentette had one daughter and seven sons, all of whom had terrific voices, and were in demand all across the country, and forever were on tour. Most notable among the singers was the quintet composed of Joseph, Rudolph, James, Alexander and Thomas. "At one time," Neal says, "the late Col. Arthur Rankin made a very flattering offer to take the quintet to Europe, so sanguine was he of the great success that was in store for them there." However, they received no remuneration for their work, thus making it imperative to end the touring—or as Neal puts it, they had "to attend to the business connected with their worldly welfare."

## 3118 Sandwich

This next place looms large on the street. I have been anticipating this white, timber-framed house with covered clapboard, sitting on a stone foundation, boasting shuttered, 6-over-6 sash windows, some with original hand-blown panes. You might not notice at first, but if you look closely, you can see the key architectural feature: the unique French-Canadian chimney arrangement on the lateral gable roof. There are two brick chimneys, one on either side of the ridge at opposite ends of the roof. They work independently to warm separate halves of the house. Although it bears the name as a bakeshop and tea place, heritage people know this building better as the McGregor-Cowan House—derived, at least in part, from James McGregor who first owned it. According to *Canada's Historic Places* register, the building is "a rare surviving example of a fine Georgian-style home… its simplicity, symmetry and solidity are representative of Georgian design." It was constructed in 1808 on property that was part of a land grant from the Crown at the turn of that century. It might be the second oldest residential structure in the Border Cities. The Duff-Baby House, farther west at the corner of Mill and Russell Streets, facing the river, was finished in 1798.

Now operating as the Olde Towne Bake Shoppe, this house was once Zoli Antiques before the Cuderman family bought it in 2001. I often step into this shop on Sundays for breakfast. Mary Cuderman bakes the most scrumptious scones, and every Saturday and

Sunday serves breakfasts with heritage flavour: "The Simon Girty," and another called "The Loyalist" or there's the "Upper Canada." It was here that I first met Terrence Kennedy, that stalwart Sandwich Town archivist. He knows more about this neighbourhood than most. To hear him speak of this part of Windsor is so colourful and engaging, lending you the impression that it can't possibly be true. He speaks of dates as if he actually *lived* through them.

Kennedy recalls July 6, 1669, as if he was among this party of twenty-one that clambered into seven birchbark canoes in Montreal. These vessels were laden with beaver skins and provisions that would take them through the fall. As Kennedy spins this story, you can almost hear what he calls "the joyous notes of the *Te Deum* and the sound of arquebus," as this convoy departed for the settlement here on the river south of what would become Detroit. The expedition included Sulpician missionaries, Brehant de Galinee, and Francois Dolliar de Casson. Galinee's jottings tell that story clearly: how they wintered at Long Point on the northern shore of Lake Erie and feasted on local grapes, from which they made wine for mass. The two finally landed on Detroit's shore in early spring, 1670. However, the tale that I love is the one about the missionaries coming ashore at Belle Isle and finding a rudimentary sculpture of the Great Manitou of which many native guides had spoken. The missionaries smashed it to pieces, and in its place, installed a massive cross and France's coat of arms. They then loaded a larger fragment of the idol into

The McGregor-Cowan House, built in 1808, stands on the north side of Sandwich Street. Note the two chimneys, the result of French-Canadian influence blended with the house's Georgian-style architecture.

a canoe and sailed off shore to drop it into an appropriately deep spot in the river. When the natives returned to discover the statue had been shattered and left strewn on the shoreline, they scooped up the fragments and returned these to their own canoes, as ordered by the spirit of Manitou. They then placed these remnants around their own abodes. And so the myth persists, these stones were instantly transformed into rattlesnakes, there to protect them from any further incursions by the white explorers.

As I said, Kennedy has a million stories. If you run into him over brunch at the Bake Shoppe, be prepared to listen, it'll be worth it. But back to the McGregor-Cowan house, it is in some ways, the real gateway to Sandwich. You come around the curve and you spot it on the north side of the street. But more than a physical landmark, it is the gateway to Sandwich's hidden stories—a sign of its long history. For a brief time during the War of 1812, General William Henry Harrison commandeered this house and used it to hold prisoners. One can still see the etching, or scratching on the hand-hewn beams in the basement where these inmates were shackled—evidence of their captivity. The shackles were still there when the present owners bought the place.

The second half of the house's name comes from the Cowans, who bought it in 1836. The family remained there for 113 years. John Cowan produced one of the area's first newspapers here. It was called *The Canadian Emigrant and Western District Advertiser*. The house was also a "station" in the Underground Railway. James Mays writes in *The Scoop* in June 2007:

> Under the cover of darkness, boats rowed up the creek to the jetty. Many a slaves' first step on free Canadian soil was here. No longer fettered, slaves still required shielding from American bounty hunters who roamed the streets in search of quarry. The McGregor House gave that shelter.

Right: The Dominion House (DH), pictured in 1901, with Amadee Marentette, son of one of the early owners, standing out front.

Below: The DH is still up and running, pictured as it looks today, making it the oldest pub in the border region.

## The Dominion House

You don't have to go far from here to find the next important heritage building. It's next door—the beloved Dominion House (3140 Sandwich), affectionately known as the DH. My memories are from the 1960s and 1970s, when this pub—the oldest continuously run tavern in the Windsor-Detroit region—sheltered the best of the best when it came to the literature scene in Windsor. Eugene McNamara, Len Gasparini, Rick Hornsey, John Ditsky, Joyce Carol Oates, Alistair MacLeod, and so many others gathered here, sometimes after classes at the university. It was at night in the basement where literature was developing. At the same time in Windsor, Black Moss Press started publishing. Among our first was Eugene McNamara's *Dillinger Poems*. *Mainline* magazine probably had its beginnings over a few beers at the DH. It operated under the guidance of McNamara, with cartoonist and artist Bob Monks doing the illustrations. In some ways, you might say the DH was the headquarters for such literary planning.

The DH that I remember was Sid Walman's place. He hailed from Toronto, hoping to use his business acumen to good use into turning this 19th century place into one of the more popular spots for the university crowd. It worked. Even unofficial English Lit classes were held there. After nearly half a century, Sid sold the Dominion House to a long-term employee and bartender.

The Dominion House is the oldest tavern of the five towns. Originally, it was a stagecoach stop for a route that began in Amherstburg and ended in Windsor. Sixteen different innkeepers have owned it. Frank Dent was the one who christened the place "The Dominion House" in 1878. Before that, when it was across the street, it had operated primarily as a hotel from about 1869, and was owned by Charles Askin. The hotel, however, burned to the ground on February 23, 1883. After that, Albert Lininger, who was the current operator, decided to rebuild it but upon the present site. It became a favoured drinking spot for many farmers who were transporting fresh produce to the Eastern Market in Detroit. During Prohibition, it was said to have basement tunnels—though I've never seen the cavernous routes that apparently led to the river. Then again, I've heard whispers of other places along the river having the same network of tunnels. Indeed, some exist; others are apocryphal. As far as the Roaring Twenties, the DH was not as popular as the roadhouses, especially the high-flying Chappell House

owned by the Trumbles, farther along Sandwich Street. During the 1920s, Capt. John McCarthy purchased the Dominion House and later Lorne White, and still later William and Jean Boyer. The latter could tell stories of the construction of the Ambassador Bridge, and how they housed many of the bridge workers.

As I stroll down Sandwich Street, I imagine what it was like to live here in the 18th and 19th centuries, or even ten years before this historic tavern was built, when the British Government bought a one-mile square portion of land from the chiefs of the Wyandottes or Hurons, Chippewas, and Ottawas. This was the original parish boundaries of Assumption Church. Indeed, before the British ever arrived here, this territory along the riverfront was called "L'Assomption," and not Sandwich. Frederick Neal says "it is quite evident Detroit and L'Assomption were one community politically, religiously and socially." Sandwich

Sandwich Street, looking east, c. 1880. The Dominion House is visible at left.

A group photograph of First Nations from Walpole Island, who came to Sandwich to re-enact the Jesuits landing, in 1909.

He suggests taking a look at Windsor's lengthy track record of removing historic buildings. Sandwich, he points out, may have been ignored and cut off when the Ambassador Bridge went up, but its people cared about their neighbourhood. That's why, Kennedy argues, finding curious gems is possible. Several years ago, for example, he found himself embroiled in a fight with the Kentucky State Museum over a cannon that had been at the Battle of Fort Detroit. He had written to authorities asking if it could be "borrowed" for a display in Windsor, but the request was turned down. Newspapers in Kentucky got hold of the story and sensationalized it, saying a Canadian was asking for the cannon to be returned to its rightful owners. Kennedy laughs about all the fuss. The story is that the weapon was turned over to General Brock when the American Commander General Hull surrendered to the British. It was Benjamin Knapp of the British who captured the cannon, and he was given a cash reward for his efforts. Col. Proctor of the British forces then took the cannon with him along the Maumee and Detroit Rivers. The cannon wound up at the Battle of Thames, and the British soldiers readied it for firing, but suddenly realized that somehow they had forgotten to bring along ammunition for it. That's when the weapon was abandoned, and soon after seized by some Kentuckian soldiers. From there, it made its way to Frankfort, Kentucky, and sits on display in the state museum. A curious story. Maybe the journalists were on to something—Kennedy realizes that he is probably the only one who refers to this cannon as

itself was not incorporated as a town until 1858—four years after Windsor, even though it had been settled earlier.

Neal's book, an early 20th-century document, is interesting for what it reveals about the community here in the early 1900s. They seemed to exhibit an appreciation for Sandwich's history—Neal in particular. He is careful to note how homesteads had been altered, acknowledging that these buildings bore importance.

What also caught my attention in Neal's book was a photograph of Walpole Island First Nations people, who in 1909 came to Sandwich to participate in the Old Boys' Reunion in August. They did a re-enactment of the Jesuits landing on the south shore of this river. There were thirty-two of them, and they had their photograph taken that day in Sandwich. History was significant.

According to Terrence Kennedy, Sandwich may have possessed a greater sense of its importance than others along these river communities.

the Knapp Family Cannon. As it turns out, Knapp was his great, great grandfather.

From time to time, other relics surface, and not all from the War of 1812 or earlier. Some divers I met reported that near Peche Island in the Detroit River, they discovered an old car lodged sideways and nearly buried in the sand underwater—still loaded into half-destroyed wooden whiskey cases. It had probably fallen through the ice during the 1920s, with the rumrunners losing their supply. Years later these divers, who had happened upon this great find, retrieved a half dozen uncorked bottles, and they were back a few times, but on several return visits to that site, they were unable to locate the automobile.

The Solomon Wigle House (Hanaka Cottage), still occupied at 3164 Sandwich Street, dates back to the 1890s.

## 3164 Sandwich

Not far, between Detroit and Mill, is a Georgian-style cottage, owned by the Hanaka family. Greg Hanaka, a dentist who settled in Sandwich in the 1970s, has been a prominent vocal community booster. This two-storey brick home, set far back beyond a wooden fence, is on the north side of the street. In 1801, Francois Baby was the owner of this property. A magistrate of the Court of Quarter Sessions, and member of the Legislative Assembly of Upper Canada, he hailed from one of Windsor's founding and most influential families. However, according to *Canada's Historic Places,* there is no evidence of a house being built here before 1890. That's when Solomon Wigle purchased the property from

Baby. Wigle was from a prominent local family, worked as a land speculator, served as reeve Sandwich Township and was a member of the Provincial Parliament from 1866 to 1869. He probably never lived there, but found others to rent it. What is curious about this house is how the floor plan "aligns the front and rear entrances, allowing shotgun pellets to be fired through one door, passing through the house without hitting any barriers, and exiting through the opposite door."

## 3165 Sandwich

Across the street is the James McKee House (3165 Sandwich Street), built in 1875. It sits sideways on the property, and is obscured almost entirely

Above: The James McKee House is pictured here in 1913. It still stands today, pictured below, but has been incorporated into Wigle's storefront, visible at the back.

by a storefront. Some claim that it originally faced Sandwich Street, and was moved. Underneath a veneer of paint is a red-brick structure. James was the grandson of Colonel Alexander McKee. Like many in these founding families, James was also politically involved, serving as the Sandwich Reeve in 1863 and from 1869–75. He was also warden of Essex in 1877.

A story that I raised earlier—and it is connected to this property that faces the DH—is that of Moses David, considered the first Jewish settler in the Windsor area. Moses David, born in 1768, son of a wealthy Montreal fur trader, was dispatched to this area by his father to represent the family business. He arrived across the river in 1793. By the following year, David was living in Sandwich. Oddly enough, even though he had established a thriving fur-trading business here, and had volunteered for the Upper Canada militia, his application for a 200-acre crown land grant was denied. No one knows for certain why David was turned down, but Jonathan V. Plaut contends in his history, *The Jews of Windsor,* that "a deeper and more insidious explanation emerged in the aftermath of his rejection when Chief Justice Elmsley issued his opinion that Jews could not be granted Crown lands in Upper Canada."

Accepting this judgement, David applied for a Crown land grant in Quebec, but also was turned down. He returned to Sandwich, resolved to right this wrong. This time he pursued the purchase of a town lot from one of the original grantees, Jean Baptiste Barthe, a brother-in-law of John Askin. This purchase involved a payment plan, and that proposal nearly did not go through. David had reasoned that once he was a landowner, his application for a Crown lot in Sandwich would be easier to acquire. He was shocked and angry when this petition was again ignored, and he decided to go over Elmsely's head directly to the Lieutenant Governor. Only then did David find success. He was awarded 27 acres of land in the Township of Sandwich in February, 1804.

From this point on, David enjoyed success on the south shore of the Detroit River, continuing with fur trading. He was also appointed coroner of the Western District by the Lieutenant Governor. This was the first instance of a Jew being chosen for a government office in Upper Canada. And while there was no place for worship in his own faith in this area, Plaut points out that his friendship with Richard Pollard, first rector of St. John's Anglican Church, led him to be a member of that Christian denomination. Indeed, David attended church meetings, and even held a pew seat in the sanctuary. Plaut says that despite this apparent devotion to the Christian church, David remained committed to the Jewish faith, evidenced by the fact that he was buried in the backyard of his Sandwich home, rather than in the cemetery adjoining St. John's Church.

David's house was on Lot #3. This is where he lived, and where he died September 26, 1814. He was 46. The cause of his death is unknown. It was local historian Kirk Walstedt who discovered his gravesite in 1978, after a developer sketched out plans for a high-rise complex opposite the Dominion House. Walstedt, who had heard rumours of Moses being buried on this property, got Rabbi Plaut involved. The two then pushed the developer to permit them to search for it. Beneath a pile of brush, vines, garbage, bricks, canisters and bottles, and four feet deep in the soil, were the remains of Moses David. Walstedt told Fred Groves of the *Essex Free Press,* "I got lucky, it was the easiest place to dig. I got near the bottom of it and the corner of the tombstone appeared. It was a light kind of stone."

The historian dug furiously, but carefully, using a small trowel. He was careful not to damage the pine box. "It became obvious to me that at one time it was a mausoleum," he said. "We had to be very careful; we couldn't touch it. The rabbi wanted the grave protected." Eventually, the two arranged for the transfer of Moses David's remains and tombstone to the Shaar Hashomayim cemetery on Pillette Road, where today stands a monument and a testimonial to the first Jewish settler in this area. What actually preserved the tombstone under four feet of earth was all that trash. Walstedt has kept some of its more interesting items, notably the bottle collection, among them a Lansbury Drug Store bottle dating back to 1830.

Plaut says that three years before his passing, David had bought the adjacent Lot #4 to his residence. There is no evidence that he had ever intended it as a burial plot, but later documents confirm that his internment was on this property. When Adolphe S. Gignac acquired the land from Jane Phyllis McKee in October 1913, this clause was included: "Northerly 50 feet with lot number three on the east side of Bedford Street by the full depth of the said lot, accepting there from the Jew Cemetery at the east corner thereof." As Plaut pointed out, there was only one grave there—that of Moses David. It becomes clear that Charlotte, David's wife, did not want to travel to Montreal to bury him, so she opted for the backyard of their residence. The tombstone for David was actually written about in the *Amherstburg Echo* in June 1880. Plaut says the reporter errored in the date of his death, but the article states that "an old relic in the shape of a tombstone was erected to the memory of Moses David by his wife Charlotte David." The stone fence is 6 feet wide by $5^{1/2}$ feet long. On the tombstone are engraved the following words: "In memory of Moses David, who departed this life… Aged 46 those wishing to see, can do so by asking Mr. Dentz of the Dominion House or James McKee."

The Barrel House restaurant, at the southeast corner of Sandwich and Mill, was home to John Spiers' general store in the late 19th century.

Just as passersby would likely never realize that this storefront obscures a historic home, it turns out that even the land bore secrets. Typical of this town, a rich history hides just below the surface.

## Sandwich & Mill

Continuing west, I am at the corner of Sandwich and Mill. On the southeast side is the Barrel House Draught Co. & Grill (3199 Sandwich Street), but in the 19th century, it was owned by John Spiers who was made the town's postmaster in August, 1885. He kept his office in this building, and the place also served as his general store. The Spiers building was apparently built by a man by the name of George Washington Mason, a Sandwich magistrate, grocer, and builder who hailed from Indiana. He served as mayor, and also built, and lived in the Mason-Girardot house (3203 Peter Street) at Mill and Peter. That house, a short detour south on Mill, dates back to 1875, and is done in that Victorian Italianate design—a jewel for Sandwich. It retains much of the original exterior. I knew it when it was a fabulous restaurant. It was a favourite of the Canadian playwright James Reaney. He always wanted to go there whenever he was in town.

Adjacent to the Spiers building is Wally's (3195 Sandwich), a bait shop. This was actually the original site of the post office before it was moved next door to Spiers' building. Ironically, during the 1920s, the upper floor was a den of prostitution. In the 19th century, it was housed by E. Lassaline Furniture Dealer and Undertaker. Mr. Lassaline would coordinate his work with the funeral home across the street.

I pause in this intersection; this corner holds special meaning to me. It was in the Spiers Building that several literary readings took place when the bar/restaurant was the Sandwich Mill. One in particular that I recall was when the Port Dover-based poet John B. Lee, one of the most renowned poets in Canada, nearly came to blows with an angry mob of beer-league baseball players. They had funnelled into the bar, grubby and sweaty from a game they had just won, thirsty for some cold suds. Lee, the featured reader, who should have started much earlier except other poets on the roster that night—one in particular—had performed well beyond the time limit. This caused a major delay for Lee's appearance, and so when he rose to deliver his own work, these bad boys from a nearby park sailed in. Lee asked politely if they might settle down and permit him to read for just a few minutes. It was a reasonable request, but such a promise wasn't about to be secured from the ballplayers. Sparks flew back and forth, and the reading came to an abrupt end. I had my car waiting around the corner to bear my friend safely away.

The other fact about the Spiers Building is that just around the corner on Mill, the city installed new sidewalks in the 1990s, and covertly removed one section that had remained since 1907. Stamped into the concrete of that sidewalk section were the words "Post Office." Another travesty was when they removed the

section in the sidewalk in front of Brock School that read "Bedford Street" which was the original name of Sandwich Street. What still remains embedded in the crosswalk at the intersection of Sandwich and Mill, and right in front of the Barrel House are the remnants of the streetcar tracks that once existed here. The streetcar line—The Sandwich, Windsor & Amherstburg Railway—ran from 1887 for 90 years.

In 1907, John Spiers went to work across Mill at the new post office—a three-storey redbrick and stone building with a mansard roof and gabled dormers. The building was designed by David Ewart, chief architect of public works, the same man who designed the Windsor Armouries. The new public building cost $15,000 to build. It also meant the removal of the two-storey clapboard homestead of Thomas McKee that stood on this property. Spiers and

Wally's Bait Shop, at 3195 Sandwich, once housed a bawdy house on the second floor, and an undertaker.

The remnants of the S.W. & A. streetcar tracks are still visible at the intersection of Sandwich and Mill.

Below: The Sandwich Post Office in 1920. It was renovated in 2016 and now operates as the Sandwich Post Café.

his daughter, Miss Jessie Spiers, the assistant postmistress, were put in charge. The second floor of the new post office building accommodated Inland Revenue & Customs House. John McLean was the Customs Inspector. McLean was later given the job of janitor and lived with his family on the third floor.

The Sandwich Post Office closed in April 2013. Alistair MacLeod told the *Windsor Star* at that time how wrong, and "terrible" it was that it was being closed down. There was a photograph of him in front of it, holding Easter packages he was mailing to grandchildren. The *Star* article read: "The Canadian literary great said there may be more conveniently located postal outlets nearer to his home, but 'this is the best—it's a real post office.'" MacLeod said he made trips there on a weekly basis.

The Sandwich Post Office lay vacant for three years until the spring of 2015 when it was purchased with the idea of transforming it into a café. Among the first things done was to restart the water fountain in front—a replica of one donated by William P. Leech, president of the Evening American Publishing Company and publishers of the *Chicago American*. He had lived in Sandwich and on the occasion of the Old Boys' Reunion in August 1909, donated the fountain to the town.

I turn south down Mill, for a quick detour. On the west side is the former Sandwich Fire Hall (363 Mill), considered "the oldest surviving example in Windsor of an early fire station." The actual fire hall, called Fire Hall No. 6, was put up in 1921, designed by a well-known Windsor architect, Gilbert J. P. Jacques. It was fashioned in the Classical Revival style. The stable that had once housed the horses that hauled the fire wagons was constructed long before that, probably before 1915. Writers for *Canada's Historic Places* note the building's unique details: "the hipped roof corner tower where water hoses were hung to dry," and "the large, multi-paned windows on the second storey… in keeping with its use as a dormitory." Also there is the "gabled hayloft dormer, original horse stall windows and a distinctive small doorway… notable features of the pre-1915 rear brick stable." In 1941, a fire broke out while the firefighters were on a call, and destroyed the second floor and upper part of the hose tower. This was rebuilt four years later. The station continued to serve Sandwich until 1964.

Next door to the north is another plain-looking dwelling at 351 Mill called "The Langlois House," built in 1888. According to city records, Albert Reaume appears to have taken possession of it in 1904. His daughter married Arthur Langlois, and the couple owned and lived in the house. The original "fish-scale" shingles remain on the building—a hint to its historic past.

I return to the intersection of Mill and Sandwich. Kitty-corner to the Barrel House and Wally's was the Jules Robinet Winery. It is now Yum Yum Pizza (3200 Sandwich Street). I knew it as the CIBC bank. This is where I first

Sandwich Fire Hall No. 6, built in 1921, sits empty today.

borrowed money to attend university. I never realized that this place was where the wine industry started in Essex Country. Robinet, in 1883, began using grapes harvested from nearby vineyards—between Felix and Mill—to make wine for commercial purposes. The

The Langlois House, at 351 Mill Street, dates back to 1888. Note the fish-scale shingles on the front facade.

Right: The north side of the intersection of Sandwich and Mill, including the Jules Robinet Winery on the northwest corner, in 1906.

Below: Rock Bottom Bar & Grill is located in the McKee Block, built in 1921, as indicated by the nameplate at the top.

winery was called Robinet et Frères. He also operated a brick and cement block business. Robinet's biggest client was Assumption. His brick workers lived in a two-storey set of row houses—still on Peter Street. These residences were located at the back of the Robinet brick-yard. A 12-page autobiography that he tapped out on a typewriter survives in the archives at the University of Windsor.

Farther along on the same side of the street is Rock Bottom (3236 Sandwich), a painted yellow-brick building. If you look up at this two-storey building just above the windows, you will see that it reads "McKee Block 1921." This was owned by Alex McKee, another descendant of Alexander McKee; he was the former Mayor of Sandwich and Warden of Essex County. He lived next door. But before the

McKee Block went up, the building that was here was the first ladies' college in Western Ontario, according to an October 3, 1930, article in *Border Cities Star* by reporter H. L. Macpherson. He said it was constructed by Captain Risk of the British army and was run by his wife and three daughters. It burned to the ground in 1871. Upon its foundation, the new McKee Block sits.

Next door is a red-brick building, and according to Macpherson's article, this is where the home of Alexander McKee was located. In the *Star* article, it is mentioned that the former mayor treasured a sword and two stone clubs found beside Tecumseh's body after he fell at Moraviantown. "While there is no direct proof that Tecumseh carried these weapons," said the *Star* reporter, "indications are that he did." The fact remains, however, that McKee might have come by these items because of the family connection to Tecumseh, that I mentioned earlier.

Across the street is the building that once housed Sandwich Towne Hall (3255 Sandwich Street). The name remains above the doorway. It's now a rooming house, no longer owned by the town, or even used by the town for official purposes. Designed by C. Howard Crane with Windsor's J.C. Pennington in 1911, this Georgian edifice that once had a slate roof, cupola, and balustrade went up in 1912. It was originally planned for use exclusively as the Town Hall, but it also wound up housing the police station and library.

Next to this is Mackenzie Hall Park. This was also the site of the former Western Hotel, a

Sandwich Towne Hall, built in 1921, operates today as a rooming house.

place where politicians congregated and where decision-making over the town's future was thrashed out. It is also the place where Sir John A. Macdonald, then prime minister, got into a debate during the federal election of 1873, and vomited partway through the speech of his opponent Alexander Mackenzie. After wiping his mouth, the prime minister remarked that it wasn't the drink that made him sick, but the political policies laid out by the contender.

Looking east down Sandwich Street, the Western Hotel is visible, c. 1860s. Behind it is Mackenzie Hall.

Who knows whether the story is true, but it has been ascribed to this meeting in Sandwich at this hotel.

## Sandwich & Brock

Mackenzie Hall (3277 Sandwich), built by Canada's second prime minister, Alexander Mackenzie from Sarnia, went up in 1855 and opened in 1856—though Mackenzie did not lead the Liberals to power until 1873. Probably the most notorious trial to take place in southwestern Ontario occurred here in the 1920s when Rev. Leslie Spracklin, the gun-toting Methodist preacher and Ontario liquor licence inspector, shot and killed roadhouse owner Beverly "Babe" Trumble in a raid of his Chappell House, located down the street at the corner of Chappell

Mackenzie Hall Cultural Centre, located at 3277 Sandwich.

and Sandwich. The Trumbles claimed it was cold-blooded murder. The Crown argued that the roadhouse owner held up a hot-water bottle in his defence, not a pistol, which is what Spracklin claimed. No weapon of any kind was ever found at the Chappell House. Rumours abounded that it was tossed overboard into the Detroit River by Trumble's friends. Spracklin's lawyer masterfully defended the colourful clergyman, and when all was said and done, the Methodist preacher was found to be not guilty.

I wrote a play about this incident called *The Fighting Parson*, and it was performed a number of times in the Windsor area, and also at the Bathurst Street Theatre in Toronto. When the play opened at Essex Hall Theatre at the University of Windsor, both the Spracklin and Trumble families showed up. They were seated on opposite sides of the theatre. Howard Spracklin, son of the late Leslie Spracklin, boldly walked up to introduce himself. He remarked, "That's my old man up there—that's his story." I had already met with the Trumbles, and they remained resentful of the historic altercation, naturally. The presence of both families sent chills into the cast.

Mackenzie Hall was the county courthouse till 1963, when it then came under the jurisdiction of Essex County. There was talk of demolishing it, but a group calling itself Friends of the Court formed in 1981 to save it. By 1983, the city bought the building and began restoration.

Before Mackenzie Hall, a brick courthouse served the area. By 1853, it was deemed "dilapidated" and in need of demolition, and plans were drawn up for a replacement by

Albert H. Jordan, a Detroit architect. His work was well known, having designed Fort Street Presbyterian Church in 1855, and St. John's Episcopal in 1861. Mackenzie and two brothers, Hope and Robert, put in a bid and won the contract to erect a new courthouse in Sandwich. In 1855, the cornerstone was laid. This took place on May 24, the Queen's birthday. The courthouse was finished the following year, with jail cells located on the first floor, below the council chambers. Over the main entrance is a carving done of the County seal. It depicts a pioneer with an axe and a felled tree.

Alfred Young is another name that arises in the courthouse stories. He was tried in September 1858, and was sentenced for hanging in February 1859. Young had come from Michigan and took his wife to a secluded place in Windsor, and shot her. The day before his execution, he managed to escape prison, allegedly by burning a hole in the floor of his cell, then digging his way out from under the building. Young also left a message to the sheriff bidding him goodbye, indicating how he had made his departure. The truth however, according to Neal, is that the jailor may have had something to do with the escape.

"The hole in the floor would scarcely admit of a child passing through it," says Neal "and the actions of the jailor in charge at that time were considered not above suspicion and it was openly hinted that he had a hand in the supposed escape."

Young was the first sentenced to be hanged after the new jail and courthouse were built. But the first public execution to take place in

Sandwich was January 3, 1862, when George Williams, an escaped slave, was hanged for murdering his wife. This 38-year-old lake steamer cook killed his wife with an axe when she insisted upon going to a dance against his wishes. Right after killing his wife, Williams then slit his own throat, but had a change of heart, and found the means to save himself. The day he was hanged, says Neal, was "a Friday afternoon and the weather was bitter cold."

The last execution to take place at Mackenzie Hall was in August 24, 1943. The public was not permitted to view the hanging of Bruno Kisielewski and Stefan Ogrodowski.

It was in 1975 that the courthouse was sold to the Ministry of Government Services for $123,000. It was then boarded up. Windsor's Architectural Conservation Advisory Committee recommended designation under the Ontario Heritage Act. City Council agreed, and the designation was made in 1978. The following year, the Ministry declared Mackenzie Hall "redundant" and offered it to the city and county "for a nominal sum." This offer was declined by the county, but Windsor decided to study the possibility of acquiring it, and doing restoration. There was a lot of conversation back-and-forth over its future, with then-Mayor Bert Weeks at one point saying Mackenzie Hall was "not worth one dollar."

It was about this time that Friends of the Court stepped forward and made recommendations to Council. From there, Council went ahead with the purchase, and the work at saving the building and raising funds for restoration from the provincial and federal governments was initiated. The public was on side with this plan and the *Windsor*

*Star* came out in support of saving it. The election of Mayor Elizabeth Kishkon—someone who cared deeply for the arts and heritage—also gave more impetus to this happening. From that point on, the grants and private funding started to pour in. Today, Mackenzie Hall is a veritable cultural centre in Sandwich.

Around the corner is the former Essex County Registry Office (356 Brock) that was designed by Detroit architect G.W. Lloyd. This stone structure, built between 1876 and 1877, is situated on the site of the original old brick court building that pre-dated Mackenzie Hall. The builder was Hypolite Reaume, who was also involved in the construction of Hôtel-Dieu Hospital. There was an addition, designed by Sheppard & Masson, which tripled its length. This was put on during the Roaring Twenties.

## St. John's Anglican Church

On the south side of Sandwich at the corner of Brock, right across the street from Mackenzie Hall, is St. John's Anglican Church (3305 Sandwich Street). It was founded in 1802, and became the first Protestant church in the area. Its first pastor, Richard Pollard, also served as Sheriff and registrar of the Western District. The original church building was made of logs and built in 1806. The present building is actually the third structure on this site. The first was torched in 1813 by the Americans during the War of 1812. Five years later, a brick building was put up and that remains part of the third and final structure, which was rebuilt in 1871. The 1819 design was done in the Norman style, and the tower was added in 1852. The main sanctuary had to be rebuilt in 1871 because the congregation's outreach had soared. According to *Canada's Historic Places* site, the architects opted for a more "Gothic style."

Pollard was an interesting character. He was raised in England, trained in law and business. He first landed in Quebec in the spring of 1775, and when the Americans invaded during the War of Independence, Pollard joined the local forces to fight the invaders. His involvement led to a deal with the British government to export "gunpowder, arms, and ball" to Quebec in 1776. By the following year, Pollard became an Indian trader at Cataraqui (Kingston, Ont.) and Niagara. By 1783, he was stationed here in Sandwich, trading with the First Nations at the British settlement of Detroit. Pollard soon had enough resources to buy land at

The third and final St. John's Anglican Church building is visible in this postcard of Bedford Street (Sandwich Street) looking east, c. 1918.

Petite Côte, near Amherstburg. His influence grew, and in 1792, Lieutenant Governor John Graves Simcoe named him sheriff of Essex and Kent counties. He also served as postmaster, registrar of deeds for Essex and Kent counties, justice of the peace, member of the land board of the Western District, and trustee of the district school. Ironically, Pollard remained relatively poor all his life, and forever in debt. How he came to land at St. John's was the result of a search for a minister who could effectively "combat republicanism, Methodism, and other evils threatening law and order, as well as perform marriages for the new settlers," says Christopher Headon in his biography of Pollard in *Dictionary of Canadian Biography*. Pollard had already conducted Church of England services in Detroit and Sandwich as a layman since the early 1790s, and so it seemed appropriate that he be awarded this post. He was ordained deacon in Quebec in 1802. Two years later, he was ordained a priest. He then began to put his attention on developing St. John's.

The War of 1812 disrupted his plans, as Pollard had to accompany the soldiers and act as their chaplain. He was taken prisoner at the Battle of Moraviantown in October 1813, but was released and sent back to Sandwich. His church, however, had been burned by the Kentucky Mounted Riflemen in his absence, his furniture was gone, and his house was beyond repair. Pollard set about rebuilding. When he died in 1824, says his biographer, "his finances were in disarray." This statement makes this crazy tale of him all the more

believable. Pollard was living in constant penury—mostly because there were perpetual delays in paying him for the jobs he did. Sometimes these impediments took up to a year. The story goes that one day, as Pollard was waiting impatiently for the delivery of his wages, Walter Roe, a clerk of the Court at Detroit, set out in a boat to cross the river to Sandwich to pay him. Apparently, Pollard gazed up at the heavens and pleaded with God to let him "see" the money, meaning, of course, receiving it, not just *seeing* it. As Roe was approaching the shoreline, but still about mid-river, he stood up in the boat he was travelling in, and held up the sacks of money to prove he was keeping his word about bringing it. Suddenly, Roe lost his balance, and toppled overboard into the Detroit River and drowned. Of course, the money he was to deliver to Pollard was lost with him.

The two-storey brick house at 3474 Sandwich, commonly called "The Richard Pollard House" was never occupied by this legendary cleric. This building with its 10-inch thick walls and a timber foundation sitting very low on the property, was built in 1850, long after his death. Its association with his name is because Pollard owned the property upon which it sits. According to the old Sandwich Town map of 1797, Pollard's name is listed as the landowner of Lot 15, the site of this house. It is possible that he lived at this address on what was then called Bedford Street. You can't help but notice it, because it differs greatly from the other homes in the neighbourhood.

The Richard Pollard House, at 3474 Sandwich Street, was built in 1850.

St. John's Anglican cemetery, located next to the church, is the oldest west of Niagara Falls.

But more interesting than St. John's Anglican Church itself is the graveyard, the oldest west of Niagara Falls. Its flat and weathered tombstones date back to 1793. The bones of an estimated 3,500 individuals are entombed here. The names inscribed on their crumbling and nearly washed-clean headstones are pioneers, politicians, escaped slaves, tycoons, magistrates, sheriffs and soldiers from the War of 1812. Also buried here, albeit unmarked, say the writers for *Canada's Historic Places*, are the "indigents and executed criminals" who were interred in a Potter's field adjacent to the original cemetery.

Notable among those buried include Sgt. William Lees who served under the Duke of Wellington at the Battle of Waterloo in 1815, another from the American Revolutionary "Battle of Bunker Hill," and another who fought at the Battle of Gettysburg in the U.S. Civil War as a captain in the 5th Michigan Infantry. As I strolled through the cemetery, I couldn't help but spot the marker for Dr. James Hume. The large flat stone had fallen over. Its words revealed the story of how he was murdered during the Battle of Windsor in 1838 by a ragtag militia calling themselves "patriots." These were zealous soldiers seeking the seizure of Southern Ontario between Detroit and Niagara Rivers with the intention of overthrowing the government. In the cemetery, I pull back some of the grass that has obscured Hume's grave to decipher the faded and decorative lettering. The inscription tells how Hume's body on December 4, 1838, in a "cowardly and shameful" act was "mangled by a gang of armed ruffians of the United States styling themselves as patriots," when in fact they were nothing more than "pirates." In that Battle of Windsor, about an hour after midnight, 250 of these soldiers in Detroit seized the steamer, *Champlain*, and by 3:00 a.m. they landed about a mile above Walkerville at the farm of Alex Pelette. Within a short time, they had burned the Windsor barracks at City Hall Square and set fire to the steamer *Thames*. By that time, they had already murdered Hume.

It wasn't long before Col. John Prince,

The Battle of Windsor mural that adorns the side of the Barrel House Bar & Grill on Mill Street.

who had rallied his battalion of Essex Militia and other combatants, met these rebels face to face in the Baby orchard in what is now downtown Windsor. It was an easy victory, but Prince didn't stop there. He ordered four of the prisoners shot without a trial of any kind—an action that was sternly criticized, and went so far as a debate in England's House of Lords. The Duke of Wellington defended the measure, but it didn't quash an inquiry launched in Canada. In the end, Prince was found innocent of all charges. Besides that, he was hailed as a hero wherever he went. The patriots, of course, threatened to assassinate him. Frederick Neal writes: "To show the state of feeling at that time against the Col., placards were posted up along the public streets in Detroit, offering a reward of $800 for his dead body and $1000 for his living body, and to protect himself after dark, he had to have an advertisement in the public papers warning all persons against coming to the park farm after night as he brings guns and manned traps set for his protection."

In Canada, Prince was also a popular political figure, serving in the Legislature for the riding of Essex from 1836 to 1860. One question that is often asked about the cemetery at St. John's is the whereabouts of the grave of John Prince. But you will not find his grave in that cemetery yard, or even anywhere near Windsor. You would have thought it would be because his involvement in this region is so legendary. But it's not here—it's hundreds of miles away near Sault St. Marie.

Some point the finger at Sir John A. Macdonald as the reason for his burial in the far North of Ontario. The two figures never did see eye-to-eye. And Prince kept pestering Macdonald for a judgeship. Finally, in 1860, when Macdonald was the Attorney General for Upper Canada, he appointed Prince as a judge in Sault St. Marie. By then, the legendary colonel was sixty-four, but apparently the northern part of Ontario was the last place on earth that he wanted to be. Prince described the Algoma District as "the Siberia of Canada."

Just before he died in 1870, Prince made his final wishes clear—that he was to be buried a few hundred feet from his house on Prince Island near the banks of the St. Mary's River. He wrote the following: "In the accursed soil must rest and rot my miserable remains and on that solitude island opposite, for I will not allow my dust to mingle with the human race, whom I hate."

As I pause here in the cemetery, I think of Mill Street wall at the Barrel House and its depiction of the Battle of Windsor, and Prince's involvement. One can stand across the street in front of the old post office. and watch as commuters wait for the bus. Almost no one looks up at the mural, or reads the account of this battle. I sometimes wonder if I asked if they knew the name Col. Prince, it probably wouldn't mean anything to them. Yet, it is all there on the brick wall right behind them.

Another famous figure buried in this American cemetery is Margaret Arnold McEwan, the granddaughter of Benedict Arnold, the notorious Revolutionary War General and avowed traitor. According to

*Historical Narratives of Early Canada*, McEwan was awarded "a gold watch for her kindness in aiding travelers on the Great Western Railway who suffered from the cholera epidemic of July 1854." Historian Neil Morrison wrote about her in *Garden Gateway to Canada*. I mentioned this story earlier. These are the same Norwegians who were thought to have been buried in a mass grave under the Peabody Bridge. The story, from Margaret's perspective, goes like this. Her husband John was the station agent at the Great Western Railway in July 1854, when he was confronted by Norwegian immigrants, sickened with cholera from drinking polluted water en-route, getting off the train in Windsor. A temporary hospital was set up at the ferry docks near the station. "From early in the day to late at night day after day, she [Mrs. McEwan] was to be found ministering to their wants," stated the officials from the Great Western Railway when they presented her with a gold watch for her service.

McEwan was a fascinating woman. She also wrote editorials for the *Windsor Herald* newspaper when her husband operated the paper in the mid-1850s. When she died in 1885, she was buried in St. John's Cemetery. McEwan Avenue is named for her.

## Bedford United

Bedford United is not far—across the street. If you walk in through the front door, you will see a photograph of the gun-slinging Methodist cleric Spracklin who was here from

1918 to 1921. Most parishoners, who knew Spracklin, are long dead. Years ago, I spoke to older members of the congregation, one in particular, who worked as correspondent for the *Detroit News* reporting on stories from this side of the river. He was there the night the church held a kangaroo court to deal with Spracklin's advances on some of the female members of the congregation. This was the same year that Spracklin had been acquitted of murdering Babe Trumble. This man reported it, and the Methodist minister fled Sandwich for Northern Michigan where he died.

In an article, *Sad Reality of Bedford United,* Meagan Anderi quotes Bruce Trothen, the last surviving connection to the original families who started this church: "It's part of my life. Ever since I can remember this has been my church." His parents were members here in 1928. This

church has been a part of his life since the day he was born in 1933: "I was baptized here. I was married here. My children were baptized here and married here. There are four generations of us connected to this church."

Bedford United Church, designed in Gothic Revival style with a Romanesque style tower, was first known as the Sandwich Methodist Church when it opened in 1907. Its roots, however, date back as early as 1838, to the spread of Methodism in this region. In April 1879, the church operated out of a building on Mill Street that it finally sold to the town for its council chamber. By 1904, the congregation was meeting in private homes. In 1906, church members raised enough to build their own sanctuary. It cost $6,500. Thompson Brothers of Windsor was hired to do the brick and stonework, while Frank B. Tofflemire

Left: Bedford United, then called Sandwich United, is pictured in 1956.

Right: The church remains largely unchanged today, save that the new name "Bedford" has been added to the stained glass above the entrance.

was contracted for the woodwork. In 1925, this red-brick church became the Sandwich United and in 1992, Sandwich United and Calvary United Church joined together to form Bedford United. In 2007, the church celebrated their 100th year anniversary. It now has heritage designation. In its heyday, the church could seat 125 and have upwards of 300 children at Sunday school. Now, seeing 50 or 60 on a Sunday would be treasured.

## Sandwich Street

Still farther west down the street, there are a couple of other places worth noting. At 3330 Sandwich is a two-storey red brick building that once housed the offices of J.H. Bishop Fur Company. The cornice and flat-arched labelled windows along the side of the building are the

This plain building at 3330 Sandwich once housed the J.H. Bishop Fur Company in the 1800s.

only remaining features of this 1890 building. This American fur company, renowned for their high-quality coats, went out of business during the First World War. Not far from there at 3402 Sandwich is another modest brick building that was the Bedford Scoop Ice Cream Parlour. Originally, it was built on land granted to Baptiste Baby by the Crown in 1801. But from 1905 to 1943, it was the home of the Lajeunesse family. This was where Father E.J. Lajeunesse, the authority on the history of the French settlement here and author of *The Windsor Border Region*, grew up. I met this Basilian priest at Assumption Church. We talked for hours about the families that landed on the south shore in the 18th century to farm and raise their families. His words betrayed such a love for the French families who lived here, as if he knew them personally.

## Chappell and Sandwich

It's a long walk to the end of Sandwich, or what I deemed the end. The Tim Hortons (3901 Sandwich Street), situated at the corner of Chappell and Sandwich, is my unofficial boundary. A large empty lot sits across the street from the coffee shop. I spent a good amount of time in that empty lot, during the 1970s, when it was the location of the former Chappell House, then called The Lido, and later the Rumrunner Bar. The first time I was there was the winter of 1979. It was a burned-out shell. I stepped into the charred back end of the building, and tiptoed through its cavernous interior. My heart leapt when I spotted an old iron safe with the lettering

The Lido Tavern, pictured here in 1949, was once the Chappell House. This is where Babe Trumble was shot and killed by Rev. J.O.L. Spracklin in 1920.

*B. Trumble.* As I mentioned earlier, this was the spot where one of the most exciting stories from the Prohibition period played out: it was here that Trumble was killed by the fire brand Methodist minister, J.O.L. Spracklin. The clergyman shot him dead in the wee hours of the morning.

So there I was, stepping among the rubble of this old roadhouse, my head filled with those final moments of its owner. My heart soared at spotting the old safe, and of course I considered scheming a way of removing it to a museum. I let some time go by before I did return to remove the scorched safe, but mysteriously someone else had already retrieved it. Years later, in 2007, I heard John Paquette of Central Hotel and Restaurant Supplies told me that when he was 16 he was dispatched to the fire-damaged Lido to haul that old strongbox away in a truck. He knew nothing of its origins, and certainly nothing about Babe Trumbull—at least until he read my column in the *Windsor Star*. The safe eventually landed at the Rockhead Pub on Ottawa Street, but Trumbull's name had been filed off. If you want to see it, take a jaunt over to the bar, and you will agree that this strongbox's significance is its ties to our history that shows our resourcefulness. The safe stands as a reminder that Windsor was a magnet for the likes of Al Capone and the Purple Gang. We were in the headlines.

Not far from old Chappell House was the Mineral Springs Spa. In the mid-1860s, there was such a flurry about digging for salt and oil deposits, but it was difficult finding the financial support for its undertaking. It was finally John B. Gauthier's efforts that won the day. He owned a general store, brickyard, and potash business, and also a piece of property in what was for years called Brighton Beach. He

The Sandwich mineral springs, c. 1880.

best in the world," wrote Frederick Neal in 1909. It led to the creation of a canal to accommodate ferry boats from Detroit. The fare for the round trip from Woodward Avenue, Detroit, to Sandwich was .25 cents. "For a time Sandwich became quite a resort for visitors. It was a common occurrence to see from 20 to 25,000 people here on a Sunday." People trekked from all over North America to the spa that developed here. Neal wrote:

> Among the visitors were many afflicted who found the sulphur water most beneficial for the elimination from the system of such diseases as rheumatism, neuralgia and asthma, scrofula, and liver complications, nervous prostration and allied diseases. This class of visitors took the baths regularly and with such good results that many were completely cured, returning home without their sticks and crutches.

had wanted the town to sink an oil well. It was Mayor Charles Baby that finally succumbed to his imploring. The decision arose out of a meeting that occurred at the Western Hotel in 1866. It led to the formation of the Sandwich Petroleum Oil Company with shares selling for $100 each. Gauthier bought the engine and well boring machinery, and digging started on his property. As Elaine Weeks and David L. Newman say in "The Sandwich Mineral Spring & Lagoon," an article in the *Walkerville Times:*

> Day after day, locals were on pins and needles anticipating the oil strike. Finally, at 900 feet, a giant plume shot 30 feet into the air. They had struck something all right! It wasn't oil, but would prove to be almost as valuable… News of the strike spread like wildfire through town.

The workers had tapped into a mineral spring that would test to be "the most valuable and

By 1891, however, it appeared the springs were drying up. The property soon reverted back to Gauthier. Today there is no sign of what once existed. The disappearance of the old Chappell House was the last connection to it. The road-house survived long after the spa closed, along with the Lagoon Park Hotel, a three-storey hotel on Bedford Street with street cars stopping right in front.

Before I depart Sandwich, I take a one-block walk south on Chappell Street to the corner. There sits a small house with a humped roof, and gingerbread-like verandah. Its architecture defies anything I've ever seen. A modest place, to be sure, but it has an air of mystery. It is featured in the book, *The Houses of Buxton: A Legacy of African Influences in Architecture* by Patricia Lorraine Neely-McCurdy. The writer makes the case that there is the presence of African influences in North American architecture—that shouldn't come as a surprise, considering their larger cultural impact. Neely-McCurdy suggests that this west side house reflects the *poteaux-en-terre* design, a palisaded house with features rooted in Normandy and Louisiana. She says the African influence with bell-shaped roofs probably hails from 18th-century Louisiana. Neely-McCurdy says when French settlers made their way north to settle here, they brought with them their black slaves who were involved in building houses here. She said the slaves built these homes, or homes like this one on Chappell, without blueprints.

They combined European elements handed to them by their slave owners, with the memory of how they built their structures in Africa. "They built what they knew," said Neely-McCurdy, who, however, isn't certain when the house on Chappell was constructed. It is possible that it hails from the 19th century.

The journey is over. I have covered quite a bit of ground. I've peeled back a small portion of Windsor's past, and walked its neighbourhoods. And as I stand here, in the last of the five towns, Sandwich seems forgotten. This part of my odyssey shows a place that seemingly few visit, that few—at least outside its borders—cherish or choose to find out more about it. Terrence Kennedy, my trusty source in Sandwich, has said time and time again, "There are so many secrets about this place—all you need to do is take a longer look." True enough.

The last stop on my walk, this house bears the influence of African slaves who built it in the 1800s.

## POSTSCRIPT
*September, 2016*

I'm sitting at Tim Hortons across from the empty lot where the Chappell House once stood. I am thinking now of this odyssey that has taken me from one end of the city to the other. I began this really on a lark, wondering if I might simply abandon it. But the stories were too good to be true. And not entirely surprising, even as I walked the five towns, our heritage was being erased. As I made my way through Sandwich, Abars, where I had started the journey, was bulldozed to the ground. You would never know that the last of the old rumrunning roadhouses once stood here. Before I started along Sandwich, I had taken a break to travel to Ireland. When I returned, I found the gap-tooth look on the main street as developers moved in to erase the Vanity Theatre from Ouellette Avenue. Gone. And one day in September, driving through Riverside, I glanced at Our Lady of Guadalupe Catholic Church and noticed the rectory was now gone. There were others along the way. I call them "The Disappeared."

# ADDRESSES

## Riverside

Abars: 7880 Riverside Dr. E.

Riverside Bar-B-Q (Walk-In Clinic): 7885 Wyandotte St. E.

Riverside Arena: 6755 Wyandotte St. E.

St. Rose of Lima Roman Catholic Church: 891 St. Rose Ave.

Riverside Public Library: 6305 Wyandotte St. E.

Glidden Dairy Bar: 5989 Wyandotte St. E

Esdras Parent Farm House: 827 Esdras Place

Edith Cavell School: 5955 Ontario St.

Dr. M.F. Gallagher – Madison's: 5850 Wyandotte St. E.

Dr. F.D. Linton: 5720 Wyandotte St. E.

Shanfield's Dry Goods (Serenity Salon): 5720 Wyandotte St. E.

Constantine's + Esquire Barber & Beauty Shop (Royal Canadian Legion): 5645 Wyandotte St. E.

Frank's Lunch (Pat & Hank's Fish & Chips): 5622 Wyandotte St. E.

Baker's Bar & Grill: 5570 Wyandotte St. E.

Marty's Childhood Home: 942 Prado Place

St. Thomas Separate School: 900 Block Thompson Blvd.

Janisse-Schade House: 5325 Riverside Dr. E.

Our Lady of Guadalupe Roman Catholic Church: 834 Raymo Rd.

Centre Theatre (Pillette Walk-In Clinic): 4900 Wyandotte St. E.

## Ford City

Frank H. Joyce House: 3975 Riverside Dr. E.

Stanislas Janisse House: 4219 Wyandotte St. E.

Drouillard Road Underpass: Drouillard Rd. & Wyandotte St. E.

Walkerville Wagon Works: West of Drouillard Rd., near 3001 Riverside Dr. E.

Holy Rosary Catholic Church (Water's Edge): 2879 Riverside Dr. E.

Ford City Town Hall: Southeast corner of Drouillard Rd. & Riverside Dr.

Ford Power House: 3001 Riverside Dr. E., between Belleview Ave. & Cadillac St.

International Tavern: 928 Drouillard Rd.

Ford City Community Garden: 971 Drouillard Rd.

Floyd Zalev's Office (New Song Church): 993 Drouillard Rd.

Ford City Parkette: Corner of Whelpton St. & Drouillard Rd.

Border City Boxing Club: 1072 Drouillard Rd.

Atelier Virginianne: 1078 Drouillard Rd.

St. John the Devine Orthodox Church: 1094 Drouillard Rd.

Drouillard Place: 1102 Drouillard Rd.

Fred Lazurek Mural: 1118 Drouillard Rd.

Holy Rosary School (Gino and Liz Marcus Community Complex): 1168 Drouillard Rd.

Prohibition Mural: 1207 Drouillard Rd.

## Walkerville

Walkerville Transfer Station (Suede Productions): 1057 Walker Rd.

Bank of Montreal: Northwest Corner of Walker Rd. & Ottawa St.

W.E. Seagrave Fire Apparatus Co.: 900 Block of Walker Rd., between Richmond St. & Niagara St.

Metropole Supper Club (Walkerville Eatery): 911 Walker Rd.

700 Block Walker Road

St. Mary's Anglican Church: 1983 St. Mary's Gate

C.C. Ambery House ("Foxley"): 811 Devonshire Rd.

Harrington E. Walker House: 1948 St. Mary's Gate

Stephen Griggs House: 889 Kildare Rd.

Willistead Manor: 1899 Niagara St.

Kenneth Saltmarche House: 995 Chilver Rd.

Leila "Danny" Pepper House: 709 Tuscarora St.

Strathcona Block: Northwest Corner of Wyandotte St. E. & Devonshire Rd.

John Bott House: 547 Devonshire Rd.

Hiram Walker & Son's Semi's: 546-548 Devonshire Rd.

Thomas Reid House: 511 Devonshire Rd.

Former Walkerville Post Office: 420 Devonshire Rd.

Crown Inn (Taloola Café and Printworks): 378-396 Devonshire Rd.

Barclay Building: 350 Devonshire Rd.

Flat Iron Building: Southeast Corner of Riverside Dr. & Devonshire Rd.

Walker Power Building: 325 Devonshire Rd.

Peabody Building: Next to Walker Power Building

Victoria Tavern: 400 Chilver Rd.

King Edward Public School: 853 Chilver Rd.

Pat Sturn House: 1875 Ontario St.

Cooper Court: 1875 Kildare Rd.

Low-Martin Building: 2021 Ontario St.

Russell Farrow House: 1219 Devonshire Rd.

Bank of Montreal (Gourmet Emporium): 1799 Wyandotte St. E.

Walkerville Theatre: 1564 Wyandotte St. E.

Biblioasis: 1520 Wyandotte St. E.

## Windsor

The Barn (Windsor Arena): 572 McDougall Ave.

Frank's: Across from the Barn, on Wyandotte

Central United: 628 Ouellette Ave.

Windsor Fire and Rescue Headquarters: 815 Goyeau St.

Patterson Collegiate, demolished: 880 Goyeau St.

Central Branch, Windsor Public Library: 850 Ouellette Ave.

HMCS Hunter: 900 Ouellete Ave.

Windsor Masonic Temple: 986 Ouellette Ave.

Medical Arts Building: 1011 Ouellette Ave.

Windsor Regional Hospital, Ouellette Campus: 1030 Ouellette Ave.

Grayson House: 1077 Ouellette Ave.

Former Essex County War Memorial: East side of Ouellette Ave. and Giles Blvd.

Shaar Hashomayim Synagogue: 115 Giles Blvd. E.

Vanity Theatre: 673 Ouellette Ave.

Lazares & Co.: 493 Ouellette Ave.

Metropolitan Store: 439-457 Ouellette Ave.

Henry Birks & Sons (City Grill): 375 Ouellette Ave.

Prince Edward Hotel (ScotiaBank): 388 Ouellette Ave.

Palace Theatre (Windsor Star): 300 Ouellette Ave.

Coles Books (South Detroit): 255 Ouellette Ave.

Windsor Armouries: 30 University Ave. E.

Top Hat Supper Club (Burger King): 73 University Ave. E.

All Saints' Anglican Church: 330 City Hall Square

Ouellette Family Homestead (Bank of Montreal): 200 Ouellette Ave.

Kresge (Royal Bank of Canada): 245 Ouellette Ave.

Dominion Building/Paul Martin Sr. Building: 185 Ouellette Ave.

C.H. Smith's: northeast corner of Pitt and Ouellette Ave.

Manning House Hotel (TD Canada Trust): 156 Ouellette Ave.

Riverside Drive One West/Norwich Block (1 Riverside Drive)

Elias Deli (CIBC Building): 114 Ouellette Ave.

British American Hotel: north of Riverside Drive, west of Ouellette Ave.

Windsor Star (School of Social Work): 167 Ferry St.

Alexander Bartlet House (Coach & Horses): 156 Chatham St. W.

La Belle Terrace: 309 Chatham St. W.

Canadian Tire (Windsor International Transit Terminal): 300 Chatham St. W.

François Baby House: 254 Pitt St. W.

Capitol Theatre: 121 University St. W.

Our Lady of the Assumption Catholic Church: 350 Huron Church Rd.

## Sandwich

Ambassador Bridge

William McKee House: 3020 Sandwich St.

Pierre Marentette House: 3066 Sandwich St.

McGregor-Cowan House (Olde Towne Bake Shoppe): 3118 Sandwich St.

Dominion House: 3140 Sandwich St.

Solomon Wigle House: 3164 Sandwich St.

James McKee House: 3165 Sandwich St.

John Spiers General Store (The Barrel House): 3199 Sandwich St.

E. Lassaline Furniture Dealer and Undertaker (Wally's Bait & Tackle): 3195 Sandwich St.

Mason-Girardot House: 3203 Peter St.

Sandwich Post Office (Sandwich Post Café): 3201 Sandwich St.

Sandwich Fire Hall: 363 Mill St.

Langlois House: 351 Mill St.

Jules Robinet Winery (Yum Yum Pizza): 3200 Sandwich St.

McKee Block (Rock Bottom): 3236 Sandwich St.

Sandwich Town Hall: 3255 Sandwich St.

Western Hotel (Mackenzie Hall Park): 3277 Sandwich St.

Mackenzie Hall Cultural Centre: 3277 Sandwich St.

Registry Office: 356 Brock St.

St. John's Anglican Church: 3305 Sandwich St.

Pollard House: 3474 Sandwich St.

Bedford United Church: 3340 Sandwich St.

J.H. Bishop Fur Company: 3330 Sandwich St.

Chappell House (Lido Tavern): 3885 Sandwich St.

# BIBLIOGRAPHY

Brandon R. Dimmel, *Engaging the Line: How the Great War Shaped the Canada-US Border*, University of Washington Press, 2016.

*Canada's Historic Places*, http://www.historicplaces.ca/.

Chris Edwards, "The Walkerville Exchange, aka 'The Vic,'" *The Times Magazine*, 2000.

Chris Edwards and Elaine Weeks, *Walkerville: Whisky Town Extraordinaire*, Walkerville Publishing, 2015.

Currie Bednarick, "The Great Bank Robbery of '59," *The Times Magazine*, 2002.

Daniel J. Brock and Michael Power, *Gather up the Fragments: A History of the Diocese of London*, Diocese of London, 2001.

Elaine Weeks, "The Curse of Peche Island," *The Times Magazine*, 2001.

Frederick Neal, *The Township of Sandwich: Past and Present*, 1909.

G. A. Rawley, "Aspects of the Canadian Evangelical Experience," McGill-Queen's University Press, 1997.

G. Mark Walsh, "Bishop Fallon and the Riot at Ford City, 8 September 1917,"*Archivaria 29*, 1989-90.

Herb Colling and Carl Morgan, *Pioneering the Auto Age*, Benchmark Publishing, 1993.

Holly M. Karibo, "Ambassadors of Pleasures: Illicit Economies in the Detroit Windsor Borderland, 1945 – 1960," PhD thesis, 2012.

Jack D. Cecillion, *Prayers, Petitions, and Protests: The Catholic Church and Ontario Schools Crisis in the Windsor Border Region, 1910- 1928*, McGill-Queen's University Press, 2013.

Joan Magee, *A Scandinavian Heritage: 200 Years of Scandinavian Presence in the Windsor-Detroit Border Region*, Dundurn Press, 1996.

Joanne and Conrad Reitz, *Into the New Millennium: All Saints' Anglican Church, Windsor, Ontario, 1852 – 2002*, 2002.

Judy Jacobson, *Detroit River Connections: Historical and Biographical Sketches of the Eastern Great Lakes Border Region*, Clearfield, 2009.

Julia Biris, "Suburbia, The Automobile, and Obesity," https://medium.com/historical-musings/suburbia-the-automobile-and-obesi ty-af7e072ce165.

Kayla Dettinger, "Mary: The Life and Times of Mrs. Edward C. Walker of Willistead Manor, Walkerville," 2015.

Larry Kulisek and Trevor Price, *Windsor, 1892 – 1992: A Centennial Celebration*, Chamber Publications, 1992.

Mary E. Baruth-Walsh and Mark Walsh, *Strike! 99 Days on the Line,* Penumbra Press, 1995.

Natalie Atkin, "From Learning to Living: Edith Cavell School," *The Times Magazine*, 2001.

Neil F. Morrison, *Garden Gateway to Canada: One Hundred Years of Windsor and Essex County, 1854 – 1954*, Ryerson Press, 1954.

Patrick Brode, *Unholy City: Vice in Windsor, 1950*, Essex County Historical Society, 2013.

Paul Dickson, "Sputnik's Impact on America," http://www.pbs.org/wgbh/nova/space/sputnik-impact-on-america.html.

Philip Marchand, *Marshall McLuhan: The Medium and The Messenger*, Vintage Canada, 1998.

*Postcards from the Past: Volume 1: Windsor and the Border Cities from the David L. Newman Collection*, Walkerville Publishing, 2005.

Richard A. Fullerton, *Our Town: A History of Riverside, Ontario, 1921 – 1966, Volume One*, R.A. Publishing, 2008.

Richard A. Fullerton, *Our Town: A History of Riverside, Ontario, 1921 – 1966, Volume Two*, R.A. Publishing, 2009.

Rosemary Donegan, *Ford City/Windsor: A Multi-Media Exhibition,* Art Gallery of Windsor, 1994.

Stephen Schneider, *Iced: The Story of Organized Crime in Canada*, Wiley, 2007.

The Mayor of Monmouth Blog, http://themayorofmonmouth.blogspot.ca/.

Windsor Architectural Conservation Advisory Committee, *Walkerville Walking Tour*, 1997.

# ACKNOWLEDGEMENTS

There are so many who need to be thanked when it came to the inspiration and the writing of this book. I'm sure I'll miss some in the following list, and I must apologize for that. At the top these would include the staff at the Windsor Public Library and the University of Windsor Library. The *Windsor Star*, as always, was a tremendous source, and I am grateful for their permission to use their photographs in this book.

Without the help of Madelyn Della Valle and Heather Colautti, and Hugh Barrett of the Windsor Community Museum, and John Calhoun, heritage planner for the City of Windsor, I think I might have lost my way. Their assistance was invaluable. I also need to bow to the Biblioasis gang from the bookstore counter to the back rooms to the upstairs offices, all of whom helped with advice and encouragement. Special thanks to my cheery editor, Sharon Hanna, for meticulous attention and guidance, to Dan Wells who runs the press and knows better than anyone that there's a story or two to tell about Windsor. Big applause goes to the amazing Owen Swain for the delightful sketches that grace the pages of this book. And the hard-working and sensitive Ellie Hastings of Biblioasis for the exceptional design and layout skills that turned this manuscript into a published book. I also can't forget those who helped out in the beginning stages: two University of Windsor English Literature students, Izza Eirabie and Malak El-Tahry, for reading earlier versions and providing fresh ideas and an honest appraisal. Also supporting me was Aaron Jonsson and Alisha Adraktas for mapping out and proofing the original manuscript. My gratitude is also directed to Rick Fullerton for his Riverside stories; Terrence Kennedy, Sandwich Town's indefatigable freelance historian, for his tireless work and generosity; Councillor Jo-Anne Gignac for the wonderful details about her Riverside pioneer family; and to all those over the years who spun wonderful tales of the five towns when I was writing *My Town* for the *Windsor Star*. Also of note is Taylor Campbell, a young videographer and photographer who was instrumental in documenting photographically the places I mention in this book.

Much of this book was written in the wee hours of the morning at a corner table at Tim Hortons at the corner of Walker Road and Ypres. I barely walked through the side door when a mug of steeped tea and a toasted bagel would be presented to me. Stalwart Vicki was ever smiling and cheerful, and now I spot her on the day shift and trade stories with her. Tanya and Cheri are the night crawlers, and are ever mindful of my eccentricities. I bless them for their kindness. Later in the day, it is Anthony who would come over and take a peek at what I was doing. The process is important. The place is important. This is my second office. That environment just a few blocks away from my house helps keep the engine firing on all cylinders. And in the wee hours, there's always Ray to chat with, or Jimmy who interrupts me with baseball stories. I applaud both for keeping me grounded. It's all important—the process, people, neighbourhood, friends, the breakfast pals who meet with me in diners and tell me stories. All of this shapes the way I think. Their belief and support are there at all times. Among these are Peter Hrastovec and Roger Bryan, both good friends and people whose ideas resonate in ever meaningful ways. Others of note include: Alan Wildeman, Carol Davison, Blake Roberts, Tom Dilworth, Suzanne Matheson, Margaret Mrozowski, André Narbonne, Christopher Menard, Vanessa Shields, Mary Ann Mulhern, John B. Lee, Bruce Meyer, Nadine Deleury, Pamela Goldstein. Finally, I want to thank my wife, Donna, who is always trying to get me to exercise.

Photo: Donna Gervais

Marty Gervais is a teacher, journalist, historian, photographer and writer. His book *The Rumrunners* was a Canadian bestseller. In 1998, Gervais received the prestigious Harbourfront Festival Prize for his work in advancing the careers of other writers. Gervais has also taught numerous courses in English Literature, Creative Writing and Journalism. With his journalism he has interviewed a wide assortment of figures, from Mother Teresa and Muhammad Ali to Arthur Miller and Jimmy Carter. His journalism has taken him all over the world, from covering the war in Iraq and Holy Week in Jerusalem to championship boxing in Bosnia and Argentina. His column, My Town, published in the *Windsor Star*, won him numerous journalism awards, and an honourary Doctor of Laws from Assumption University. In 2012, Gervais was named Windsor's first Poet Laureate. He also received the Queen's Jubilee Medal.